The Rise
of the
Welfare State

Readings in Politics and Society

GENERAL EDITOR: Bernard Crick
Professor of Politics, Department of Politics and Sociology, Birkbeck College, University of London

Already Published

W. L. Guttsman, *The English Ruling Class*
A. J. Beattie, *English Party Politics* (two volumes)
Frank Bealey, *The Social and Political Thought of the British Labour Party*
Krishan Kumar, *Revolution*
Edmund Ions, *Modern American Social and Political Thought*
W. Thornhill, *The Growth and Reform of English Local Government*
J. B. Poole and Kay Andrews, *The Government of Science in Britain*

Forthcoming Titles

N. D. Deakin, *Race in British Politics*
Louis Blom-Cooper and Gavin Drewry, *Law and Morality*

Previously published in this series by Routledge & Kegan Paul
David Nicolls, *Church and State in Britain Since 1821*

The Rise
of the
Welfare State

ENGLISH SOCIAL POLICY, 1601–1971

Edited and Introduced by
MAURICE BRUCE
Director of Extramural Studies,
University of Sheffield

World University
WEIDENFELD AND NICOLSON
London

Editorial and introductory material
© 1973 by Maurice Bruce

ISBN 0 297 76546 9 cased
ISBN 0 297 76547 7 paperback

Printed in Great Britain by
Cox & Wyman Ltd,
London, Fakenham and Reading

Contents

List of Documentary Sources   vii
General Editor's Introduction   xxiii
Foreword   xxv
Acknowledgements   xxvii
Introduction   1

1   The Poor Law Background   39
2   The Victorian Poor Law   50
3   Public Health in the Nineteenth Century   69
4   Housing in the Nineteenth Century   88
5   The Local Government Board at Work   105
6   The Rising Tide of Social Concern   115
7   Turning Away from the Poor Law   129
8   Between the Wars   166
9   The Impact of Total War   234
10 The 'Welfare State' Arrives   250
11 New Practice and New Concepts   270
12 Poverty Continues   289
13 Statistics of Social Policy   293

List of Documentary Sources

1 The Poor Law Background

1.1   CONTINUITY
1.1.1   Poor Relief Acts, 1601–1930
        From the Poor Relief Act, 1601
        From the Poor Law Act, 1930

1.2   THE LAW OF SETTLEMENT
1.2.1   Settlements and Removals, 1662
        From the Poor Relief Act, 1662
1.2.2   Removable Only If Chargeable, 1795
        From the Poor Removal Act, 1795
1.2.3   Irremovability, 1846
        From the Poor Removal Act, 1846
1.2.4   A Case of Removal, 1861
        From the Law Times, *May 1861*
1.2.5   Settlement, Irremovability and Removal
        From the Poor Law Act, 1930

1.3   THE WORKHOUSE AND OUT-RELIEF
1.3.1   The Origins of the 'Workhouse Test', 1723
        From the Poor Relief Act, 1723
1.3.2   A New Approach, 1782
        From 'Gilbert's Act', 1782
1.3.3   Encouraging Out-Relief, 1795
        From the Poor Relief Act, 1795
1.3.4   Welfare and Speenhamland, 1795
        From the Reading Mercury, *11 May 1795*
1.3.5   What the Labourers Felt
        From the First Annual Report of the Poor Law Commissioners, 1835

2 The Victorian Poor Law

2.1   THE NEW POOR LAW
2.1.1   The Poor Law Report and Amendment Act, 1834
        From the Poor Law Report, 1834
        From the Poor Law Amendment Act, 1834
2.1.2   The Franchise and the Poor Law, 1832–1918
        From the Representation of the People Act, 1832
        *From the Medical Relief Disqualification Removal
        Act, 1885*
        From the Representation of the People Act, 1918

2.2   THE POOR LAW COMMISSIONERS AT WORK,
        1834–47; CHADWICK IN CONTROL
2.2.1   Workhouse Regulations
        *From the First Report of the Poor Law Commissioners,
        1835*
2.2.2   The Problem of Industry
        *From the Third Annual Report of the Poor Law
        Commissioners, 1837*
2.2.3   The Economics of Sickness
        *From the Fourth and Fifth Annual Reports of the
        Poor Law Commissioners, 1838 and 1839*
2.2.4   The Labour Test
        *From the Ninth Annual Report of the Poor Law
        Commissioners, 1843*
2.2.5   Controlling Out-Relief
        *From the General Out-Door Relief Prohibitory Order
        of 2 August 1841*
        From the Out-Door Labour Test Order of 30 April 1842
        *From the General Out-Door Relief Regulation Order
        of 14 December 1852*
2.2.6   A Comment on Stone-Breaking
        *From the Reports of the Select Committee on Distress
        from Want of Employment: Second Report, 1896*

2.3   OBJECTIONS TO THE NEW POOR LAW
2.3.1   The Commons Debate on the Renewal of the
        Commission, 1839
        From the House of Commons Debate, 20 July 1839

2.3.2   Letter from a Manufacturer to Chadwick, 1841
         From a Letter from Edmund Ashworth to Chadwick,
         12 November 1841
2.3.3   The Andover Report, 1846
         From the Report from the Select Committee . . .
         on the Andover Union
2.3.4   Workhouse Reality
         From George Lansbury, My Life *(1928)*

3 Public Health in the Nineteenth
  Century

3.1   THE BEGINNINGS OF ACTION
3.1.1   Reports on the State of Large Towns, etc., 1844–5
         From the First Report of the Commissioners of
         Inquiry into the State of Large Towns and
         Populous Districts, 1844
         From the Second Report of the Commissioners of
         Inquiry into the State of Large Towns and
         Populous Districts, 1845
3.1.2   The Commons Debate on the Health of Towns
         Bill, 1847
         From the House of Commons Debates,
         18 June–1 July 1847
3.1.3   The First Public Health Act, 1848
         From the Public Health Act, 1848

3.2   THE WORK OF DR (SIR) JOHN SIMON
3.2.1   The Social Condition of the Poor in London, 1849
         From the First Annual Report of the Medical Officer
         of Health to the City of London, 1849
3.2.2   Disease Investigated for the Privy Council, 1858–71
         From the Seventh Annual Report of the Medical
         Officer of the Committee of Council on Health,
         1864 (1865)
         From the Eighth Annual Report of the Medical
         Officer of the Committee of Council on Health,
         1865 (1866)
3.2.3   English Sanitary Institutions
         From Dr John Simon, English Sanitary Institutions
         (1890)

3.3   THE CLIMAX OF LEGISLATION
3.3.1 The 'Imperative Mood', 1866
       From the Sanitary Act, 1866
3.3.2 Completion of the Environmental Services, 1875
       From the Public Health Act, 1875
3.3.3 Public Hospitals, 1867
       From the Metropolitan Poor Act, 1867
       From the Public Health (London) Act, 1891

3.4   VACCINATION
3.4.1 'A Victorian National Health Service'
       From the Vaccination (Amendment) Act, 1841
       From the Vaccination Act, 1867

4 Housing in the Nineteenth Century

4.1   THE FIRST LEGISLATION
4.1.1 Back-to-Back in Manchester, 1844
       From the Manchester Police Act, 1844
       *From the Royal Sanitary Commission, First Report,
       1869*
4.1.2 The First Working Class Housing Act, 1851
       *From an Act to Encourage the Establishment of
       Lodging Houses for the Labouring Classes, 1851*
4.1.3 Loans to Local Authorities for Housing, 1866
       *From the Labouring Classes' Dwelling Houses Act,
       1866*

4.2   THE TORRENS AND CROSS ACTS
4.2.1 Clearing Single Houses, 1868
       *From the Artisans' and Labourers' Dwellings Act,
       1868*
4.2.2 Clearing Whole Areas, 1875
       *From the Artisans' and Labourers' Dwellings
       Improvement Act, 1875*
4.2.3 Report on the Working of the Acts, 1882
       *From the Report of the Select Committee on the
       Artisans' and Labourers' Dwellings Improvement
       Acts, 1882*
4.2.4 Workmen's Fares, 1883
       From the Cheap Trains Act, 1883

4.3   THE COMING OF LOCAL AUTHORITY HOUSING

4.3.1   Birmingham and the Cross Act
      From J. L. Garvin, The Life of Joseph
      Chamberlain, *Vol I (1932)*

4.3.2   'How the Poor Live', 1883
      From an article by G. R. Sims

4.3.3   The Royal Commission of 1884–5
      From the Report of the Royal Commission on the
      Housing of the Working Classes, 1884–5: Summary

4.3.4   Local Authority Powers, 1890
      From the Housing of the Working Classes Act, 1890

4.3.5   Housing Estates, 1900
      From the Housing of the Working Classes Act, 1900

4.3.6   Health and Housing, 1909
      From the Housing and Town Planning Act, 1909

4.3.7   The End of Back-to-Back, 1910
      From a Report to the Local Government Board, 1910

4.3.8   The LGB and Housing, 1915
      From the Forty-Second Annual Report of the Local
      Government Board, 1912–13, Part II

4.3.9   Birmingham after Chamberlain
      From Asa Briggs, History of Birmingham, Borough
      and City, 1865–1938 *(1952)*

5 The Local Government Board at Work

5.1   'A NEW POOR LAW'

5.1.1   The Over-Sixties in the Workhouse, 1847–1930
      From the Poor Law Board Act, 1847
      From the Divided Parishes and Poor Law
      Amendment Act, 1876
      From the Poor Law Act, 1930

5.1.2   Old People in the Workhouse
      From Flora Thompson, Candleford Green *(1943)*

5.1.3   Circular on Elderly Couples, 1885
      From the Fifteenth Annual Report of the
      Local Government Board, 1885

5.1.4 Workhouse Indulgences, 1892 and 1894
From the Twenty-Second Annual Report of the
Local Government Board, 1892–3
From the Twenty-Fourth Annual Report of the
Local Government Board, 1894–5

5.1.5 Out-Relief and Friendly Societies, 1894
From the Outdoor Relief (Friendly Societies) Act,
1894

5.1.6 The New Guardians, 1895
From the Twenty-Fifth Annual Report of the
Local Government Board, 1895–6

5.1.7 A New Policy for the Aged, 1900
From the Thirtieth Annual Report of the Local
Government Board, 1900–1

5.2 CHILDREN UNDER THE POOR LAW
5.2.1 Poor Law Recividism?
From the Twenty-Sixth Annual Report of the
Local Government Board, 1896–7

5.2.2 Getting Children Out of the Workhouse, 1900
From the Thirtieth Annual Report of the
Local Government Board, 1900–1

6 The Rising Tide of Social Concern

6.1 NEW IDEOLOGIES
6.1.1 Idealist Philosophy
From Lecture on Liberal Legislation and
Freedom of Contract, Works of Thomas Hill
Green, *Vol. III, 1880*

6.1.2 The Fabians on the Poor Law
From J. F. Oakeshott, The Humanizing of the
Poor Law, *Fabian Tract No. 54 (1894)*

6.2 THE PROBLEM OF OLD AGE
6.2.1 Booth on Old Age, 1894
From Charles Booth, The Aged Poor in England
and Wales *(1894)*

6.2.2 Pensions at Seventy
From Charles Booth, Life and Labour of the
People in London, *Vol. XVII (1902)*

6.3   THE PROBLEM OF POVERTY
6.3.1   Life and Labour in London
        From Charles Booth, Life and Labour of the
        People in London, *Vol. I (1889)*
6.3.2   Poverty in York
        From R. Seebohm Rowntree, Poverty. A Study of
        Town Life *(1901)*
6.3.3   Winston Churchill's Hair Stands on End
        From R. S. Churchill, Young Statesman, 1901–14,
        Winston S. Churchill, *Vol. II (1967)*

7 Turning Away from the Poor Law

7.1   THE CHILDREN
7.1.1   The Fear of Physical Deterioration
        *From the Report of the Interdepartmental
        Committee on Physical Deterioration, 1904*
7.1.2   School Meals and Health Services
        From the Education (Provision of Meals) Act, 1906
        *From the Education (Administrative Provisions)
        Act, 1907*
7.1.3   The First Children Act, 1908
        From the Children Act, 1908

7.2   THE UNEMPLOYED
7.2.1   The Chamberlain Circular, 1886
        *From the Sixteenth Annual Report of the
        Local Government Board, 1886–7*
7.2.2   The Political Quandary, 1905
        *From the House of Commons Debate, 20 June 1905 :
        The Unemployed Workmen Bill, Second Reading*
        *From the House of Commons Debate, 17 August
        1905 : The Unemployed Workmen Bill, Third
        Reading*
7.2.3   Beveridge on the Unemployed Workmen Act, 1907
        *From the Report of the Royal Commission on the
        Poor Laws and the Relief of Distress : Minutes of
        Evidence*

7.3   OLD AGE PENSIONS
7.3.1   Asquith's Promise and Performance, 1908
        From the House of Commons Debate, 7 May 1908

7.3.2   The Old Age Pensions Act, 1908
         From the Old Age Pensions Act, 1908
7.3.3   Pensions in the Village
         From Flora Thompson, Lark Rise *(1939)*

7.4   THE LEADING SPIRITS
7.4.1   Speeches by Lloyd George
         From Better Times *(1910)*
7.4.2   Speeches by Churchill
         From Liberalism and the Social Problem *(1909)*
7.4.3   Churchill's Tribute to Lloyd George, 1945
         From the House of Commons Debate, 28 March 1945

7.5   THE POOR LAW REPORT, 1909
7.5.1   The Reports
         From the Majority Report
         From the Minority Report
7.5.2   The Reports Compared
         From the Majority and Minority Reports:
         A Summary

7.6   EMPLOYMENT AND UNEMPLOYMENT
7.6.1   The Beveridge Analysis
         From W. H. Beveridge, Unemployment,
         A Problem of Industry *(1909)*
7.6.2   Churchill and Unemployment Insurance, 1909
         From the House of Commons Debate, 19 May 1909

7.7   NATIONAL HEALTH INSURANCE
7.7.1   Lloyd George Introduces National Insurance, 1911
         From the House of Commons Debate, 4 May 1911
7.7.2   'The Tide of Social Pity'
         From The People's Insurance. Explained by the
         Rt Hon. David Lloyd George, MP *(1911)*
7.7.3   'We Have Got L.G. There'
         From Sir Henry N. Bunbury (ed.), Lloyd George's
         Ambulance Wagon, The Memoirs of William J.
         Braithwaite, 1911–12 *(1957)*

8 Between the Wars

8.1   THE POST-WAR SETTLEMENT
8.1.1   Reconstruction and the Ministry of Health

From Reconstruction Problems (*1918*)
From the Report of the Ministry of Reconstruction
to 31 December 1918 (*1919*)

8.1.2   The Dawson Report, 1920
Ministry of Health Consultative Council on Medical
and Allied Services : From the Interim Report on
the Future Provision of Medical and Allied Services

8.1.3   Unemployment Insurance Extended, 1920
From the Unemployment Insurance Act, 1920

8.1.4   Rent Restriction, 1915
From the Increase of Rent and Mortgage Interest
(*War Restrictions*) *Act, 1915*

8.1.5   'Homes for Heroes', 1919
From the Housing, Town Planning, etc. Act, 1919
From the Housing (*Additional Powers*) *Act, 1919*

8.1.6   'The Good Old Ways'
From a Speech by Lord Halifax at Oxford
University, 27 February 1940

8.2   THE PROBLEM OF UNEMPLOYMENT

8.2.1   'The Dole'
From a Ministry of Labour Report on National
Unemployment Insurance to July 1923

8.2.2   Unemployment and The Poor Law
From the Second Annual Report of the Ministry of
Health, 1920–1

8.2.3   'Genuinely Seeking Work'
From the Unemployment Insurance (*No. 2*) *Act, 1924*

8.2.4   Benefit and Maintenance
The Official View : From the Report of the
Interdepartmental Committee on Public Assistance,
1923
Labour Policy, 1924. From the House of Commons
Debate, 9 July 1924
Conservative Policy, 1927. From the House of
Commons Debate, 6 December 1927

8.2.5   The Blanesburgh Report, 1927
From the Report of the Unemployment Insurance
Committee, 1927 (*Blanesburgh Committee*)

8.2.6   Beveridge on Unemployment, 1930

From W. H. Beveridge Unemployment: A
Problem of Industry *Vol. II (1909 and 1930)*

8.2.7 Relaxing Conditions, 1930
From the Unemployment Insurance Act, 1930

8.2.8 The Royal Commission on Unemployment, 1932
*From the Royal Commission on Unemployment,
Final Report, 1932*

8.2.9 The Unemployment Act, 1934
From the Unemployment Act, 1934

8.2.10 The Household Means Test
*From the First Report of the Unemployment
Assistance Board, 1935*

8.3 THE POOR LAW
8.3.1 The Poor Law Under Stress
*From the Third Annual Report of the Ministry of
Health, 1921–2*
*From the Eighth Annual Report of the
Ministry of Health, 1926–7*

8.3.2 The Guardians Default Act, 1926
From the Boards of Guardians (Default) Act, 1926

8.3.3 The End of the Guardians
From the Local Government Act, 1929
*From the Eleventh Annual Report of the
Ministry of Health, 1929–30*

8.3.4 The Last Poor Law Acts
From the Poor Law Act, 1930
From the Poor Law Act, 1934
From the Poor Law (Amendment) Act, 1938

8.4 CONTRIBUTORY PENSIONS
8.4.1 Contributory Pensions, 1925
*From the Widows', Orphans' and Old Age
Contributory Pensions Act, 1925*

8.4.2 The 'Black-Coated Workers' Act, 1937
*From the Widows', Orphans' and Old Age
Contributory Pensions (Voluntary Contributors)
Act, 1937*

8.5 PUBLIC HEALTH
8.5.1 National Health Insurance, 1926

From the Report of the Royal Commission on
National Health Insurance, 1926 : Majority Report
From the Report of the Royal Commission on
National Health Insurance, 1926 : Minority Report

8.5.2   Public Health
From the Public Health Act, 1936

8.5.3   The Hospitals
From B. Abel-Smith, The Hospitals, 1800–1948
(1964)
From R. Pinker, English Hospital Statistics,
1861–1938 *(1966)*

8.6   HOUSING
8.6.1   The Commons Debate, 1923
From the House of Commons Debate, 24 April 1923

8.6.2   The Chamberlain Act, 1923
From the Housing, etc. Act, 1923

8.6.3   The Wheatley Policy, 1924
From the House of Commons Debate, 3 June 1924

8.6.4   The Wheatley Act, 1924
From the Housing (Financial Provisions) Act, 1924

8.6.5   Slum Clearance
From the Housing Act, 1930

8.6.6   The End of the Wheatley Policy, 1933
From the Housing (Financial Provisions) Act, 1933

8.6.7   Overcrowding, 1935
From the Housing Act, 1935

8.6.8   Final Report, 1939
From the Twentieth Annual Report of the
Ministry of Health, 1938–9

9   The Impact of Total War

9.1   NEW POLICIES
9.1.1   Supplementary Pensions, 1940
From a Memorandum by Sir John Simon,
Chancellor of the Exchequer, to the War Cabinet,
January 1940
From the House of Commons Debate, 23 January 1940

9.1.2   The Pensions Act, 1940

From the Old Age and Widows' Pensions Act, 1940
From The Times, 14 August 1940

9.1.3   The Means Test Abolished, 1941
From the House of Commons Debate, 29 April 1941

9.1.4   Needs, Not Means, 1941
From the Determination of Needs Act, 1941

9.1.5   Statistics of Assistance
From the Annual Report of the Ministry of Health,
1939–41: Public Assistance
From the Annual Report of the Ministry of Health,
1943–4: Public Assistance
From the Annual Report of the Assistance Board,
1944–5

9.2   THE BEVERIDGE REPORT, 1942

9.2.1   The Report
From the Report on Social Insurance and Allied
Services, 20 November 1942

9.2.2   The Prime Minister's Broadcast, 1943
From the Broadcast by the Prime Minister on the
War and Future Social Policy, 21 March 1943

9.2.3   The 'White Paper Chase', 1944
From the White Paper on a National Health Service
From the White Paper on Employment Policy
From the White Paper on Social Insurance

10 The 'Welfare State' Arrives

10.1   THE FIRST LEGISLATION

10.1.1   Family Allowances, 1945
From the Family Allowances Act, 1945

10.1.2   A New Policy for Deprived Children, 1948
From the Children Act, 1948

10.2   NATIONAL INSURANCE

10.2.1   Commons Debates, 1946
From the House of Commons Debate, 6 February 1946
From the House of Commons Debate, 30 May 1946

10.2.2   The National Insurance Act
From the National Insurance Act, 1946

10.3   NATIONAL HEALTH
10.3.1 Public Health During the War
        From On the State of the Public Health During
        Six Years of War, *Report of the Chief Medical
        Officer of the Ministry of Health, 1939–45
        (Sir Wilson Jameson)*
10.3.2 The National Health Service
        From the House of Commons Debate, 30 April 1946

10.4   NATIONAL ASSISTANCE
10.4.1 The Commons Debates, 1947–8
        *From the House of Commons Debate, 24 November
        1947*
        From the House of Commons Debate, 5 March 1948
10.4.2 The End of the Poor Law, 1948
        From the National Assistance Act, 1948
10.4.3 National Assistance Board Statistics
        *From the Annual Report of the National Assistance
        Board, 1949*

11 New Practice and New Concepts

11.1   THE NATIONAL HEALTH SERVICE
11.1.1 The Cost of the National Health Service, 1956
        *From the Report of the Committee of Enquiry into
        the Cost of the National Health Service
        (The Guillebaud Report), 1956*
11.1.2 The Finances of the National Health Service, 1970
        *From the Annual Report of the Department of
        Health and Social Security, 1970*

11.2   THE END OF BEVERIDGE
11.2.1 Sharing Prosperity, 1959
        *From the House of Commons Debate,
        24 June 1959 (1)*
11.2.2 Exorcising the Poor Law Spirit, 1959
        *From the House of Commons Debate,
        24 June 1959 (2)*
11.2.3 The 'Beveridge Revolution' Ended, 1964
        *From the House of Commons Debate,
        10 November 1964*
11.2.4 Earnings-Related Benefits

From the Annual Report of the Ministry of
Social Security, 1966
From National Superannuation and Social
Insurance: Proposals for Earnings-Related
Social Security (Cmnd 3883, 1969)
From Strategy for Pensions: The Future
Development of State and Occupational Provision
(Cmnd 4755, 1971)

11.2.5 Social Security and Supplementary Benefits, 1966
From the Ministry of Social Security Act, 1966
From the Annual Report of the Ministry of
Social Security, 1966
From the Annual Report of the Ministry of
Social Security, 1967

12 Poverty Continues

12.1 THE WAGE-STOP
From Administration of the Wage-Stop,
Report by the Supplementary Benefits Commission
(1967)

12.2 FAMILY CIRCUMSTANCES
From Circumstances of Families,
Report of the Ministry of Social Security (1967)

13 Statistics of Social Policy

13.1 PUBLIC EXPENDITURE, 1951–70
13.1.1 Public Expenditure Summary: Analysis by
Function
13.1.2 Public Expenditure at 1963 Prices
13.1.3 Expenditure on Social Services, including
Housing, 1921–69

13.2 NET INCOME AND SOCIAL SECURITY, 1951–70
13.2.1 Net Income: At Work or Sick, Unemployed or
Retired

13.3 NATIONAL INSURANCE AND NATIONAL
ASSISTANCE/SUPPLEMENTARY BENEFITS,
1951–70

13.3.1 Persons Receiving National Insurance Benefits
        and Extent Supplemented

13.4   STATISTICS OF NATIONAL ASSISTANCE /
        SUPPLEMENTARY BENEFITS, 1948–70
13.4.1 Persons Receiving Supplementary Benefits
13.4.2 Supplementary Benefits: Age of Men Receiving
        Regular Weekly Payments
13.4.3 Supplementary Benefits: Age of Women Receiving
        Regular Weekly Payments

General Editor's Introduction

The purpose of this series is to introduce students of society to a number of important problems through the study of sources and contemporary documents. It should be part of every student's education to have some contact with the materials from which the judgements of authors of secondary works are reached, or the grounds of social action determined. Students may actually find this more interesting than relying exclusively on the pre-digested diet of textbooks. The readings will be drawn from as great a variety of documents as is possible within each book: Royal Commission reports, Parliamentary debates, letters to the Press, newspaper editorials, letters and diaries both published and unpublished, sermons and literary sources, etc., will all be drawn upon. For the aim is both to introduce the student to carefully selected extracts from the principal books and documents on a subject (the things he always hears about but never reads), and to show him the great range of subsidiary and secondary source materials available (the memorials of actors in the actual events).

The prejudice of this series is that the social sciences need to be taught and developed in an historical context. Those of us who wish to be relevant and topical (and this is no bad wish) sometimes need reminding that the most usual explanation of why a thing is as it is, is that things happened in the past to make it so. These things might not have happened. They might have happened differently. And nothing in the present is, strictly speaking, *determined* from the past; but everything is limited by what went before. Every present problem, whether of understanding or of action, will always have a variety of relevant antecedent factors, all of which must be understood before it is sensible to commit ourselves to an explanatory theory or to some course of practical action. No present problem is completely novel and there is never any single cause for it, but always a variety of conditioning factors, arising through time, whose relative importance is a matter of critical judgement as well as of objective knowledge.

The aim of this series is, then, to give the student the opportunity to examine with care an avowedly selective body of source materials. The topics have been chosen both because they are of contemporary importance and because they cut across established pedagogic boundaries between the various disciplines and between courses of professional instruction. We hope that these books will supplement, not replace, other forms of introductory reading; so both the length and the character of the Introductions will vary according to whether the particular editor has already written on the subject or not. Some Introductions will summarise what is already to be found elsewhere at greater length, but some will be original contributions to knowledge or even, on occasions, reasoned advocacies. Above all, however, I hope that this series will help to develop a method of introductory teaching that can show how and from where we come to reach the judgements that are to be found in secondary accounts and textbooks.

Bernard Crick

Foreword

The documents in this book have been selected to show the stages by which what we loosely, and not altogether accurately, call the Welfare State came into existence in Britain. In a broader setting the story has been told by the present editor elsewhere.[1] Here, however, the documents speak for themselves, though the historical process of which they form part is sketched in the introduction.

Considerations of space have made the choice of documents, and of the passages quoted from them, highly selective. Much has had to be omitted, but it is hoped that the material presented is sufficient to show the stages by which social legislation was developed and to illustrate at each stage how and why it was done.

The story is carried up to the 'Beveridge revolution' and the definitive legislation of 1945–8, with a final section on the fading of the Beveridge principles and the search for new policies in the light of developments since 1948.

My thanks are due, and are gratefully expressed, to my one-time colleague, Professor Bernard Crick, editor of the series in which this book appears, for offering me so congenial, if time-consuming, a task. His patience and that of the publishers, especially Julian Shuckburgh, has been tried by the time it has taken, amid other engrossing duties, to get the book within reasonable compass. I owe thanks also to B. T. Batsford, who allowed me to suspend work on another book in order to prepare this one.

Much of the material used has taken a good deal of tracking down. I have appreciated the help I have had from the library of my own university, and the trouble taken, in particular, by Miss R. L. Wells, Senior Library Assistant responsible for inter-library loans, who has spirited books for me from a variety of haunts. The staff and collections of the Sheffield City Library, the University

[1] *The Coming of the Welfare State* (Batsford, 4th ed., reprinted 1972).

and City Libraries of Manchester, the Library of the National Liberal Club and the Archives of the Greater London Council have between them contributed much. Nor should the inventor of photocopying be overlooked. The process is taken for granted now, but without it the task of copying so many documents in so many places would have been impossible for me.

Maurice Bruce

Acknowledgements

The author and publishers express their thanks to the following for permission to quote from copyright sources: the executors of the late Lord Beveridge for *Unemployment. A Problem of Industry*; Birmingham Corporation for *History of Birmingham*, vol. II, by Asa Briggs; Constable Ltd for *My Life* by George Lansbury; the Fabian Society for Tract 54; William Heinemann Ltd for *Winston S. Churchill* by Randolph Churchill, vol. II; Heinemann Educational for *The Hospitals* by B.Abel-Smith and *English Hospital Statistics* by R.Pinker; HMSO for Hansard and Command Papers, and *Social Trends*, No. 2; Macmillan for *The Life of Joseph Chamberlain* by J.L.Garvin, vol. I; Methuen Ltd for *The Life and Times of Edwin Chadwick* by S.E.Finer and *Lloyd George's Ambulance Wagon* ed. by Sir H.Bunbury; T.Nelson Ltd for *Poverty* by R.S.Rowntree; Oxford University Press for *Lark Rise to Candleford* by Flora Thompson, and Times Newspapers Ltd for *The Times* 28 February and 14 August 1940.

Acknowledgements

The author and publishers express their thanks to the following for permission to quote from copyright sources: The translation of the B:te Peel thoroughfare questionnaire [...]

Introduction

The story begins, if an actual date may be hazarded, in 1838, with the revelations in the Fourth Annual Report of the Poor Law Commissioners [2.2.3] of the financial burden to the poor law of epidemics, out of which was to spring all future legislation on public health. As the National Health Service is to most people today the aspect of the Welfare State with which they are most familiar and which they feel to be the most directly beneficial to them, so the first beginnings of a national movement of concern about public health are to be found in this report of 1838.

THE POOR LAW BACKGROUND

Concern for public health was not, however, a spontaneous development. It arose from experience of the operation of the reformed poor law of 1834, itself a move to check what was felt to be the excessive cost of the traditional system for the relief of poverty, originally established as far back as the last years of Elizabeth I. This system of poor relief was destined to remain on the statute book, much modified in practice but with its basic wording unaltered since 1601, until 1948, when the National Assistance Act formally abolished it. With the National Health Service and the new National Insurance system, as well as National Assistance, coming into operation then, 1948 was the year of the Welfare State, the year which finally saw the recognition of the community's concern for the welfare of all its members. This concern had developed gradually during the previous century and a half, as population had increased, society become more complex, and knowledge been gained of social problems and possible remedies – above all, as the growth of national resources through industrialisation had provided the means for social improvement on a scale never known in the world before. As W.W.Rostow has written, 'the emergence of the Welfare State is one manifestation of a society's moving beyond technical maturity',[1] and to be fully understood our story needs to be seen against a background which includes economic growth, amid much else.

There has been for centuries an open debate on the problems of the 'needy' in society, who they are, what their needs are, and how, if at all, they are to be helped. In recent times, as the needs and requirements of life have broadened, the debate itself has broadened to take into consideration whether the needs of any one social group can be singled out for special attention, whether, in fact, with respect to some at least of our needs, they can be adequately met at all unless the whole of society is covered.

Needs in earlier times were simple enough. The main concerns of society were to preserve order, to protect itself against marauders, whether internal or external, and, as far as it could, to prevent any of its members from perishing from want. It was to meet this last aim that there arose from the economic and social stresses of Tudor times the Elizabethan poor law, designed to provide relief for the 'lame, impotent, old and blind, and such other being poor, and not able to work', to set to work the able-bodied without occupation, to apprentice or find work for children who had no one to care for them, and to establish 'places of habitation' for the impotent poor – all within the framework of a stress on family responsibility and on the punishment of those menaces to society, the idle and vagrant who would not apply themselves to honest labour.

This analysis of the problems of social need was to endure, in almost exactly the same terms, for more than three centuries, to be restated last in 1930, and only set aside in 1948. By that time the poor law had long ceased to be the one expression of national social policy, and had been whittled down by the development of other services to the position of a last recourse for those otherwise unprotected. Moreover, the whole concept of social policy had been, and continues to be, broadened. It is now no longer merely a simple matter of work or relief: help is provided for many of the conditions and accidents incidental to life, especially, for instance, in matters of health, where few today could provide themselves unaided with treatment on the scale which medical progress has

[1] W.W.Rostow, *The Stages of Economic Growth* (1960), 11.

made possible. Hospitals need greater resources than used to be provided by charitable contributions or 'flag day' street collections, but even in matters of housing it is not merely the very poor who need assistance, while the industrial experience of recent years has shown that the risk of unemployment is not confined to the least skilled. It has been realised, in fact, that all, or almost all, at times have needs which only collective action can cope with on the scale expected by modern standards.

In the Elizabethan context, and for long after, 'the poor' were paupers, the destitute poor who had to seek relief. Most people until recent times have been poor in varying degrees, but their poverty was such a commonplace of existence that it was hardly recognised as such. Not until the nineteenth century, with its great advances in the resources of civilised living, was it realised that poverty was another problem in itself, denying to many not merely the basic needs of life but a share in the wider possibilities that civilisation was building up. No longer was it enough, therefore, to shrug off concern with the comforting biblical maxim 'the poor shall never cease out of the land'. It became increasingly obvious, especially as the advance of democracy broadened the basis of political power, that the benefits of civilised advancement were unevenly distributed. It had ceased to be a matter of charity – of the injunction (to complete the biblical quotation) 'thou shalt open thine hand wide' – and had become one of justice. Even then it could still be assumed that 'the poor' were but one section of society, however large, which further advance might in time be expected to lift into the ranks of the more affluent. What brought the final change of outlook were the economic depression of the inter-war years, with its tragedy of large-scale unemployment, the increase in medical knowledge, and consequent increase in the cost of treatment, and the enforced equality of the war years, 1940–5. After 1945, if the poor did not cease out of the land it was because all were liable to be needy in some sense at some time in their lives. The poor were no longer a race apart, to be treated as despised pauper dependents. Moreover, society itself could not afford too much poverty: the economy could not flourish on restricted resources and demand. The welfare of all was a matter of major concern to society as a whole. The Welfare State had arrived.

It is not intended to suggest by thus looking back to 1601 that it is there that the origins of the Welfare State are to be found. The aims of the Elizabethan framers of the law, except in their charitable concern for destitution, were totally different, formed in a different context, and with different social purposes in view.[1] Through its continuance into the radically changed conditions of centuries later, however, the poor law provided the base from which, in practice, social concern developed and broadened, out of it and away from it. Other countries have fashioned their welfare systems with no tradition of national poor law policy behind them, and Britain would almost certainly have developed a system of some kind – possibly one less confused and piecemeal – had there been no Elizabethan inheritance. The expectation of 1834 was that as the country developed and all classes shared in its increasing prosperity, provided that dependence was discouraged, the poor law would in time become superfluous. Later nineteenth-century experience proved, however, that without more positive intervention by the state not only would pauperism continue but large numbers of people would remain in poverty, ever in risk of slipping into pauperism. Gradually, therefore, the positive role of the state was developed, in order to ensure not merely the bare basic support of the poor law, but the establishment of all at standards acceptable to civilised society. Even then, however, it has been found essential, on various accounts, to preserve a basic minimum service – something like the poor law, though without its humiliating connotations – as a last resort, and to fill the gaps left by other services (at first called 'Assistance' but now, in more neutral terms, 'Supplementary Benefits').

THE DEVELOPMENT OF THE POOR LAW TO 1834

The Act of 1601 was the culmination of a series of fumbling attempts to deal with the widespread poverty of Tudor times. Lacking the means of central control, Tudor government looked for the operation of its policies to unpaid local officials, Justices of the Peace and others, who were in fact to dominate local government in the counties until 1888. For poor relief the basic unit of local administration was the parish, originally a medieval unit of ecclesiastical organisation, which now assumed a new significance under lay control. Each parish was to have its 'overseers of the

[1] See, for instance, J. Pound, *Poverty and Vagrancy in Tudor England* (1971).

poor', appointed by the JPs, and this principle of unpaid local service continued through the reorganisation of the poor law in 1834, which replaced the overseers by elected guardians, until the poor law itself was taken over by the County and County Borough Councils in 1930.

Despite the administrative changes of 1834, which also merged the parishes into unions, the parishes themselves retained financial responsibility for their own poor until 1865, when the burden was spread over the unions, eventually being assumed by the local authorities in 1930. In 1948 it passed to the nation as a whole with the abolition of the poor law and the establishment of the National Assistance Board.

The extent of parochial responsibility was defined by the Poor Relief Act of 1662, which set out the principles of each individual's legal 'settlement'. There was much criticism of the law as a barrier to the free movement of labour, but although removals of paupers back to their parish of settlement were numerous they affected mainly the most helpless of the poor: able-bodied men could be given certificates to enable them to look for work.

The greater humanity of the late eighteenth century limited removals to those actually in need of relief [1.2.2], but another fifty years were to pass before a limit of time was set after which a man was irremovable – five years in 1846 [1.2.3], reduced to three in 1861 and to one year in 1865, though each of these concessions left unchanged the legal settlement, and therefore the financial responsibility, until 1876, when three years' residence was declared sufficient to gain a new settlement. This three-year clause remained the law, and was restated in the Act of 1930 [1.2.5]. In the early years of the present century removals could still run into thousands (affecting as many as twelve thousand people in 1907, as the Poor Law Commission of that time found), but by 1930 they had been greatly reduced, usually by mutual agreement between authorities, though, owing to evacuation, problems of settlement still arose during the Second World War.

As the constant wrangling over settlements showed, the poor law was for long only grudgingly applied. Many attempts to recover its cost by 'setting the poor on work' in workhouses were made from the end of the seventeenth century, and, though they invariably proved futile, an Act passed in 1723 requiring that anyone claiming relief should enter the workhouse unwittingly stumbled on the principle of which so much was to be made from 1834.

Conditions in workhouses were so bad, however, that in the late eighteenth century an attempt was made to improve their administration and reserve them for people unable to look after themselves. Able-bodied men needing work were to be found work or given relief, and during the long years of war from 1793, when war prices and bad harvests kept food prices high, it was this policy that was followed. Workers were given allowances on a scale system according to the price of bread and the size of their families, and much distress was thereby prevented. The cost of poor relief rose alarmingly, however, and, with the notion that men were being paid to be idle and breed recklessly, led to a long debate[1] which culminated in the Royal Commission appointed by Lord Grey's reforming government in 1832. The cost had been some £2 million in the 1780s, but had doubled by 1803 and doubled again by 1818, after which it fell somewhat, only to rise again in the late 1820s and reach £7 million in 1832. This seemed serious enough, but the immediate occasion of the government's action was the 'Labourers' Revolt' of 1830, which particularly affected the areas in which the scale system operated. The government, alive to the political sensitiveness of the poor law issue, set up an independent inquiry, in the unusual form of a Royal Commission, to which it appointed, among others, Nassau Senior, one of the leading economists of the day, and Edwin Chadwick, who had already made a name for himself as a powerful advocate of social reform and had served Jeremy Bentham as secretary. These two were largely responsible for the Commission's report, which appeared in 1834; the proposals for future policy, which were to dominate poor law thinking until the next great investigation in 1905-9, were mainly Chadwick's contribution. Chadwick thus began a public career of social and administrative reform, first in the poor law and then in public health, which, though it lasted for only twenty years, made him one of the architects of nineteenth-century government.

[1] For this debate see J. R. Poynter, *Society and Pauperism. English Ideas on Poor Relief, 1795-1834* (1969).

THE POOR LAW RESHAPED

The influential report of 1834 is too long to be quoted at any length, but the principal recommendation and the significant sections of the Act that followed are set out in 2.1.1. The report was based on evidence of poor law practice from all over the country, but its conclusions were largely predetermined, and were put together somewhat hurriedly at the behest of a government which was anxious to allay the concern at the confusion and costliness of poor law administration. The members of the Commission were obsessed with the seeming dangers of the scale system, which they saw as 'opposed to the letter, and still more to the spirit' of the Elizabethan legislation. They therefore argued that relief should be provided only on proof of destitution, not as a bounty, and that the only convincing, and 'self-acting', proof of destitution was willingness to enter the workhouse where, as protection against 'fraudulent rapacity and perjury', the standard of maintenance should be 'less eligible than that of the independent labourer of the lowest class'. Such were the famous principles of 'less eligibility' and the deterrent workhouse test. The workhouses themselves were to be improved, and parishes to be joined together in unions to provide greater resources for their proper maintenance, while the different categories of paupers, especially the old people and children, were to be classified and admitted to separate institutions, though out-relief was still to be possible, under strict conditions. As for the new unions, they were to be served by salaried officials, and controlled by elected Guardians of the Poor, but a uniform policy was at last to be imposed by a central body of Poor Law Commissioners.

The Amendment Act did not restate poor law policy, which still stood unchanged on the statute book as in 1601, but it established a national and local administrative system for its operation. The combination of national control of policy with the reform of the local administration which had operated the poor law for more than two centuries was a revolutionary measure. It was not, however, a measure which went as far as the 'centralisation' to which nineteenth-century Britain, viewing events abroad with disfavour, was so much opposed. Yet it did create new governmental machinery, and the balance it tried to strike between the overall responsibility

7

of the central government and the desire of each locality to control its own affairs was inevitably tilted towards the former, as the growing complexity of life in the new industrialised urban society revealed the inadequacies of the local machinery of government. The story of the nineteenth century is largely the story of the realisation of the need for effective central legislation and control, and, though Chadwick and others in their plans for administrative reform constantly tried to maintain the balance, their radical empirical approach pointed the way towards the increasing scope of central government which the welfare of a rapidly increasing population demanded.

The sheet anchor of the new poor law policy was the workhouse test, a device adopted all the more readily because of the confusion of thought and policy which had so long marked poor law practice. Only the workhouse test, it was believed, could lower the rates and force the poor into self-reliance, and belief in it soon settled into a dogma. Like other reformers, too, the men of 1834 believed that the institutions they were remaking would in time 'wither away'. Once the workers had been weaned from pauperism, their self-reliance would make them independent of the poor law, even in times of sickness and old age, which could be made bearable by thrift and providence.

If these were the hopes they were hardly realised. Provident friendly societies flourished, it is true, though they barely touched any but the better-paid workers. Sickness, old age and the care of children kept the workhouses occupied however, though in the event, and for various reasons, most paupers were able to remain outside, on out-relief – no fewer than four-fifths of them in 1839, a year of depression, and still two-thirds in 1909, as the next Royal Commission noted.

The new-style workhouses themselves, deterrent and 'less eligible' as they were intended to be, speedily came to be viewed with hatred and horror [2.3.4], denounced as 'Bastilles', with a depth of feeling which still lingers today. Workhouse policy was not intended to be cruel, but the regulations issued by Chadwick as secretary of the new Poor Law Commissioners in 1835 [2.2.1] demanded, if they were to be humanely operated, a degree of administrative skill that was all too rare at the time, and laches gained in the telling, while 'less eligibility' was formidable enough when poverty was rife outside.

The most serious gap in the new policy, however, was that in its obsession with the seeming errors of the past it made no provision for the new industrial urban society that was coming into existence, with problems markedly different from those of its rural precursor. As the Sheffield *Iris* complained in 1836, 'Are the whole of the worthy poor of this kingdom to be starved to death because a set of stupid farmers [in Suffolk] choose to pay wages from the parish funds?'[1] It was, in fact, in the north that resistance to the new poor law was fiercest, eventually merging into Chartism, as one aspect of that many-sided movement. For two problems in particular – industrial unemployment, and the disease and distress that arose from urban squalor – the new system had no adequate answer, and it was from its grappling with these that reforms of the greatest significance for the future were to emerge.

At the very moment when the Commissioners were turning their attention to the north, industry there was struck by depression and unemployment, the beginnings of what were later to be called the 'hungry forties'. Chadwick found himself, without preparation, having to suggest means by which men in distress through lack of work could be relieved when workhouse accommodation was inadequate, as it almost invariably was to be in times of sudden acute unemployment. His solution was the device of the labour test, by which men could be provided with out-relief in return for work which would be a test of their need [2.2.4]. Regulations were issued to control this [2.2.6–7], the labour test usually consisting of breaking stone for road repairs. It was not until the 1880s that it began to be realised that stone-breaking was no more of a solution to unemployment than the workhouse itself, but as no alternative was devised the practice survived a further investigation by the Royal Commission of 1905–9 and lingered on into the 1920s. Only in the greatly different conditions of the 1930s was a more constructive policy adopted [8.3.3 and 8.2.9].

In areas where the labour test did not apply [2.2.5] men had to go to the workhouse, with their families if they had any, though a 'modified workhouse test' was later devised, by which if a man entered the workhouse his wife and family could be relieved outside. This procedure was another that was much resorted to in some areas during the years of unemployment in the 1920s.

[1] M. E. Rose, 'The Anti-Poor Law Movement in the North of England', *Northern History*, I (1966), 82.

Tasks were also set inside the workhouse, and it was the scandalous mismanagement of the Andover workhouse [2.3.3] which brought down the Commission in 1847, and set in its place a normal government department, the Poor Law Board, with a president in Parliament and Chadwick excluded thenceforth from poor law administration. Not until the Local Government Board succeeded the Poor Law Board in 1871 was there again a firm policy at the centre.

THE PUBLIC HEALTH PROBLEM

With his departure from the poor law began Chadwick's second career, in public health. In the 1838 Report of the Poor Law Commission he had drawn attention to the high cost of sickness and death resulting from squalid living conditions, which had already caused concern in the cholera epidemic of 1832. Chadwick's revelations now shocked opinion to such an extent that he was commissioned to undertake the wider investigations which led in 1842 to the publication of his most important work, the *Report on the Sanitary Condition of the Labouring Population*.[1] In the following year Sir Robert Peel appointed a Royal Commission, which reported in its turn in 1844–5 [3.1.1]. At the same time came the formation of a national Health of Towns Association, whose membership included such men as the great evangelical reformer, Lord Ashley, afterwards Seventh Earl of Shaftesbury, Lord Morpeth (who was to battle for sanitary reform in Lord John Russell's government from 1846), Disraeli, Dickens, Southwood Smith, and a future health official of distinction, Dr John Simon; Chadwick was active in the background.

Despite the efforts of the Association there was much resistance to government interference in local affairs, even in such a matter as public health. Morpeth introduced a Public Health Bill in 1847, but was able to carry it only in a modified form in the following year, though aided then by the alarm at the second, and more virulent, cholera epidemic, which killed eighty thousand people. Under the terms of the Act a General Board of Health was established, with Morpeth himself as chairman and Ashley and Chadwick as the other members. In the six years of the Board's life much local activity for the improvement of sanitary conditions

[1] Reprinted in 1965 with an introduction by Professor M.W. Flinn.

was stimulated, but hostile influences remained strong, and were not converted by Chadwick's well-known abrasiveness of manner. In 1854 the Board came to an end and, like the Poor Law Commission before it, was converted into a minor department with a political head. With it also ended Chadwick's career in the public service.

There followed a long period of confusion. In its new form the Board continued until 1859, less active than its predecessor but achieving one stroke of importance by bringing into government service Dr John Simon, who since 1848 had been Medical Officer of the City of London. His had been the second such appointment made in the country, preceded only by that of Dr William Duncan at Liverpool in 1847.

Simon thus began a career in national administration which was to make him the dominant figure in health matters of the years from 1855 to 1875, as Chadwick had been of the earlier period. The Board itself finally disappeared in 1859, its duties being divided between the Home Office and the Privy Council, which, with Simon to advise it, concerned itself with general health policy. There followed a long series of investigations by Simon, who presented his findings year by year in a series of pungent reports [3.2.2] which prepared opinion for the next legislative moves. In 1866, hastened by another outbreak of cholera – fortunately the last which the country was to suffer – Parliament passed a Sanitary Act which for the first time *required* authorities to improve conditions [3.3.1], and a major investigation, the Royal Sanitary Commission, followed. The Commission's report in 1871 led at last to definitive public health measures in 1872 and 1875. The first established two sets of sanitary authorities – in towns, councils, elsewhere, the guardians – all of them with the duty of appointing medical staff. The final step, the climax of Simon's career, was the consolidating Act of 1875 which was to remain the basis of sanitary legislation until 1936.

If the 1848 Act had at least recognised public health as an aspect of government in its own right, not merely as an adjunct of the poor law, the 1875 Act brought to an end the period of *environmental* sanitary legislation. Henceforth the concern was to be increasingly with *personal* health, as the advances of medicine and surgery, and especially the discoveries of the bacteriologists, opened up entirely new possibilities.

Following the Sanitary Commission's report, the central administration of public health was also reorganised. In 1871 public health and the poor law were combined in a Local Government Board headed by a ministerial president. It was a more economic and less thoroughgoing approach than the Commission had proposed, and one in which the poor law was inevitably the senior partner, while the new department was at times almost overwhelmed by the weight of its wide-ranging responsibilities. As a result the Board (LGB for short) became a byword for caution and dilatoriness and adherence to strict poor law principles. Simon retired from it in disgust in 1876, but it was to lumber on until 1919, when it was at last replaced by a Ministry of Health, though one still encumbered with the poor law, until that was abolished in 1948.

With the rise in environmental standards, public health gradually improved from the fifties onward, but the most striking success was achieved in the control of smallpox, largely by a campaign waged over the years by Simon. By the end of the century the ancient scourge had almost been eradicated.

The 1860s, which saw the Sanitary and Vaccination Acts, saw also the beginnings of an effective hospital service. An Act of 1867 [3.3.3] led to much-needed improvements in poor law hospitals, and within a few years a number of new 'infirmaries' were being built, some of them on a lavish scale. Local authorities received the power to found their own hospitals, though they built mainly for infectious diseases in 'isolation hospitals'. The creation of more poor law infirmaries raised problems at a time when other hospitals were scarce. For many people they were the only hospitals available, but their use threatened loss of voting rights [2.1.2], a serious matter after the franchise extensions of 1867 and 1884. A special Act was passed in 1885 to exempt medical relief from franchise disqualification,[1] a measure later bewailed by a LGB official as 'the first marked departure from poor law principles'.[2] The pauper disqualification itself was not removed until the next extension of the franchise in 1918. Long before this, as was pointed out to the Poor Law Commission of 1905–9, the availability of the poor law infirmaries, together with

---

[1] For an intriguing account of the political circumstances in which this Act was passed see B. Rodgers, 'The Medical Relief (Disqualification Removal) Act, 1885. A Storm in a Political Teacup', *Parliamentary Affairs*, 1955–6.

[2] Report of the RC on the Poor Law, 1909, App. I, 182, 3302.

the abrogation of the franchise disqualification, had led them to be regarded, in effect, as 'state hospitals'.

THE HOUSING PROBLEM

From health to housing – an essential part of environmental improvement, and one which was inextricably involved in health considerations. While, however, there could be resistance to public health measures in the name of local freedom, demands for housing improvements entailed interference with the sacred rights of property. As a police report of 1854 noted of one owner of insanitary dwellings, 'he thought he ought not to be dictated to, as to the way his property was to be managed'.[1] Standards could be laid down in legislation as to cleanliness, sanitation and the avoidance of overcrowding, but it was difficult to enforce them until there was a body of medical officers and sanitary inspectors, supported by their authorities in the enforcement of regulations. The 1848 Act prescribed some essential requirements, and the 1866 Act went so far as to try to check overcrowding, though without offering any definition (which was not, in fact, achieved until 1935). The main concern of legislation was with sanitary measures and the banning of the use of cellars as living accommodation, such as was only too common in Lancashire, especially among the unfortunate Irish immigrants. Regulations of this kind were consolidated in the 1875 Act, and a further Act of 1885, which empowered local authorities to make their own by-laws, rendered possible the application of an effective code of sanitary practice.

Improved sanitary standards, however, meant higher building costs. Most workingmen earned too little to meet the rent of decent housing, and houses built for them therefore tended to be small, and tightly packed in an area of land so as to bring in the maximum possible rent. They were commonly built back-to-back, or in narrow courts, and the lack of through currents of air which proved so detrimental to health was excused on the grounds that the poor were not sufficiently well-fed or well-clad to be able to withstand fresh air. As early as 1840 Lord Normanby, then Home Secretary, tried, at Southwood Smith's prompting, to ban

[1] Second Report of the Commissioner of Police on ... Common Lodging Houses, 1854, Appendix.

back-to-back building, but was foiled by building interests. Not until 1909 was a ban finally included in legislation [4.3.6], being followed then by a medical report on the health hazards of housing of this kind [4.3.7]. Meanwhile, however, some authorities had taken their own precautions – Manchester, by local legislation, as early as 1844 [4.1.1] – though at least one other town, Leeds, found ways of evading the law even after 1909.

The truth was that with wages low, and builders expecting a normal seven per cent on their outlay, decent working-class housing was impracticable except by subventions of some kind, and was to become increasingly so as standards rose. The nineteenth century saw a number of philanthropic building societies, notably the Peabody Trust in London (1862), but as they also expected some return on their capital their rents, though lower than in private building, still did not meet the needs of the really poor. Peabody Trust tenants, for instance, had an average wage of 23s a week, which was fairly high by contemporary standards, and paid between 2s 6d and 5s, which brought the Trust a return of three per cent. Aid from public funds, it was eventually realised, was essential, but this was long regarded with horror as a misuse of them, and it was an article of faith for many that private enterprise would in time do all that was necessary. Even when local authorities were given effective powers in 1890 they were slow to move, and it was not until 1919, when the scale of the problem could no longer be evaded, and Treasury grants were made available, that a public housing policy can be said to have come into existence.

The 1890 Housing of the Working Classes Act [4.3.4] was the climax of forty years of concern and legislation. Lord Ashley took the first step in 1851 by persuading Parliament to pass an Act empowering local authorities to build homes for the 'labouring classes' [4.1.2] – not to be confused with his other measure of the same year for the licensing and regulation of Common Lodging Houses. The Act proved totally ineffective, however, as no authority would spend public money for such a purpose. An attempt to stir interest in the idea was made in 1866, when the Public Works Loan Commissioners were authorised to lend money for the purpose [4.1.3], but the only authority to take advantage of the concession was Liverpool, which built St Martin's Cottages, opened in 1869, and therefore has the distinction of being the earliest municipal housing authority in the country. Liverpool borrowed only £13,000, however, of the total of more than half a million lent by the time of the Royal Commission on the Housing of the Working Classes in 1884. Most of the loans went to the philanthropic building societies, £300,000 to the Peabody trustees alone.

Two Acts that followed, the Torrens Act of 1868 and the Cross Act of 1875, tried to improve matters by giving authorities powers to clear insanitary buildings, single buildings in the one case and whole areas in the other. These achieved little, however, as authorities in general lacked both the powers and the will to replace condemned housing, and private builders could not afford to do it. Liverpool alone, having cleared land under the Cross Act and found no one willing to build on it, proceeded to move itself and erected the impressive Victoria Dwellings. Elsewhere, though sites were cleared, they often remained undeveloped, unless philanthropists were willing to act. An exception was the spectacular example of Birmingham where, under the bold leadership of Joseph Chamberlain, a new centre was created in the heart of the city.

With population increasing, and insanitary housing being pulled down, overcrowding became a serious issue. Attempts were made to encourage people to move further out, but by the 1880s it was evident that legislation was doing little to improve matters. Political opinion was roused by parliamentary investigations, and public opinion by newspaper revelations and the famous pamphlet put out by the Rev. Andrew Mearns, *The Bitter Cry of Outcast London*.[1] A Royal Commission was appointed in 1884, and disclosed most of the evils, though it prescribed no bold remedy. The 1890 Act at last made Ashley's pioneer effort of 1851 effective, and in 1900, to ease matters, authorities were enabled to develop sites outside their own boundaries, but there was still great reluctance to spend rate-funds on house building for anyone [4.3.9]. An Act of 1909 [4.3.6] extended the powers of authorities, and even banned back-to-back housing, but the last years before 1914 saw comparatively little municipal building, as the taxes levied on land development by the Lloyd George budget of 1909 kept much land off the market.

[1] A new edition of *The Bitter Cry*, edited and introduced by Professor A. S. Wohl, was published in 1970.

15

THE TURNING POINT OF THE 1880s

The LGB on its establishment in 1871 was faced with what seemed an alarming increase in out-relief, arising from the depressed years of the 1860s, and tightened its regulations, arguing that, with the sick better cared for in the new hospitals, stricter adherence to rules was possible. There followed what was later called a 'crusade against out-relief'. The 1870s were in the main easier, but economic stresses recurred in the last years of the decade, and the 1880s saw increasing public concern at social conditions. The 1880s were indeed a turning point. The realities of poverty, as of housing conditions, began to be appreciated, and policy increasingly concerned itself with its causes, rather than with the crude numerical records of pauperism.

The 1880s were also a formative period of political and intellectual activity, marked, as one young contemporary, Beatrice Potter (Webb), recorded later, by 'a new consciousness of sin among men of intellect and men of property' at the uneven distribution of Britain's increasing wealth.[1] The influence of T.H. Green's idealist philosophy began to spread from Oxford, and to lead many into social work, including the university settlements which followed the lead of Samuel Barnett at Toynbee Hall in 1884. Of greater significance for the future was the formation of Socialist groups, H.M. Hyndman's Social Democratic Federation, William Morris's Socialist League and the Fabian Society, with G.B. Shaw and Sidney Webb among its earliest members.

CAUSES OF POVERTY

Unemployment

In political circles the future seemed to be in the hands of the radical Joseph Chamberlain, who produced his 'unauthorised programme' in 1885, made the first moves in 1886 towards tackling unemployment outside the poor law, and in 1891 took up, albeit inadequately, the case for old age pensions. In both of these last Chamberlain's initiative, though he never took it further, sparked

[1] Beatrice Webb, *My Apprenticeship* (Penguin edn. 1971), 191.

off developments that were to prove decisive, if long delayed. In the matter of unemployment he was struck, during the severe winter of 1885–6, by the failure of the poor law statistics to reflect the distress which he knew to exist, and while in office at the LGB in the early months of 1886, before his split with Gladstone over home rule for Ireland, he proposed special measures of relief. In this course he may well have been influenced by the SDF riots in London in February, which brought the distress home to many among the public hitherto unconcerned. He concluded, rightly enough, that men normally in steady work were unwilling to resort to the poor law, and therefore encouraged the provision of special work for them by local authorities, to 'tide them over' until employment picked up again [7.2.1]. Thus began the twenty-year delusion which culminated in the Unemployed Workmen Act of 1905 [7.2.2]. The policy proved a failure, as it hardly affected the type of workman for whom, in periods of *un*employment, it was intended, but attracted instead a class of *under*-employed workers, whose existence had hardly been suspected. The truth was eventually exposed by William Beveridge [7.2.3 and 7.6.1], who showed that the problem was one of industrial organisation, not, as the poor law would have it, of personal moral failure. The logical answer, therefore, was insurance against unemployment, which came in 1911.

The Revelations of Booth and Rowntree

While Chamberlain was turning attention to the distress caused by unemployment, a wealthy amateur investigator, Charles Booth, was initiating an impressive inquiry into living conditions in London which he was not to complete until 1902, and which cost him in the process some £33,000. Booth had been struck in 1885 by a claim by H. M. Hyndman that a quarter of London's working-class was living in poverty, and set out to disprove it, only to find, after a campaign of meticulous investigation, that Hyndman had underestimated the proportion, which was nearer one-third. What Booth showed, in fact, was that the prevailing view of poverty in general was fundamentally at fault, as in its reliance on the shibboleths of 1834 it ascribed to moral weakness what was due no less to social and economic conditions over which the poor could have no control. Such conclusions, commented Beatrice Webb, who had worked with Booth in his researches, 'reverberated in the world of politics and philanthropy'.[1] Even before Booth had completed his seventeen-volume study of the *Life and Labour of the People in London*, however, confirmation of his findings had come from a similar inquiry undertaken in York in 1899 by Benjamin Seebohm Rowntree [6.3.2]. Rowntree's book, *Poverty. A Study of Town Life*, published in 1901, had unexpected and far-reaching consequences, since it came into the hands of a young MP, Winston Churchill [6.3.3], and shocked him into a concern with social problems which was in time to lead to the first positive government intervention against unemployment.

Old Age

Booth in his investigations was particularly struck by the high proportion of the aged among paupers [6.1.2], and from 1891 became an advocate of non-contributory pensions, paid for out of taxation, a startling notion at the time, especially at the very moment when Chamberlain was preparing his own scheme for mere state support of voluntary savings. The subject was investigated in 1893–5 by a Royal Commission, which produced little more than meagre proposals for improvements in out-relief and workhouse conditions, on which the LGB took some action. Further consultations got no further, especially after the outbreak of the South African War in 1899. Meanwhile, after New Zealand had adopted non-contributory pensions in 1897, a national movement was formed, over which Booth presided, and although the Conservative government consistently refused to move in the matter, fearing its cost, the Liberal government of 1905 eventually brought in a scheme in 1908 [7.3.1–2]. It did not provide universal coverage, as Booth would have wished, but it marked a complete break with the poor law both in granting pensions as of right, and without further investigation, to old people of narrowly limited means, and in constituting a national service, not, like the poor law, one subject to local variations. Never before had the state shown such concern for the welfare of its citizens: the fear of the workhouse in the years of decline had been lifted. Stalwarts of 1834 could only predict ruin, and hint darkly at the awful example of the bread and circuses of Imperial Rome.

[1] Webb, *Apprenticeship*, 252.

THE 'TIDE OF SOCIAL PITY'

A new concept of national concern for the well-being of the individual citizen, rather than merely for his environment, was beginning to take shape. From the 1890s, while interest in old age pensions was rising, concessions were made to old people on relief [5.1.5–8], which drew the complaint from an official of the LGB that a new poor law was being created. At the same time the realisation that pauper children were hardly responsible for their condition, and would not necessarily inherit a 'pauper taint', led to pressure for their removal from workhouses [5.2]. Then came the shock of the South African War, which revealed the low physical standard of many who volunteered for service, and raised the fear of national physical deterioration at a time when Britain was faced by a Europe of conscript armies. A committee looked into the position in 1903–4 and, while playing down the apprehensions, recommended more attention to the health of schoolchildren. Some of its recommendations were translated into the Acts of 1906–7 which provided for school meals and medical inspection [7.1.2]; others were included in the first Children Act, passed in 1908 [7.1.3]. With old age pensions these were the measures of a new age, reflecting the general concern at the inadequacies of modern society and the realisation of the expanding resources which made greater generosity possible. Lloyd George spoke in 1911 of 'a tide of social pity that was only waiting for a chance of expression' [7.7.2]: the construction of a welfare state had begun.

REMEDIES

Poor Law Reform?

One manifestation of the general concern was the appointment by the Conservative government, on its very last day in office, of a Royal Commission on the Poor Law and – significant addition – the relief of distress [7.5]. LGB officials had hoped to see a return to deterrent policies, but although the Commission spoke with two voices when it reported in 1909, there was at least agreement that the existing poor law should be brought to an end and its functions taken over in some way by the local authorities. There was agreement also that the state should be involved in the provision of

Labour Exchanges and the encouragement of insurance against unemployment [7.5.2]. Little came of the proposals on functional reform for many years, until Neville Chamberlain swept away the guardians in his reform of local government in 1929. In the meantime, however, Labour Exchanges, National Insurance against unemployment, and both insurance and medical care for sickness were introduced by Lloyd George and Churchill in the legislation of 1909–11.

Insurance

During the passage of the Bill for old age pensions Lloyd George's thoughts had turned to further measures for checking poverty, and in the summer of 1908 he visited Germany, where sickness insurance had been introduced by Bismarck in 1883 and pensions in 1889, though there was no unemployment insurance. On his return he began to prepare plans for a vast insurance scheme which would provide protection against many of the accidents of life which had driven people to the poor law – sickness, infirmity, unemployment and death of a breadwinner. Against these menaces most workers had little protection, except in the case of death, as Lloyd George showed in introducing his Bill in 1911 (7.7.1). At a very early stage of his planning he found, however, that he had to abandon any prospect of providing a death grant which might help widows and orphans. There was too much at stake for the organisations engaged in funeral insurance – the friendly societies, the trade unions, and, above all, the 'industrial assurance' companies, with their vast business – for them to permit him even to consider some kind of widows and orphans pension, such as he had had in mind. In the event that was not to come until 1925.

Sickness was another matter, however, though there again Lloyd George had to make concessions. His intention had been to work through the friendly societies, but the assurance companies, scenting possible future threats to their business, insisted on coming in, and faced by the threat of their political influence [7.7.3] Lloyd George had to create the artificial device of the non-profit-making 'approved society' in order to include them. After them there were the doctors to be placated, the most touchy and suspicious of all professional groups, and, although they were eventually to benefit most from the new service, the argument with them as to terms was strenuous and protracted. Delay was caused by the constitutional struggle over the budget of 1909, which was intended to raise money for the new policies, and it was not until 1911 that the National Insurance Act, with Part 1 devoted to health insurance, was finally carried, a notable triumph for the man who, in the famous phrase, made the nation lick stamps.[1]

Part II of the Act dealt with unemployment insurance. In their last year of office the Conservatives had brought in the Unemployed Workmen Act [7.2.2.] to encourage the help to unemployed workers in 'tiding over', without recourse to the poor law, which Chamberlain had introduced in 1886. This last desperate attempt to cure unemployment with relief was soon seen to be of little avail, but, as Lloyd George realised, it had in effect committed the country to government intervention on behalf of the unemployed. Beveridge exposed the fallacies of the situation, and both poor law reports of 1909 accepted the need for a new approach to unemployment, with labour exchanges to assist men to find work. Germany had failed to light on a test of need which would make unemployment insurance practicable, but Beveridge was able to show that the labour exchange could provide such a test through its register of work available [7.6.1], and it was his enthusiasm for exchanges that brought him into government service in 1908. Winston Churchill had entered the government as a junior minister in 1905, with an interest in social problems already stirred by Rowntree [6.3.3] and the Webbs. In 1908, when Asquith became Prime Minister, Churchill had succeeded Lloyd George at the Board of Trade, and through the Webbs had met Beveridge, who in the idea of exchanges presented him with the congenial task of setting on foot something new and striking. Labour Exchanges followed, with Beveridge as director of the new service, Trade Boards to improve conditions in 'sweated' occupations and finally, in 1911, unemployment insurance.

As Lloyd George pointed out, a good deal was known, through friendly society experience, about the incidence of sickness. Unemployment was almost an unknown quantity, however, since, although there was trade union experience to draw on, only a minority of workers were in unions, and those not the most prone

---

[1] The fullest and most up-to-date account of National Health Insurance, based on a study of the Cabinet papers, is B. B. Gilbert, *The Evolution of National Insurance in Great Britain* (1966).

to unemployment. A cautious start was therefore made with a few trades, mainly in construction and engineering, known to be particularly prone. There were Labour and trade union objections to levying contributions from the workers themselves, and these were to continue for some time, partly because it was thought that the state should provide but partly also because men who felt themselves to be in secure work resented paying for others in less secure occupations. Indeed, as was made clear on a number of occasions during the heavy unemployment of the inter-war years, the greater part of the cost of supporting the unemployed was met by the contributions of the employed and their employers [8.2.1 and 5]. Not until 1934 was the burden of long-term unemployment made a wholly national charge through the creation of Unemployment Assistance.

Unemployment insurance on Churchill's lines was launched in 1912–13, helped by conditions of rising employment. During the war, war-workers were covered, though other workers refused to be brought in. In 1920 however, in the euphoria of victory and reconstruction, and with no foretaste of what was soon to come, the scheme was extended to most workers, except groups in occupations deemed secure, public employees, domestic servants, and railway and agricultural workers, whose contributions might have been helpful in the years ahead (agricultural and domestic workers were to be covered in 1936 and 1938). The 1920 Act increased the number of workers covered to eleven million, but even before it came into effect unemployment was rising fast, and the scheme never had time to establish itself; until the fundamental overhaul of 1934 it could only stagger from expedient to expedient, in the Micawberish hope that better times were on the way.

WAR AND 'RECONSTRUCTION'

The war of 1914–18 came as a setback to projects which Lloyd George had in mind, especially for the improvement of the health services, and did not bring any general stirring of thought about social problems such as the conflict of 1939–45 was to engender. When peace came there was a widespread impression that a return to pre-war conditions was not only possible but unqualifiedly desirable [8.1.6], and financial orthodoxy proved to have learnt little from the methods of wartime finance. The Labour party, now

strong enough to form the Opposition, and since 1918 avowedly
Socialist, had other views, but Socialism was suspiciously equated
with Bolshevism, and regarded by many with horror. Lloyd
George had appointed a loyal follower, the medical politician
Christopher Addison, as Minister of Reconstruction in 1917, and
Addison struggled hopefully for new policies in health and housing [8.1.1–2 and 5]. The forces of inertia and economy were too
strong, however, while for a variety of reasons Lloyd George failed
to give the lead that was required, and in 1921 callously sacrificed
him in order to maintain the political hold which was in fact
already slipping from his own grasp.[1]

Addison and many others had hoped for the creation of a
Ministry of Health which would bring together the public health
responsibilities of the LGB and the more personal services of
National Health Insurance and give a lead to health policy in the
country. This was also the aim of Robert Morant, the brilliant
civil servant who had been given the task of running NHI in 1912,
and the two came together as Minister and Secretary when, as
part of the reconstruction policies, the LGB disappeared in 1919
and a Ministry of Health took its place. There had already been
consideration of the future of the poor law, and in 1917 the
Maclean Committee had recommended its passing to the local
authorities very much in the terms of the minority report of 1909.
Addison hoped to achieve this transference, but, weakened as he
was by Morant's premature death in 1920, and burdened by the
pressing problems of the new Ministry, he was unable to make any
move before his fall. Moreover, by that time the onset of heavy unemployment had rendered the existing organisation too useful to
be scrapped in a hurry. The poor law therefore remained with the
guardians until Neville Chamberlain took the decisive step in
1929. Meanwhile, in the mood of economy which prevailed from
1921, the Ministry was unable to make any significant developments in health policy, such as had been proposed in 1920 by the
report of a committee chaired by Dr Bertrand Dawson [8.1.2].
What might have been a great measure of reform therefore remained hardly more than the LGB writ large.

---

[1] Lloyd George never again held office after 1922, but Addison joined the
Labour party, held office twice, and became a peer and the first Labour Knight
of the Garter.

HOUSING POLICY FROM 1919

Addison's greatest defeat, and the immediate cause of his downfall, came over housing. In the election campaign that followed the armistice in 1918 Lloyd George had promised 'a fit country for heroes to live in'. As shown above, housing progress had been slow before the war, and while wartime conditions had necessitated control of rents [8.1.4] the very fact of control deterred the private builder from the construction of working-class houses which, at least until the 1930s, necessarily meant houses for renting. The need for a great programme of building was recognised in 1919, but its scale was underestimated and it was regarded as largely a temporary means of filling the gap until private building could rise to the task. Moreover, the building industry itself was disorganised, materials were scarce, and the competition for money for post-war developments of all kinds was keen.

However, a crash programme of local authority building was agreed on, and Addison carried the Housing and Town Planning Act, 1919 [8.1.5], which both imposed on authorities, for the first time, the duty of meeting the needs of their areas, and offered them Treasury grants towards repaying the loans they would have to raise for the purpose. Thus began the direct involvement of the central government with housing needs, and the acceptance of the principle of local authority building. The shock of the cost of the Addison experiment caused both to falter after his removal, but they were restored in 1923–4 and have continued since, never more than in the years after 1945.

What brought the Addison programme to a sudden halt in 1921 was the high cost of the loans which local authorities were left to negotiate for themselves in the face of much competition, combined with the strain on the Treasury from the fact that its contribution was a global sum, with no limit to the share absorbed by each individual house built. Addison was denounced for inefficiency, but by the time he fell the situation was already easing, though John Wheatley, Minister of Health in the Labour government of 1924, was able to show how much the cost of houses was due to interest charges [8.6.3].

A second Act of 1919 provided grants for private building, and the two together produced in all some 113,000 houses, at a cost to the Treasury alone of £130 million by 1939, representing about two-thirds of the total amount of £208 million provided for nearly a million and a half houses between the wars [8.6.8]. It was 1923 before building was resumed, and Neville Chamberlain, true to the spirit of Conservative housing policy, then provided Treasury grants, to be administered by the local authorities, principally for private building and without any charge on the rates, but with a limit on the grant for each house [8.6.1–2]. Because of the uncertainties of demand and finance, however, the building industry was slow to move, and it was Wheatley who in 1924 set it on a new path by guaranteeing a fifteen-year programme which was to make possible not only the continuance of local authority building but the immense programme of private building that ensued in the 1930s. In addition, Wheatley restored Addison's combination of local authority building with rate support and Treasury backing, all at vastly less cost, even though he also increased the grant on each house. Building was then able to go steadily ahead, to such an extent, indeed, that by 1930 it was possible to turn attention again to slum clearance and rehousing. This was a more acceptable task for the Conservative policies of the 'National' government from 1931 than the encouragement of new local authority housing, and in 1933 the life of Wheatley's Act was cut short. A drive on slums and, from 1935, on overcrowding was then launched, though the vast amount of clearance that had to be undertaken after 1945 is evidence that, as many observers maintained at the time, the scope of the drive was too narrow. As it was, by 1939 only half of the officially-declared slums had been cleared in what had been announced as a five-year programme. With all the new houses built since 1919, some four million in all, the contrast with remaining squalor was more marked than ever, and unfortunately was to be protracted by war. However, the country had come a long way since Addison's first bold move.

UNEMPLOYMENT BETWEEN THE WARS

Housing was a preoccupation throughout the 1920s and 1930s, but the dominant concern was with unemployment. Many were the devices adopted to stretch the notion of insurance cover for workers who had technically lost – or, as in many cases, had never been able to earn – their right to benefit, and to check whether there was a real will to work if work were available. The failure to achieve recovery in the economy, or rather in those sections of industry which were manifestly declining, defied all efforts at reducing unemployment to acceptable levels, and many among the unemployed had to turn to the poor law. Guardians were under heavy pressure, both financial and social, while the strain on local finances in the areas of high unemployment was in painful contrast to the comparative affluence and – it has to be admitted – the common incredulity and indifference of other parts of the country. Small wonder that in some parts the guardians themselves, hitherto jealous of their position, called for a national policy of relief.

The Unemployment Act of 1927, based on the recommendations put forward by the Blanesburgh Committee [8.2.5] in the hopeful expectation of economic revival, had introduced 'transitional benefits' for men out of insurance benefit, and these were continued from 1931 on a different basis, as part of the economy measures of the 'National' government, in the form of 'transitional payments' made through the new Public Assistance committees of local authorities but financed by the Treasury, and subject to a means test adapted from the poor law. They implied, in effect, the recognition of a national responsibility for the long-term unemployed. In 1930 the Labour government had appointed a Royal Commission on Unemployment, and the Commission's final report, which appeared in 1932, advocated a similar system of relief, local in administration and assessment of need, but under the general supervision of the Ministry of Labour. The Treasury was already uneasy, however, at the local distribution of national funds, and Chamberlain in any case was thinking on different lines. There followed in 1934 the division of the problem of the unemployed into two sections, the insurable risks and the long-term needs, the former administered by an Unemployment Insurance Committee, the latter cared for by a separate Unemployment Assistance Board. The UAB was accompanied by the economical device of the household means test, which was to be the cause of so much personal and political bitterness until it was abolished by the wartime government, at Labour's insistence, in 1941. After a bad start, however, the UAB settled down, and both parts of the new system were aided by a revival of employment. With all but the worst cases of unemployment now in the care of the UAB, the poor law was left only with the social residuum for which there was as yet no other statutory provision.

THE END OF THE GUARDIANS

During the 1920s the poor law had struggled on, while the Ministry of Health, true to its LGB origins, endeavoured to maintain strict standards, and called to order – even sometimes suspended [8.3.2] – boards of guardians whose 'extravagance' in relief exhausted their credit. It became obvious that the financial areas on which the guardians could draw needed enlarging, and when Chamberlain became Minister of Health again in Baldwin's second government he prepared an ambitious programme of reform on several fronts. He planned to improve local government by introducing a system of block grants based on need, and by increasing the area of resources, which meant, among other things, moving the poor law to the authorities. Across his plans, however, swept those of Churchill, now Chancellor of the Exchequer. Churchill's aim, after the now notorious return to the gold standard in 1925, was to stimulate industrial recovery first by lowering taxation and then by 'derating' industry – relieving it of a great part of its responsibility for rates by lowering assessments – while compensating local authorities for their loss of revenue. As a one-time Councillor and Lord Mayor of Birmingham Chamberlain was horrified at this suggestion of Treasury interference in local finance, but he had no alternative but to agree, though the inevitable effects of derating in reducing the resources of boards of guardians strengthened his case for their abolition. Derating followed, as did the Local Government Act 1929, which finally put an end to the narrowly local control of the poor law and transferred it to public assistance committees of local authorities. The days of *ad hoc* authorities, commented the annual report of the Ministry of Health, were now past [8.3.3(2)]. The Act made no changes, however, in the law itself, which was restated in 1930, in the event for the last time, and in its historic terms [8.3.4]. On the other hand, a new and more constructive relief policy was introduced [8.3.3(2)]. A few minor poor law Acts followed, the last of them, in 1938 [8.3.4], an apt comment in itself on nearly 350 years of history.

The most obvious result of the change in poor law administration was the opportunity given to local authorities by the absorption of the poor law hospitals, and the extension of their own powers under the 1929 Act, to develop their hospital services. Their powers were further increased in 1936, by the first major public health Act since 1875 [8.5.2], but the depression prevented much hospital building [8.5.3] and it was not until the demands of war and the revelations of wartime evacuation struck home that the country came to realise how serious its needs were in hospital provision. Hence the attention to plans for improvement during the war years which was to lead to a newly constituted National Health Service.

CONTRIBUTORY PENSIONS

With his plans for changes in local government Chamberlain had included in 1924 pensions for widows and orphans and for old people at sixty-five, both of them earlier projects of Lloyd George. Widows and orphans still lacked protection, and the steadily increasing proportion of old people in the population was making non-contributory pensions a heavy burden. The principle of social insurance had by now become widely accepted, and Chamberlain therefore proposed an extension of the contributory system to pensions. Churchill agreed, as pensions would 'do something for the working classes', to balance reductions of taxation for others. The 'approved societies' were still opposed, but realised that some pension development was inevitable, and preferred Conservative action to what they might expect from Labour. The Contributory Pensions Act was therefore carried in 1925 [8.4.1], and was extended to cover lower-paid non-manual workers in 1937 [8.4.2].

CONTINUING PROBLEMS

National Health

The approved society system had now solidified in National Health Insurance, and effectively stultified progress because of the inequality of resources among societies. A thoroughgoing reform was out of the question, both financially and because of the powerful political interest of the societies, especially through the industrial assurance companies. A Royal Commission had been appointed by Wheatley in 1924, and presented in 1926 majority and minority reports, both of them critical of the societies [8.5.1]. Chamberlain had hoped to make some changes but was unable to move, and the reports remained of purely historical interest, though objections to the approved societies built up until in the rethinking that Beveridge touched off in 1942 they were set aside.

Old Age Pensioners

When introducing his pensions Bill, Chamberlain claimed that 'the circle of security' for the workers had now been closed, but experience was to show that for old people at least the new pensions were hardly adequate. The number of people over sixty-five applying for poor relief (from 1930 'public assistance') increased gradually but steadily, and the introduction of supplementary pensions in 1940 [9.1.1–2] revealed how many others there were who needed help but would not seek it from sources associated with the poor law. The 750,000 pensioners, unknown to public assistance, who then came forward were, as *The Times* commented, a revelation of 'secret need' [9.1.2]. The offer of supplementary pensions to meet the wartime increase in the cost of living, together with the payment of the pensions through the restyled Assistance Board instead of through the poor law, therefore to some extent introduced new principles, and the effect was immediately noticeable in poor law statistics [9.1.5].

Benefits and Earnings

Much evidence had already been gathered to show how necessary new principles were. In all the payments made, from the first pensions of 1908, the assumption had been that what was offered was not adequate in itself, but was to serve as a significant supplement to other resources. This was made clear, for instance, in connection with unemployment benefit [8.2.4]. Where other resources were lacking, only the poor law could help. Yet there were anomalies in the situation. Thus, in the case of unemployment benefit, whether 'standard', 'extended' or 'transitional', there were allowances for dependents. These had arisen in part from the connection with soldiers' pay and the 'donation' given to demobilised soldiers in 1919–21 to aid their resettlement. But there were no such allowances attached to sickness insurance. This confused situation was still further confounded by the low standards of wages of many workers, some of whom would have been no worse off on Assistance than when in work, and might indeed have been better off, especially if they had children, as Assistance included allowances. During the thirties a number of social investigations were undertaken which brought out the distress caused by unemployment, low wages, housing costs or families that were large by the standards of a period of declining birthrate. Seebohm Rowntree, indeed, wrote a sequel to his *Poverty* of 1901; *Poverty and Progress*, published in 1941, showed that on the basis of minimum standards of healthy life worked out by the BMA nearly one-third of the workers of York were to some degree in poverty. (Beveridge was to use the same standards in 1942 for the calculation of his national minimum of subsistence.) By 1939 the demand for better standards was increasing, and the idea of family allowances for the support of children, which was eventually adopted in 1945, was much in the air.

Family Allowances

Concern for children was heightened by the war and, with the prospect of heavy casualties, by the realisation of the effect upon the population of the lower birthrate of recent years. There seemed to be an inevitable likelihood of a high proportion of old people in a rapidly diminishing population, and Beveridge pointed out in his report of 1942 that unless population trends were reversed, by 1971 the proportion of the aged in the population (twenty-one per cent) would substantially exceed that of the young (sixteen per cent) – a prospect happily invalidated by the higher birthrate of the post-war years, which has produced, in 1971, corresponding percentages of sixteen and twenty-four respectively. It was in order to encourage the reversal of this trend, and to ease the circumstances of families with children, especially in times of unemployment and disability, that Beveridge insisted in his report on the necessity for family allowances [9.2.1].

Child Care

The case for better child care was pressed still further by the revelation of the condition of many children evacuated from areas of high poverty, which shocked people in the wartime reception areas. Their reactions were conveyed to the rest of the country by a notable publication of 1943, *Our Towns. A Close-Up*. Although there were inadequate parents, it was clear that the condition of the children and the standards of conduct some of them exhibited were at least as much the result of social as of personal failure. As with Booth's findings many years before, the case for new social policies was evident enough. Hitherto the adequate care of children had been regarded as essentially a personal responsibility, with the community involved only in cases of destitution or family breakdown, and intervening then only to divide and separate the family. Family allowances introduced a new concept of communal, as well as personal, responsibility for adequate family life, while wartime experience reinforced the recognition of the importance of the family, which was reflected in post-war policies aimed at keeping families together or, where there was breakdown, at restoring the family or providing the nearest substitute. This last aim underlay the Children Act of 1948 [10.1.2].

THE IMPACT OF TOTAL WAR

Care for children was but one aspect of the sense of social unity and responsibility which was engendered by the war, and still more by the disasters of 1940, which made of Britain a beleaguered fortress, and proved a catalyst for social policies. In the circumstances of total war, with so much at stake, unity existed in the nation as never before, and equality could not be restricted to the equalities of sacrifice. A new spirit was abroad. Great though the sacrifices of all classes had been in 1914–18, government was then still narrowly based. The year 1940, however, saw the Labour party brought into government as an equal partner, and its impact on policy was felt immediately. The Chamberlain government had already lowered the pension age for women to sixty and introduced supplementary pensions. The Labour ministers now insisted on the abolition of the household means test and the assessment of relief on the basis of individual need rather than of household means [9.1.3–4].

With this narrowing of family responsibility, which effectively restricted clauses 7 and 14 respectively of the Acts of 1601 and 1930 [1.1.1], the Elizabethan poor law, as Bevin pointed out in introducing the measure, was almost buried. Wartime needs for manpower had almost eradicated unemployment, and supplementary pensions relieved the elderly. Meanwhile a complex system of rationing, and concern for the welfare of mothers and children through the provision of essential foods of many kinds, which no

31

one associated with pauper relief, pushed poor law ideas still further into the background. Churchill hailed putting milk into babies as the finest national investment, and the results of all these measures were seen in the remarkable standard of public health during the war [10.3.1].

THE BEVERIDGE REPORT

What was needed, however, amid all these developments, was a rationalisation and improvement of the existing confused system of social security, with all its evidence of *ad hoc*, piecemeal growth. This rationalisation the Beveridge report was to provide, and with it the basis for further development.

Beveridge had since 1935 been chairman of the Unemployment Insurance Committee, but in his search for wartime occupation was invited to lead an inter-departmental committee on the inter-relation of the national schemes of social insurance and their allied services, which he soon turned into a vehicle for his own proposals for 'making all the immense good that has been accomplished into something better still'. The result was the great document which seized the country's imagination in November 1942 and, for all its length, proved a best-seller [9.2.1].[1]

Beveridge's case was basically a simple one, an argument for 'a natural development from the past ... a British revolution' [para. 31]. Taking the existing services, and the surveys of living standards and conditions made in the 1930s, he showed how, without any extreme measures, want could be abolished and a 'national minimum' assured to all, provided that the scheme were universal and that three assumptions could be accepted – children's allowances, a comprehensive health scheme and the prevention of mass unemployment. Insurance was to continue to be the basis of social security, 'giving in return for contributions benefits up to subsistence level, as of right and without any means test'. 'Subsistence level' only, be it noted, so that, as Beveridge maintained, 'individuals may build freely upon it', but the level was to be carefully calculated (Beveridge's calculation was based on 1938 figures, with an allowance for inflation) and to be adequate. Contributions and benefits would be at a flat rate, assuring security but again leaving individuals to add what they could. The plan was not one

[1] The report was reprinted in 1966.

providing 'something for nothing' [para. 455], but all would receive benefits for unemployment and disability, pensions on retirement, medical treatment and – an old proposal at last made practicable – funeral expenses. The national health service would cover everyone, though the details of its financing lay outside the scope of the report. Family allowances, however, were to be non-contributory and paid from taxation. In the matter of funeral insurance Beveridge exposed the costliness of 'industrial assurance', and proposed a state 'death benefit', which would cost only 6d in the £ as against 7s 6d for the industrial companies [para. 158]. For old age the proposal was for 'retirement pensions'. To overcome the problem presented by the increasing proportion of the elderly, Beveridge wished to encourage old people to stay at work. Pensions were therefore to be paid on retirement, though due from a particular age, and would be increased by the deferment of retirement. Moreover, as funds for the payment of these new pensions needed to be built up, Beveridge proposed the gradual introduction of the pensions over a period of twenty years, an impractical notion which political considerations brushed aside in 1946.

All this was reasonable enough – a matter, as Beveridge insisted, of common sense, not of politics. The political implications were all too clear, however, not least because of the threat posed to the unity of the coalition government by raising controversial issues of policy. Churchill himself, in a broadcast in 1943, deplored the attention that was being given to an uncertain future. He reminded his hearers of his own earlier association with unemployment insurance and, though promising developments in national insurance, urged them to get on with the war [9.2.2]. The government's coolness and tardiness in responding to the report aroused suspicions which were probably not without their effect on the unexpected result of the general election in 1945, which turned Churchill out of office, and there was much protest from back-benchers of all parties. Nevertheless, plans began to be prepared towards the end of 1943, under Lord Woolton as Minister of Reconstruction, and White Papers on *A National Health Service, Employment Policy* and *Social Insurance* (soon to be renamed National Insurance) followed in 1944 [9.2.3], the year which also saw a new Education Act. Beveridge, piqued at being excluded from discussions on the implementation of his ideas, characterised the appearance of the government's statements as the 'White Paper chase', but received a tribute of appreciation for his work in the Social Insurance paper [para. 186].

THE 'WELFARE STATE' ARRIVES

Even before the war ended Family Allowances were introduced [10.1.1], and the Labour government of Atlee carried measures for National Insurance [10.2] and the National Health Service [10.3] in 1946, and for National Assistance [10.4] in 1948. Of these, only that for the NHS caused serious difficulty, owing to a long and bitter wrangle with the doctors. The White Paper had been produced in 1944 by the coalition Minister of Health, Henry Willink, after an abortive attempt by his predecessor, Ernest Brown, who had been the first minister since Lloyd George to encounter what one distinguished medical authority was later to describe as the 'paranoid fears' of some doctors.[1] The British Medical Association had declared itself in favour of a comprehensive health service, but as soon as practical planning began its powerful trade union attributes asserted themselves. The notion of health centres and a salaried service became particular matters of dispute, and there was disagreement also over the position of the voluntary hospitals and as to how much private practice was acceptable within a comprehensive service. As earlier, too, there was strong opposition to any suggestion of local authority control. 'Rabid appeals and provocative allegations'[2] became the order of the day. Even more than with Lloyd George, however, the confrontation arose from suspicion rather than actual menace: it is significant that, for all its distant links with his own proposals of 1920 [8.1.2], Dr (now Lord) Dawson, by this time a very old man, did not approve of the government's scheme. Yet by a shrewd stroke Bevan, the Labour Minister of Health, won over the consultants by granting them a privileged position, and the leaders among them then exercised a moderating influence behind the scenes while Bevan himself made mollifying statements that could be regarded as concessions. The only major concession, in fact, was the assurance that there would be no salaried service, which was ratified by an Amending Act in

---

[1] Lord Platt, *Doctor and Patient. Ethics, Morale, Government* (1963), 53.
[2] A. Lindsay, *Socialized Medicine in England and Wales. The National Health Service, 1948–61* (1962), 47.

1949, though conditions and payments have continued to be a fruitful source of dissension since.

Political differences presented less difficulty, since there was a considerable measure of agreement among the parties on the broad principles of a comprehensive scheme, and the argument on details took place almost as much within the parties as between them. The Conservatives disliked the absorption of the local authority and voluntary hospitals, but were overridden. What finally emerged was a skilful compromise between conflicting needs and interests which, though it far from satisfied elements in both the major parties, and left the doctors in a more independent position than was intended by earlier proposals, such as those of the coalition government, nevertheless almost certainly represented the best arrangement that could be made.

When, finally, in the summer of 1948 the 'appointed day' arrived for the launching of the NHS, Bevan's message of goodwill to doctors hailed the liberation of the doctor-patient relationship from its dependence on the collection and payment of fees. Since Lloyd George had first assured a limited medical service to a substantial section of the population in 1911, there had been much discussion, both lay and medical, of its possible extension and improvement. Now at last the service was assured to all, on the basis of medical need rather than of capacity to pay. The rest, as Bevan said, lay with the skill and judgement of the doctors. It was still primarily a service of cure rather than prevention – though prophylaxis was to be greatly extended, especially for children – and still somewhat fragmented, with public health and the school medical services organised apart. Moreover, progress in the provision of health centres and hospitals was to be painfully slow. Yet the NHS was, and remains, one of the 'notable achievements of the twentieth century',[1] to all those who use it the most obvious and beneficial aspect of the Welfare State, even if now, with charges and contributions producing, in all, some fifteen per cent of the cost [11.1.2], rather less 'free' than when it began.

NEW PROBLEMS AND POLICIES

With the passage of the National Assistance Act in 1948 [10.4.2] the Elizabethan poor law finally disappeared from the statute

[1] Lindsay, *Socialized Medicine*, 474.

book, and the machinery of the Welfare State was largely complete. It had been confidently expected that National Assistance would have only a limited function, but in the event the numbers involved have been large, both for Assistance itself and for its successor service since 1966, Supplementary Benefits [13.4(1)], mainly because of the inadequacy of normal benefits, particularly for the elderly [13.4(1–3)]. The change to National Assistance from Public Assistance and the Assistance Board encouraged some to apply who had not come forward before [10.4.3], but old people in particular could not so easily expunge the memory of the poor law, and frequent appeals were made to encourage them to take advantage of a service to which no pauper taint any longer attached [11.2.2].

What the various services were to cost, and what they could mean to individuals, are shown in tables in chapter 13. The most difficult service to cost in 1946 was the NHS, and only a tentative estimate of £180 million could be made. The hope was even expressed (and occurs in the Beveridge report) that the service would in time diminish the demands made on it by improving general health standards. There was great leeway to be made up, however, especially in the dental and ophthalmic services, while medical care was in every way becoming more sophisticated and costly, and the general expectation of high standards of treatment, which rose with medical advances, imposed heavy demands. Inflation also took its toll. By 1950 expenditure had reached £350 million: a ceiling was set, and in the following year the Labour government decided to introduce certain charges, though it was the Conservative government which actually imposed them. The Conservative government, led by Churchill, succeeded Labour in 1951, and was confronted with much criticism of the cost of the service. In 1953 it appointed the Guillebaud committee to consider the possibilities of reductions in cost, but the committee's report [11.1.1] which appeared in 1956, disposed of any charges of extravagance, and in fact showed that the proportion of the national product spent on health had declined. More recent investigations have suggested that since 1948 Britain has also fallen behind other countries in this respect: nevertheless, the service now costs more then £1600 million a year [11.1.2].

The years since 1948 have made it clear that what was achieved then was not, in fact, anything particularly new, but a fulfilment of hopes and plans long since adumbrated, reaching back for their origins, as has been shown, through nearly a century and a half. To Ernest Bevin in 1943 the Beveridge proposals represented no more than a coordination of 'the nation's ambulance services',[1] and in general this was what Beveridge himself, as a good Liberal, had intended. The experience of a quarter of a century, however, has shown how inadequate this concept is for modern needs: inflation and rising standards of living have together destroyed the relevance of the 'national minimum' and the insurance principle. By the late 1950s it was already clear that subsistence standards were no longer a satisfactory basis for benefits, and in 1957 the Labour party produced plans for earnings-related pensions. Before the election of 1959 the Conservative government, in a shrewd political move, raised National Assistance rates to enable recipients to share in the increasing national prosperity [11.2.1], for these were the days of Harold Macmillan's famous, and oft misquoted, remark that 'most of our people have never had it so good'. When it returned to power, having, in Disraeli's historic phrase, caught the Opposition party bathing, Macmillan's government introduced its own modest – and, as it proved, clumsy and inadequate – scheme for earnings-related pensions, but went no further. The Labour government in 1964 acknowledged that the 'Beveridge revolution' had spent itself, and declared its intention of relating all benefits to earnings [11.2.3]. The first step came in 1966 with earnings-related supplements to unemployment and sickness benefits [11.2.4(1)], and an ambitious scheme for superannuation and social insurance was proposed in 1969 [11.2.4(2)], only to be foiled by the election of 1970. The Conservative government that then succeeded Labour put forward its own more limited plans for superannuation in 1971 [11.2.4(3)].

Meanwhile, in pursuance of the policy of unifying and simplifying services which had been put forward in 1964, the Labour government in 1966 brought pensions, insurance and assistance together in a new Ministry of Social Security, to which the NHS was later added. In order to overcome the reluctance of many to apply for help, it reshaped and renamed National Assistance as Supplementary Benefits [11.2.5]. It was possible, however, for a man on supplementary benefit to qualify, because of his needs, for benefits greater than his normal earnings, a condition familiar

[1] A. Bullock, *The Life and Times of Ernest Bevin*, II, 242.

from the experience of the thirties, and a 'wage-stop' was therefore imposed. Concern at the results of this policy [12.1] coincided with increasing awareness of the amount of poverty which remained in an affluent 'welfare' society, especially among families [12.2], and led to much discussion of the problems of 'need' and low wages, leading up to the Conservative government's introduction of 'family income supplements' in 1971. At the same time the increase in unemployment, on a scale far greater than at any time since the war, has imposed the first serious test on the 'insurance' scheme, and points the question as to how much of the general welfare of the population can be ascribed to the Welfare State, and how much to the high level of employment since the war and the government policies which have hitherto sustained it – and thereby helped to impose the countervailing strain of inflation. But these are questions of current concern which go beyond an historical examination of the rise of the Welfare State.

1 The Poor Law Background

1.1 CONTINUITY

1.1.1 Poor Law Acts: 1601–1930

From the Poor Relief Act, 1601: An Act for the Relief of the Poor

1. Be it enacted by the authority of this present Parliament, that the churchwardens of every parish, and four, three or two substantial householders there, as shall be thought meet ... to be nominated yearly ... under the hand and seal of two or more justices of the peace in the same county ... shall be called overseers of the poor of the same parish; and they ... shall take order from time to time ... for setting to work the children of all such whose parents shall not ... be thought able to keep and maintain their children; and also for setting to work all such persons, married or unmarried, having no means to maintain them, use no ordinary and daily trade of life to get their living by; and also to raise weekly or otherwise (by taxation of every inhabitant ... in such competent sum or sums of money as they shall think fit) a convenient stock of flax, hemp, wool, thread, iron, and other ware and stuff, to set the poor on work; and also competent sums of money for and towards the necessary relief of the lame, impotent, old, blind, and such other among them being poor, and not able to work; and also for the putting out of such children to be apprentices ...

4. And be it further enacted, that it shall be lawful for the said churchwardens and overseers ... to bind any such children as aforesaid to be apprentices, where they shall see convenient, till such man-child shall come to the age of four and twenty years, and such woman-child to the age of one and twenty years, or the time of her marriage.

5. And to the intent that necessary places of habitation may more conveniently be provided for such poor impotent people, be it

enacted by the authority aforesaid, that it shall and may be lawful for the said churchwardens and overseers . . . by the leave of the lord or lords of the manor whereof any waste or common within their parish is or shall be parcel . . . to erect, build, and set up, in fit and convenient places of habitation in such waste or common, at the general charges of the parish . . . convenient houses of dwelling for the said impotent poor, and also to place inmates or more families than one in one cottage or house ; . . . which cottages and places for inmates shall not at any time after be used or employed to or for any other habitation, but only for impotent and poor of the same parish. . . .

7. And be it further enacted, that the father and grandfather, and the mother and grandmother, and the children of every poor, old, blind, lame, and impotent person, or other poor person not able to work, being of a sufficient ability, shall at their own charges relieve and maintain every such poor person.

From the Poor Law Act, 1930

The Act restated the poor law for the guidance of the local authorities which had assumed responsibility for it under the Local Government Act, 1929 [8.3.3].

Here the duties of those concerned are set out, much in the terms of 1601. For other sections of the Act see 1.2.5, 5.1.1 and 8.3.4.

DUTIES OF FAMILY AND LOCAL AUTHORITY RESPECTIVELY

14. It shall be the duty of the father, grandfather, mother, grand-mother, husband or child, of a poor, old, blind, lame or impotent person, or other poor person not able to work, if possessed of sufficient means, to relieve and maintain that person.

15. It shall be the duty of the council of every county and county borough

    (a) to set to work all such persons, whether married or un-married, as have no means to maintain themselves, and use no ordinary and daily trade of life to get their living by;

    (b) to provide such relief as may be necessary for the lame, impotent, old, blind, and such other persons as are poor and not able to work;

    (c) to set to work or put out as apprentices all children whose parents are not, in the opinion of the council, able to keep and maintain their children . . .

1.2 THE LAW OF SETTLEMENT

1.2.1 Settlements and Removals, 1662
From the Poor Relief Act, 1662

1. Whereas the necessity, number, and continual increase of the poor, not only within the cities of London and Westminster, with the liberties of each of them, but also through the whole kingdom of England and dominion of Wales, is very great, and exceedingly burdensome, being occasioned by reason of some defects in the law concerning the settling of the poor, and for want of a due provision of the regulations of relief and employment in such parishes or places where they are legally settled . . . be it enacted . . . that whereas by reason of some defects in the law, poor people are not restrained from going from one parish to another, and therefore do endeavour to settle themselves in those parishes where there is the best stock, the largest commons or wastes to build cottages, and the most woods for them to burn and destroy; and when they have consumed it, then to another parish, and at last become rogues and vagabonds, to the great discouragement of parishes to provide stocks, where it is liable to be devoured by strangers; be it therefore enacted by the authority aforesaid, that it shall and may be lawful, upon complaint made by the churchwardens, or overseers of the poor of any parish, to any justice of peace, within forty days after any such person or persons coming so to settle as aforesaid, in any tenement under the yearly value of ten pounds, for any two justices of the peace . . . of the division where any person or persons, that are likely to be chargeable to the parish, shall come to inhabit, by their warrant to remove and convey such person or persons to such parish where he or they were last legally settled, either as a native, householder, sojourner, apprentice, or servant, for the space of forty days at the least, unless he or they give sufficient security for the discharge of the said parish . . .

3. Provided also, that (this Act notwithstanding) it shall and may be lawful for any person or persons to go into any county, parish, or place, to work in time of harvest, or at any time to work at any other work, so that he or they carry with him or them a certificate from the minister of the parish, and one of the churchwardens, and one of the overseers for the poor for the said year, that he or they have a dwelling-house or place . . . in which he or they inhabit,

and hath left wife and children, or some of them there (or otherwise, as the condition of the person shall require) and is declared an inhabitant or inhabitants there . . .

1.2.2 Removable Only If Chargeable, 1795

From the Poor Removal Act, 1795

1. . . . Whereas many industrious poor persons, chargeable to the parish, township or place where they live merely from want of work there, would in any other place where sufficient employment is to be had maintain themselves and families without being burthensome to any parish, township or place . . . and whereas the remedy intended to be applied thereto, by the granting of certificates in pursuance of the Act passed in the eighth and ninth years of the reign of King William the Third . . . hath been found very ineffectual and it is necessary that other provisions should be made relating thereto: Be it therefore enacted that . . . so much of the . . . Act of the thirteenth and fourteenth years of King Charles the Second as enables the justices to remove any person or persons that are likely to be chargeable to the parish, township or place into which they shall come to inhabit, shall be and the same is hereby repealed; and that from henceforth no poor person shall be removed by virtue of any order of removal from the parish or place where such poor person shall be inhabiting to the place of his or her last legal settlement, until such person shall have become actually chargeable to the parish, township or place in which such person shall then inhabit.

2. And whereas poor persons are often removed or passed to the place of their settlement during the time of their sickness, to the great danger of their lives: For remedy thereof, be it further enacted . . . that in case any poor person shall from henceforth be brought before any justice or justices of the peace for the purpose of being removed from the place where he or she is inhabiting . . . and it shall appear to the said justice or justices that such poor person is unable to travel by reason of sickness or other infirmity, or that it would be dangerous for him or her so to do, the justice or justices making such order of removal . . . are hereby required and authorised to suspend the execution of the same until they are satisfied that it may safely be executed without danger to any person who is the subject thereof.

1.2.3 Irremovability, 1846

As some compensation for the agriculturalists who feared ruin for themselves from the repeal of the corn laws, Sir Robert Peel relieved them of part of their poor law liability by limiting the period of removability. The concession particularly affected industrial areas, which found themselves no longer able to remove unemployed workers.

From the Poor Removal Act, 1846

1. No person shall be removed, nor shall any warrant be granted for the removal of any person, from any parish in which such person shall have resided for five years next before the application for the warrant. (Time spent in prison, or as a soldier etc. to be excluded.)

2. No woman residing in any parish with her husband at the time of his death shall be removed . . . for twelve calendar months next after his death, if she so long continue a widow.

3. No child under the age of sixteen years, whether legitimate or illegitimate, residing in any parish with his or her father or mother, stepfather or stepmother, or reputed father, shall be removed . . . in any case where such father etc. may not be lawfully removed from such parish.

1.2.4 A Case of Removal, 1861

From the Law Times, *n.s., IV, 244, May 1861*

Removal cases in the records are legion but one may be cited as an example of the human tragedies that so often occurred from attempts to apply the settlement laws with equal regard for the law and the rates. It concerned a Mrs Lambert, left a widow in Leeds with three small daughters, Sarah, aged six, and Ann and Emily, twins of four.

A widow whose parish of settlement was Aughton, but who was irremovable from Leeds by a five years' residence, had three children, and being unable to maintain them, the Leeds board of guardians made an order for the admission of such three children to the workhouse. A few weeks afterwards the overseers of Leeds obtained an order for the removal of the children to Aughton. The object of the board of guardians in sending them to the workhouse was to obtain their removal to their place of settlement. They were sent there with the consent of their mother, but she was not informed that the result of separating her children from her would be their removal to Aughton. Each of the children at the time of removal was under seven.

Held that in the circumstances the separation of the children from their mother was a fraud upon her, and that the order of removal was bad; also that as the children were within the age of nurture the mother could not consent to their separation from her.

1.2.5 Settlement, Irremovability and Removal
From the Poor Law Act, 1930

84. A person shall be deemed to be settled in the county or county borough in which he was born until it is shown that he has derived or acquired a settlement elsewhere, or is presumed to be settled elsewhere, and the county or county borough in which a person is last settled shall be deemed to be his county or county borough of settlement . . .

86. Where a person has resided for the term of three years in a county or county borough in such manner and in such circumstances in each of those years as would, in accordance with the provisions contained in this Act, render him irremovable, he shall be deemed to be settled in that county or county borough . . .

93. (1) No person shall be removed, nor shall any order be made for the removal of any person, from any county or county borough in which he has resided for one year next before the application for the order . . .

94. A person who is in receipt of relief, unless rendered irremovable by virtue of the foregoing provisions of this Act, may be removed . . . to his county or county borough of settlement.

95. Upon complaint made by the council or any county or county borough that a person has become chargeable to the county or county borough, two justices of the peace having jurisdiction in any part of the county or county borough, if satisfied of the truth of the complaint and that the person is not settled within or irremovable from the county or county borough, may order him to be removed to his county or county borough of settlement.

Provided that
no order shall be made for the removal of any person becoming chargeable in respect of relief made necessary by sickness or accident, unless the justices making the order state therein that they are satisfied that the sickness or accident will produce permanent disability . . .

99. If it appears to the justices making a removal order that any person named therein is unable to travel by reason of sickness or other infirmity, or that it would be dangerous for him to do so, they shall by an endorsement on the order signed by them suspend the execution of the order until satisfied that it may safely be executed without danger to that person.

1.3 THE WORKHOUSE AND OUT-RELIEF

1.3.1 The Origins of the 'Workhouse Test', 1723
This Act was passed in the early months of 1723, which to contemporaries was still 1722. It is sometimes referred to, therefore, as the 1722 Act.

From The Poor Relief Act, 1723
For the greater ease of parishes in the relief of the poor, be it further enacted, that it shall and may be lawful for the church-wardens and overseers of the poor in any parish, town, township, or place . . . to purchase or hire any house or houses in the same parish, township, or place, and to contract with any person or persons for the lodging, keeping, maintaining, and employing any or all such poor in their respective parishes, townships, or places, as shall desire to receive relief or collection from the same parish, and there to keep, maintain, and employ all such poor persons, and take the benefit of the work, labour, and service of any such poor person or persons . . . and in case any poor person or persons of any parish, town, township, or place, where such house or houses shall be so purchased or hired, shall refuse to be lodged, kept, or maintained in such house or houses, such poor person or persons so refusing shall be put out of the book or books where the names of the persons who ought to receive collection in the said parish, town, township, or place, are to be registered, and shall not be entitled to ask or receive collection or relief from the church-wardens and overseers of the poor of the same parish, town, or township.

1.3.2 A New Approach, 1782
Thomas Gilbert (1720–98) represented Lichfield for over thirty years, for the last eleven of which he was Chairman of the Committee of Ways and Means. He was deeply concerned with poor law matters, and this Act is always known by his name.

From 'Gilbert's Act', 1782 : An Act for the Better Relief and Employment of the Poor

1. Whereas notwithstanding the many laws now in being for the relief and employment of the poor, and the great sums of money raised for those purposes, their sufferings are nevertheless very grievous; and by the incapacity, negligence or misconduct of Overseers, the money raised for the relief of the poor is frequently misapplied, and sometimes expended in defraying the charges of litigations about settlements indiscreetly and unadvisedly carried on: and whereas ... power is given to the Churchwardens and Overseers to purchase and hire houses, and contract with any person for the lodging, maintaining and employing the poor, and taking the benefit of their work, labour and service, for their maintenance ... which provisions, from the want of proper regulations and management in the poorhouses or workhouses ... and for want of control over the persons who have engaged in those contracts, have not had the desired effect but the poor, in many places, instead of finding protection and relief, have been much oppressed thereby ... be it enacted ... that so much of the said clause as respects the maintaining and hiring out the labour of the poor by contract ... is hereby repealed ...

2. Provided nevertheless ... that it shall be lawful for ... any parish, township or place ... from time to time to make agreements with any person or persons for the diet or clothing of such poor persons who shall be sent to the house ... and for the work and labour of such poor persons ...

29. No persons shall be sent to such poor house or houses, except such as are become indigent of old age, sickness or infirmities, and are unable to acquire a maintenance by their labour; and except such orphan children as shall be sent thither by order, and except such children as shall necessarily go with their mothers for sustenance ...

32. Where there shall be, in any parish, any poor person or persons who shall be able and willing to work, but who cannot get employment, it shall be lawful for the Guardian of the Poor of such parish to agree for the labour of such poor person or persons, at any work or employment suited to his or her strength and capacity, in any parish near the place of his or her residence, and to maintain ... such person or persons ... until such employment shall be procured, and during the time of such work, to receive the money

earned by such work or labour, and apply it in such maintenance, as far as the same will go, and make up the deficiency, if any.

33. The Guardian of the Poor for any parish adopting the provisions of this Act shall provide, at the expense of such parish, suitable and necessary clothing for the persons sent by him to such poor house as aforesaid . . .

39. Nothing herein contained shall . . . alter or affect the settlement of any person or persons whomsoever . . .

1.3.3 Encouraging Out-Relief, 1795
From the Poor Relief Act, 1795

1. Whereas the Provision contained in the Act (of 1723) has been found . . . inconvenient and oppressive, inasmuch as it often prevents an industrious Poor Person from receiving such occasional Relief as is best suited to the peculiar Case of such Poor Person, and inasmuch as in certain Cases it holds out Conditions of Relief injurious to the Comfort and domestic Situation and Happiness of such Poor Persons . . . from and after the passing of this Act, it shall and may be lawful for the Overseer or Overseers of any Parish . . . to distribute and pay Collection and Relief to any industrious Poor Person or Persons, at his, her or their Homes, House or Houses, under certain Circumstances of temporary Illness or Distress, and in certain Cases respecting such Poor Person, or his, her or their Family, or respecting the Situation, Health or condition of any Poor House . . . although such Poor Person or Persons shall refuse to be lodged . . . within such House; anything in the said Act to the contrary notwithstanding.

1.3.4 Welfare and Speenhamland, 1795
The resolutions of the magistrates at Speenhamland were by no means unique, but achieved notoriety through being printed in the First Annual Report of the Poor Law Commissioners, 1835,[1] from a report by Richard Hall, Assistant Commissioner for Berkshire, who had quoted the original newspaper report.

Hall's report also included the revealing comments of a group of roadmenders [1.3.5],[2] which were obviously quoted as a vindication of the new poor law policy.

[1] Pp. 207–8.
[2] Ibid., p. 212.

From the Reading Mercury, *11 May 1795*

At a general meeting of the justices of this county, together with several discreet persons, assembled by public advertisement, on Wednesday the 6th day of May 1795, at the Pelican Inn, in Speenhamland (in pursuance of an order of the last court of general quarter sessions), for the purpose of rating husbandry wages by the day or week, if then approved of: Present –

Charles Dundas, Esq. in the Chair, &c. &c.

Resolved unanimously – That the present state of the poor does require further assistance than has been generally given them.

Resolved – That it is not expedient for the magistrates to grant that assistance by regulating the wages of day labourers ... but the magistrates very earnestly recommend to the farmers and others throughout the county to increase the pay of their labourers in proportion to the present price of provisions; and agreeable thereto the magistrates now present have unanimously resolved, that they will in their several divisions, make the following calculations and allowances for the relief of all poor and industrious men and their families, who, to the satisfaction of the justices of their parish, shall endeavour (as far as they can) for their own support and maintenance; that is to say, when the gallon loaf of second flour, weighing 8 lbs. 11 oz. shall cost 1s. then every poor and industrious man shall have for his own support 3s weekly, either procured by his own or his family's labour, or an allowance from the poor rates; and for the support of his wife and every other of his family, 1s 6d.

When the gallon loaf shall cost 1s 6d then every poor and industrious man shall have 4s weekly, for his own support, and 1s 10d for the support of every other of his family.

And so in proportion as the price of bread rises or falls (that is to say) 3d to the man, and 1d to every other of his family on every penny which the loaf rises above 1s.

By order of the meeting,

(signed) W. Budd, Deputy Clerk of the Peace.

1.3.5 What the Labourers Felt

From the First Annual Report of the Poor Law Commissioners, 1835

I passed six or seven men professedly working on a road, about 10 o'clock in the morning: returning about four in the afternoon, I found them reposing in various attitudes near the spot where I had

seen them before. After some introductory observations, I asked
'Do you think you earn your money at this work?'
– 'If I do, said one, it is by walking here and back morning and
evening.' 'Why, do you do the road no good?' – 'Not a morsel, sir,
I think we rather do it harm.' 'Then what do you think you are
put here for?' – 'Oh, sir, we know the overseer only puts us here
to *suffer* [i.e. punish] us, and I have often told him he had better
give us our money for nothing.' 'But why not get employment from
the farmers?' – 'The farmers will not give us any just at present,
they keep us here like potatoes in a pit, and only take us out for
use when they can no longer do without us.'

2 The Victorian Poor Law

2.1 THE NEW POOR LAW

2.1.1 The Poor Law Report and Amendment Act, 1834

After a lengthy impressionistic account of what was thought to be wrong in the administration of the poor law, the Royal Commission of 1832–4 recommended a new administrative structure and a strict return to the policy of relieving the able-bodied only in the workhouse.

The Act that followed deliberately broke with tradition by requiring the election of guardians, instead of, as hitherto, their appointment by the JPs. It was hoped in this way to attract a more conscientious type of person to serve, and one more careful of the rates. The right to vote and to serve as a guardian was inevitably biased towards property owners, and JPs were allowed to serve *ex officio*. Not until 1894 were any changes made in the qualifications prescribed [5.1.6].

From the Poor Law Report, 1834

227. The most pressing of the evils which we have described are those connected with the relief of the Able-bodied ... If we believed the evils stated ... to be necessarily incidental to the compulsory relief of the able-bodied, we should not hesitate in recommending its entire abolition. But we do not believe these evils to be its necessary consequences. We believe that, under strict regulations, adequately enforced, such relief may be afforded safely and even beneficially ...

262. The chief specific measures that we recommend ... are:–
First, that except as to medical attendance ... all relief whatever to able-bodied persons or to their families, otherwise than in well-regulated workhouses (i.e. places where they may be set to work according to the spirit and intention of the 43rd of Elizabeth) shall be declared unlawful, and shall cease.

From the Poor Law Amendment Act, 1834

1. Whereas it is expedient to alter and amend the Laws relating to the Relief of poor Persons in England and Wales: . . . It shall be lawful for His Majesty, His Heirs and Successors, by Warrant under the Royal Sign Manual, to appoint Three fit Persons to be Commissioners to carry this Act into execution . . .

2. The said Commissioners shall be styled 'The Poor Law Commissioners for England and Wales'; . . .

7. The said Commissioners shall and they are hereby empowered from Time to Time to appoint such Persons as they may think fit to be Assistant Commissioners for carrying this Act into execution . . . Provided always, that it shall not be lawful for the said Commissioners to appoint more than Nine such Assistant Commissioners to act at any one time . . .

15. From and after the passing of this Act the Administration of Relief to the Poor throughout England and Wales . . . shall be subject to the Direction and Control of the said Commissioners . . .

26. It shall be lawful for the said Commissioners, by Order under their Hands and Seal, to declare so many Parishes as they may think fit to be united for the Administration of the Laws for the Relief of the Poor, and such Parishes shall thereupon be deemed a Union for such Purpose, and thereupon the Workhouse or Workhouses of such Parishes shall be for their common Use: and the said Commissioners may issue such Rules, Orders, and Regulations as they shall deem expedient for the Classification of such of the Poor of such united Parishes in such Workhouse or Workhouses as may be relieved in any such Workhouse, and such Poor may be received, maintained, and employed in any such Workhouse or Workhouses as if the same belonged exclusively to the Parish to which such Poor shall be chargeable; but notwithstanding such Union and Classification, each of the said Parishes shall be separately chargeable with and liable to defray the Expense of its own Poor, whether relieved in or out of any such Workhouse . . .

38. Guardians of the Poor for each Union shall be constituted and chosen, and the Workhouse or Workhouses of such Union shall be governed, and the Relief of the Poor in such Union shall be administered, by such Board of Guardians, and the said Guardians shall be elected by the Ratepayers, and by such Owners of Property in the Parishes forming such Union as shall have their Names entered as entitled to vote, as Owners in the Books of such Parishes;

and the Commissioners shall determine the Number and prescribe the Duties of the Guardians to be elected in each Union, and also fix a Qualification without which no Person shall be eligible as such Guardian, such Qualification to consist in being rated to the Poor Rate of some Parish or Parishes in such Union, but not so as to require a Qualification exceeding the Annual Rental of Forty Pounds, and shall also determine the Number of Guardians which shall be elected for any one or more of such Parishes . . . Provided always, that one or more Guardians shall be elected for each Parish included in such Union; . . . and every Justice of the Peace residing in any such Parish shall be an ex-officio Guardian . . .

40. In all cases of the Election of Guardians under this Act . . . the Votes of Ratepayers shall be given or taken in writing . . . and in every case the Owners, as well as the Ratepayer, in respect of any Property in such Parish or Union, shall be entitled to vote . . .

52. And whereas a Practice has obtained of giving Relief to Persons or their Families who, at the Time of applying for or receiving such Relief, were wholly or partially in the Employment of Individuals . . . From and after the passing of this Act it shall be lawful for the said Commissioners, by such Rules, Orders, or Regulations, as they may think fit, to declare to what Extent and for what Period the Relief to be given to able-bodied Persons or to their Families in any particular Parish or Union may be administered out of the Workhouse of such Parish or Union . . . and all Relief which shall be given by any Overseer, Guardian, or other Person having the Control or Distribution of the Funds of such Parish or Union, contrary to such Orders or Regulations, shall be and the same is hereby declared to be unlawful, and shall be disallowed . . .

56. . . . Nothing herein contained shall discharge the Father and Grandfather, Mother and Grandmother, of any poor Child, from their Liability to relieve and maintain such poor Child in pursuance of the Provisions of a certain Act of Parliament passed in the Forty-third Year of the Reign of Her late Majesty Queen Elizabeth intituled An Act for the Relief of the Poor.

2.1.2 The Franchise and the Poor Law, 1832–1918

The first Reform Act of 1832 denied the use of the vote to men on poor relief, and the disqualification was restated in the further Acts of 1867 and 1884. Vaccination under the guardians' powers was exempted in 1841 [3.4.1], and use of the poor law medical services, where no relief was involved, by a special Act in 1885. The disqualification was finally removed in the further widening of the franchise in 1918.

From the Representation of The People Act, 1832

36. No person shall be entitled to be registered in any year as a voter in ... any city or borough who shall within twelve calendar months next previous ... have received parochial relief or other alms.

From the Medical Relief Disqualification Removal Act, 1885

2. (1) Where a person has in any part of the United Kingdom received for himself, or for any member of his family, any medical or surgical assistance, or any medicine at the expense of the poor rate, such person shall not by reason thereof be deprived of any right to be registered or to vote either –

 (*a*) as a Parliamentary voter; or

 (*b*) as a voter at any municipal election ...

but nothing in this section shall apply to the election –

 (*a*) of any guardian of the poor ...

4. The term 'medical or surgical assistance' in this Act shall include all medical or surgical attendance, and all matters and things supplied by or on the recommendation of the medical officer having authority to give such attendance and recommendation at the expense of any poor rate.

From the Representation of the People Act, 1918

9. A person shall not be disqualified from being registered or from voting as a parliamentary or local government elector by reason that he or some person for whose maintenance he is responsible has received poor relief or other alms.

2.2 THE POOR LAW COMMISSIONERS AT WORK, 1834–47; CHADWICK IN CONTROL

Chadwick as Secretary of the Poor Law Commissioners drew up regulations which were circulated to boards of guardians and printed in his annual reports. The quotations that follow are from regulations affecting major aspects of policy – the conduct of workhouses, industrial unemployment, the heavy cost of sickness and the labour test.

 The three doctors who gathered evidence of unhealthy conditions for Chadwick are quoted in 2.2.3:

Neil Arnott (1788–1874) was Chadwick's own doctor, and a pioneer of smoke prevention.

James Phillips Kay (1804–77) had practised in Manchester, where he published in 1832 a report on social conditions, *The Moral and Physical Condition of the Working Classes*, and had joined Chadwick as an Assistant Commissioner. He turned his attention increasingly to education, becoming the first secretary of the Privy Council Committee for Education and, as Sir James Kay-Shuttleworth (a change of name following an inheritance), a pioneer advocate of teacher training and a national education system.

Thomas Southwood Smith (1788–1861) was on the staff of the London Fever Hospital. He had been a close friend of Bentham, whose skeleton he left to University College, London. He was active in the Health of Towns Association and in housing projects, and from 1849 to 1854 was the medical member of the General Board of Health.

2.2.1 Workhouse Regulations
From the First Report of the Poor Law Commissioners, 1835

ORDERS AND REGULATIONS TO BE OBSERVED IN THE WORK-HOUSE OF THE — UNION
Admission of paupers

IV. As soon as a pauper is admitted, he or she shall be placed in the probationary ward, and shall there remain until examined by the medical officer of the workhouse.

V. If the medical officer, upon such examination, pronounces the pauper to be labouring under any disease of body or mind, the pauper shall be placed either in the sick ward, or the ward for lunatics and idiots not dangerous, as the medical officer shall direct.

VI. If the medical officer pronounces the pauper to be free from disease, the pauper shall be placed in that part of the workhouse assigned to the class to which he or she may belong, and shall thereafter be treated according to the regulations hereinafter contained.

VII. Before removal from the probationary ward, the pauper shall be thoroughly cleansed, and shall be clothed in the workhouse dress; and the clothes which he or she wore upon admission shall be purified, and deposited in a place to be appropriated for that purpose, to be restored to the pauper on leaving the workhouse, or else to be used by the pauper as the Board of Guardians shall direct.

VIII. The clothing of the paupers shall be made of such materials as the board of guardians shall determine, and shall, so far as possible, be made by the paupers in the workhouse.

Classification of paupers

IX. The in-door paupers shall be classed as follows:

1. Aged or infirm men.
2. Able-bodied men, and youths above 13.
3. Youths and boys above seven years old and under 13.
4. Aged or infirm women.
5. Able-bodied women, and girls above 16.
6. Girls above seven years of age and under 16.
7. Children under seven years of age.

X. To each class shall be assigned by the board of guardians that apartment or separate building which may be best fitted for the reception of such class, and in which they shall respectively remain, without communication, unless as is hereinafter provided.

XI. Provided . . .

Secondly. If for any special reason it shall at any time appear to the majority of the board of guardians, to be desirable to suspend the above rule, on behalf of any married couple, being paupers of the first and fourth classes, the guardians shall be at liberty to agree to a resolution to that effect [which had to be approved by the Commissioners] . . .

Fifthly, the children of the seventh class shall be placed either in a ward by themselves, or in such of the wards appropriated to the female paupers as the board of guardians shall direct. The mothers of such children to be permitted to have access to them at all reasonable times. With the foregoing exceptions, no pauper of one class shall be allowed to enter the wards or yards appropriated to any other class . . .

Discipline and diet

XIII. All the paupers in the workhouse, except the sick, the aged and infirm, and the young children, shall rise, be set to work, leave off work, and go to bed, at the times mentioned in the accompanying table, and shall be allowed such intervals for their meals as herein are stated; and these several times shall be notified by ringing a bell; and during the time of meals, silence, order and decorum shall be maintained . . .

XIX. The diet of the paupers shall be so regulated as in no case t
exceed, in quantity and quality of food, the ordinary diet of th
able-bodied labourers living within the same district . . .

XXIII. No person shall be allowed to visit any pauper in th
workhouse, except by permission of the master . . . and provide
that the interview shall always take place in the presence of th
master or matron, and in a room separate from the other inmate
of the workhouse, unless in case of sickness; provided also, tha
any licensed minister of the religious persuasion of any inmate o
such workhouse, at all times in the day, on the request of suc
inmate, may visit such workhouse for the purpose of affordin
religious assistance to such inmate, and also at all reasonable time
for the purpose of instructing his child or children in the principle
of their religion . . .

2.2.2 The Problem of Industry

*From the Third Annual Report of the Poor Law Commissioners, 1837
Letter from the Commissioners to the Board of Guardians of th
Mansfield Union, in Reply to their letter of 25 May 1837*

POOR LAW COMMISSION OFFICE, SOMERSET HOUSE, 27 MA
1837

The Poor Law Commissioners for England and Wales have t
acknowledge the receipt of your letter of the 25th instant, statin
by direction of the Board of Guardians of Mansfield Union, tha
in the parish of Mansfield there are at present upwards of 300 able
bodied men out of employment in a state of destitution, relieve
or employed by a private subscription, that the workhouse is quit
full, and requesting the Commissioners' Instructions and advice a
to whether relief should be given to them out of the workhouse.

The Commissioners are of opinion that under the circumstance
stated, great care should be taken to adhere to sound principles i
the administration of relief on all occasions of pressure arising fro
revulsions of trade or other causes.

The distress which actually ensues is always accompanied by
demonstration of a large amount of fictitious distress, and the id
and the fraudulent are forward to avail themselves of the sympath
which is then called forth . . . It is, therefore, of the highest impo
tance that the operative classes should be taught lessons of frugali
and forethought at those times when they are able to earn mor

than is actually necessary for their immediate support, and that they should then save up the surplus to meet emergencies like the present . . .

The Commissioners are aware that until the new workhouse is completed . . . it will be necessary for [the guardians] to deal with the existing distress by the administration of out-door relief of some kind . . . it is desirable that out-door relief should, as far as circumstances will permit, be given only in return for work performed.

However . . . a state of circumstances may arise . . . in which the number of applicants for relief may be such as to render it impossible to make immediate arrangements for setting them to work.

The mode of relief which appears least liable to objection, under such circumstances, is, that the relief, or the greatest portion of it, should be administered in kind, and in such manner as to render it acceptable to those only who are really in want of it. To this end it may be advisable that soup kitchens should be opened . . .

> Signed by order of the Board,
> E. Chadwick, Secretary.

2.2.3 The Economics of Sickness
From the Fourth and Fifth Annual Reports of the Poor Law Commissioners, 1838 and 1839

REPORT AS TO PAYMENT OF CERTAIN EXPENSES OUT OF THE POOR RATES

Amongst the charges which have been unavoidably disallowed are many which increasing experience proves it necessary to submit for the sanction of the Legislature for their allowance. The chief charges which we feel it our duty to recommend for allowance are:–

1. Those charges found necessary for the prevention of burthens upon the rates, occasioned by the desertion of children by their parents, or by the refusal of natural relations to contribute their proper charges; and those charges caused by nuisances by which contagion is occasionally generated, and persons reduced to destitution . . .

The most prominent and pressing of the first class of charges for which some provision appears to be required, are for the means of averting the charges on the poor-rates which are caused by nuisances by which contagion is generated and persons are reduced to destitution.

In general, all epidemics and all infectious diseases are attended with charges, immediate and ultimate, on the poor-rates. Labourers are suddenly thrown, by infectious disease, into a state of destitution, for which immediate relief must be given. In the case of death, the widow and the children are thrown as paupers on the parish. The amount of burdens thus produced is frequently so great as to render it good economy on the part of the administrators of the poor-laws to incur the charges for preventing the evils, where they are ascribable to physical causes, which there are no other means of removing . . .

During the last two years the public has suffered severely from epidemics . . . We have . . . directed local examinations to be made, in parts of the metropolis where fever was stated to be the most prevalent, by Dr Arnott, by Dr Southwood Smith [the chief physician of the London Fever Hospital], and by Dr Kay, our Assistant Commissioner. The more important communications of the medical officers are comprehended in the medical report prepared by Dr Kay, with the concurrence of Dr Arnott . . . given in a Supplement to this Report . . .

We shall adduce a few of the illustrative facts which have occurred to Dr Arnott in the course of his professional engagements.

1. In the field behind Euston-square . . . there was until lately, near some very extensive cow-sheds, the meeting of several public drains or sewers in an open ditch, which often overflowed and covered a considerable space with a lake of the most odious filth. In the neighbourhood of this field typhoid fevers were frequent, and in a school of 150 female children in Clarendon-square, Somers Town, every year, while the nuisance was at its height, the malaria caused some remarkable forms of disease . . . Since the covering of the drains all these diseases have disappeared. . . .

FROM THE REPORT BY DR ARNOTT AND DR KAY (1838)

. . . The extirpation of the evils arising from defects in the sanatory police of large cities cannot be effected unless powers are confided to some authority selected by the Legislature for the prevention of those grievous defects to which our attention has been drawn. The imperfect drainage, or the absence of all drainage whatever, the want of a proper pavement in the street, etc. are frequently found in districts which have been recently covered with masses of new habitations huddled together in confused groups, with streets so narrow, and courts so completely enclosed, as to prevent the dilution of the malaria arising from various sources within their precincts by the ventilation of free currents of air.

Many of the most recently erected suburbs of our great cities exhibit so complete a neglect of the most common and obvious precautions, that it can be attributed only to the fact of the increase of the population being so rapid that the owners of such property can command tenants, notwithstanding the absolute neglect of sewerage, and the absence of many precautionary arrangements absolutely necessary to insure health. . . .

REPORT ON FEVER IN THE METROPOLIS (1839)

There is no disease which brings so much affliction into a poor man's family as fever. It most commonly attacks the heads of the family, those upon whose daily labour the subsistence of the family depends. The present returns afford melancholy evidence of the pauperising influence of this prevalent and fatal disease. They show that out of the total number of persons in London who received parochial relief during the last year, more than one-fifth were the subjects of fever. In Bethnal Green the proportion was one-third, in Whitechapel it was nearly one half, and in St George the Martyr it was 1,276 out of 1,467. Placing out of consideration the suffering of the individual attacked with fever, which is one of the most painful maladies to which the human being is subject, placing out of view also the distress brought upon all the members of the family of the sick, it is plain that this disease is one of the main causes of pressure upon the poor-rates. That pressure must continue, and the same large sums of money must be expended year after year for the support of families afflicted with fever, as long as those dreadful sources of fever which encompass the habitations of the poor are allowed to remain. . . . These neglected places are out of view, and are not thought of; their condition is known only to the parish officers and the medical men whose duties oblige them to visit the inhabitants to relieve their necessities, and to attend their sick; and even these services are not to be performed without danger. [Local conditions of hygiene are so bad that] during the last year, in several of the parishes, both relieving officers and medical men lost their lives in consequence of the brief stay in these places which they were obliged to make in the performance of their duties. Yet in these pestilential places the industrious poor are obliged to take up their abode; they have no choice; they must live in what houses they can get nearest the places where they find employment. By no prudence or forethought on their part can they avoid the dreadful evils of this class to which they are thus exposed. No returns can show the amount of suffering which they have had to endure from causes of this kind during the last year; but the present returns indicate some of the final results of that suffering; they show that out of 77,000 persons 14,000 have been attacked with fever, one-fifth part of the whole; and that out of the 14,000 attacked nearly 1,300 have died. . . . It is notorious that this disease has been very prevalent during the last year among the industrious classes who have never received parochial relief, and that it has found its way even into the dwellings of the rich, where it has proved extremely mortal. . . . There can be no security against the constant recurrence of this calamity, but the adoption of measures adequate to diminish very materially, if not entirely to prevent, the generation of the febrile poison in every district. The expenditure necessary to the adoption and maintenance of these measures of prevention would ultimately amount to less than the cost of the disease now constantly engendered. . . . It follows, that the prevention of the evil, rather than the mitigation of the consequences of it, is not only the most beneficent but the most economical course.

I am etc.
Southwood Smith

2.2.4 The Labour Test

From the Ninth Annual Report of the Poor Law Commissioners, 1843
The Poor Law Commissioners have, during the present year, issued to several Unions an order prescribing the mode of administering relief, with the offer of out-door labour to able-bodied men under certain circumstances.

They took this course either because the imperfect state of workhouse accommodation made it impracticable to issue the order prohibiting out-door relief to able-bodied persons, or because, in cases where this order had been issued, they had been obliged to sanction large exceptions to its provisions. . . .

The main object of prescribing a task of work to be performed in exchange for relief out of the workhouse, is to supply a test of the reality of destitution on the part of the applicant, and thereby to afford him an inducement to seek for independent employment. . . .

Every payment made by Guardians to paupers ought to assume the form of relief, not of wages; and, consequently, be measured by the wants of the family, and not by the quantity of labour done. A single man, or a man with a wife and one child, ought not to receive as much as a man with a wife and eight children. . . .

Allowances so made should be treated as relief, proportioned to the wants of the applicant and his family, and should not be deemed remuneration for work done. The language should be, 'The Guardians allow you so much, because you are in want of so much; and they require you to break a certain quantity of stone, and to work a certain number of hours, not to harass you, but because without this condition they cannot be sure that the money which they are intrusted with is given to those who are really in want, and who are not working elsewhere'.

It may, indeed, be objected to this plan, that it involves a return to the 'scale system', as formerly practised in the pauperised counties of the South and East of England; viz. of making up wages according to a certain scale, dependent on the numbers of the family.

The true objection to the scale system, as formerly practised, is, that it involved an interference with wages, and that, by this interference, it converted the wages of nearly the entire labouring class, which ought to have depended upon the value of the labour, into relief dependent on the wants of the labourer, and the numbers of his family. This objection does not apply to the plan above considered; inasmuch as it is assumed that the paupers relieved work exclusively for the Guardians, and that their wages are not 'made up' out of the rates. . . .

2.2.5 Controlling Out-Relief

By 1841 it was felt that enough workhouses had been constructed to make it possible to issue a general order prohibiting out-relief. Exceptions were made for certain industrial Unions, where out-relief was permitted under labour-test conditions.

After the Relief Regulation Order of 1852 no further order was issued until 1911, following on the report of the Royal Commission in 1909.

2.2.6 provides a later comment on stone-breaking as a labour test. It appeared in a report on the distress that accompanied the severe winter of 1895–6.

From the General Out-Door Relief Prohibitory Order of 2 August 1841

We do hereby order, with respect to each of the Unions named in the schedule:

1. Every able-bodied person, male or female, requiring relief from any parish within any of the said unions shall be relieved wholly in the workhouse of the Union, together with such of the family of every such able-bodied person as may be resident with him or her, and may not be in employment . . . except in the following cases:

1st. Where such person shall require relief on account of sudden and urgent necessity.

2nd Where such person shall require relief on account of any sickness, accident, or bodily or mental infirmity affecting such person, or any of his or her family.

3rd Where such person shall require relief for the purpose of defraying the expenses of the burial of any of his or her family.

4th Where such person, being a widow, shall be in the first six months of her widowhood.

5th Where such person shall be a widow and have a legitimate child or legitimate children dependent upon her, and incapable of earning his, her, or their livelihood, and no illegitimate child born after the commencement of her widowhood.

This order was re-issued in December 1844, with certain amendments, including prohibition of the payment of rent for paupers.

From the Out-Door Labour Test Order of 30 April 1842

1. Every able-bodied male pauper receiving relief from any parish within the Union, and not relieved in the workhouse, shall be relieved in the following manner:

Half at least of the relief given to such pauper shall be given in food, clothing, and other articles of necessity.

No such pauper shall receive relief from the Guardians of the Union, while he is employed for wages or other hire or remuneration by any person; but every such pauper so relieved shall be set to work by the Guardians.

2. The place or places at which able-bodied male paupers shall be so set to work in the Union; the sort or sorts of work in which they or any of them shall be employed; . . . and all other matters relating to the employment of such able-bodied paupers, shall be fixed and regulated in such manner as the Poor Law Commissioners shall direct. . . .

13. It shall not be lawful for the Guardians of the Union to pay the rent, wholly or in part, of any pauper.

From the General Out-Door Relief Regulation Order of 14 December 1852 (issued to unions not covered by prohibitory orders)

1. Whenever the Guardians allow relief to any able-bodied male person, out of the workhouse, one half at least of the relief so allowed shall be given in articles of food or fuel, or in other articles of absolute necessity.

2. In any case in which the Guardians allow relief for a longer period than one week to an indigent poor person . . . without requiring that such person shall be received into the workhouse, such relief shall be given or administered weekly.

3. It shall not be lawful for the Guardians or their officers –

To establish any applicant for relief in trade or business;

Nor to redeem from pawn for any such applicant any tools, implements, or other articles;

Nor to purchase and give to such applicant any tools, implements, or other articles, except articles of clothing or bedding where urgently needed.

Nor to pay, wholly or in part, the rent of the house or lodging of any pauper. . . .

5. No relief shall be given to any able-bodied male person while he is employed for wages or other hire or remuneration by any person.

6. Every able-bodied male person, if relieved out of the workhouse, shall be set to work by the Guardians, and be kept employed under their direction and superintendence so long as he continues to receive relief.

2.2.6 A Comment on Stone-Breaking

From the Reports of the Select Committee on Distress from Want of Employment: Second Report, 1896

THE GUARDIANS' LABOUR TEST OF DESTITUTION (STONE-BREAKING, ETC.)

Much has been said by witnesses . . . in reference to the difficulties experienced by boards of guardians in the administration of the stone-breaking test of destitution during periods of exceptional pressure. Not only is the demoralising nature of the test . . . insisted on, but it is said that the test is of too arduous a character. Witnesses, however, admit that stone-breaking is an industry against which less objection can be raised on the score of competing with independent labour than any other, and it has further the advantage that it is not interrupted during periods of frost.

Further objection to the stone-breaking test is to the effect that it is more eligible than an offer of admittance to the workhouse. . . . Perhaps, however, the principal objection . . . consists in the premium on idleness that it involves. No specified task can be enforced. The capability of the persons employed varies, and it can only be required that each person shall perform the amount of work that he appears to be able to accomplish. . . . The amount of work per man . . . tends to a minimum. The standard of accomplishment is practically fixed by the unwilling worker.

The Chairman of the Board of Guardians of the Wandsworth and Clapham Union has told your Committee that an experienced man can break one ton of stone per day. . . . Within his experience, however, the average weight broken . . . has not exceeded from 2 to 3 cwts. per day. Again, the Chairman of the St Olave's Board of Guardians has informed your Committee that, whereas the cost of breaking stone where competent stone-breakers are employed is about 4s. per ton, every ton of stone broken in the guardians' stoneyard during the winter of 1894–95 cost the union £7.

2.3 OBJECTIONS TO THE NEW POOR LAW

2.3.1 The Commons Debate on the Renewal of the Commission, 1839

Two extracts are given from the debate on the renewal of the Poor Law Commission after its initial period of five years. Both bear on aspects of poor law administration which were to be taken into account in the framing of the regulations for outdoor relief.

Sir James Graham (1792–1861) was MP for Dorchester, and had been a member of Lord Grey's reforming Ministry, but was moving over to the Tories and served, not very successfully, as Home Secretary under Peel, 1841–6.

Edward Baines (1774–1848) had succeeded Macaulay as MP for Leeds in 1834, and as proprietor of the influential *Leeds Mercury* was a prominent citizen of the town.

From the House of Commons Debate, 20 July 1839
Sir J. Graham . . . was quite satisfied, that, upon the whole, [the poor law] had not been more beneficial to the rate-payers than to the independence of the labourer. It had encouraged the industrious, while it secured to the really destitute those advantages of relief which were formerly enjoyed by the idle and vicious. At the same time the working of the measure had established, that in certain particulars, it had borne with hardship on some meritorious classes. He particularly alluded to widows left with large families, suddenly deprived of their husbands, not perhaps advanced in life, but struck to the earth by some unexpected blow. To compel such at once to remove from the cottage to the workhouse, when, by a little support for a short time, they might, by industry, be enabled to maintain their families in independence, would be cruel in the extreme. The practical working of the measure had also proved to him, that in times when provisions were dear, when the demand for labour was slack, and families large, relief must, at times, in special cases, be given to the able-bodied man. . . .

Mr Baines . . . In the manufacturing districts with which he was acquainted, it was quite impossible that they could, by any means, carry into effect the denial of all out-door relief. Circumstances occasionally occurred there which threw 400 or 500 persons in a single parish out of employment. In such cases could they enforce the rule; or were they prepared to build new workhouses enough to carry it out?

2.3.2 Letter from a Manufacturer to Chadwick, 1841

This letter echoes Baines's case of 1839. Henry and Edmund Ashworth were mill-owners of Bolton, paternalistically concerned about the welfare of their workers, and supporters of the new poor law. They contributed material about the housing of their workers to Chadwick's *Sanitary Condition*, and were visited by Disraeli, who portrayed them in *Coningsby* and *Sybil*. (A study of the Ashworths and their business is given in R. Boyson, *The Ashworth Cotton Enterprise. The Rise and Fall of a Family Firm, 1818–80*.)

From a Letter from Edmund Ashworth to Chadwick, 12 November 1841 (quoted in S.E.Finer, The Life and Times of Sir Edwin Chadwick, p. 182)

... When we who live amongst it, see a thousand families brought to poverty by mere want of employment, the Poor Rates doubled, and parties asking for relief or pining in want who never asked for relief before, we cannot stand silently by or stamp them all as imposters ... the patient endurance of the people hitherto is beyond belief and deserving all praise.

2.3.3 The Andover Report, 1846

The Andover scandal brought down the Poor Law Commissioners and Chadwick with them. For a variety of reasons, including its lack of direct accountability to Parliament, the Commission was unpopular, and this case revealed its failure to exercise effective control. A political storm broke, a Select Committee investigated the case, and the Commission was wound up, to be replaced by a Board with a political head.

From the Report from the Select Committee ... on the Andover Union

WORKHOUSE DIETARY

Resolved, That it is the opinion of this Committee:

1. That in the month of February 1836 several Forms of Dietary were sent down by the Poor-law Commissioners, of which one, marked No. 3, was selected by the Board of Guardians for adoption in the Workhouse, and was in use from that time until December 1845.

2. That in their Second Annual Report, published in 1837, the Poor-law Commissioners published six Forms of Dietary, as actually in use in Workhouses, but that No. 3 of such Forms differs in several respects from Form No. 3, as sanctioned at Andover, and is in fact a superior Dietary.

3. That the Committee have not received any Evidence in answer to their inquiries which can enable them to explain satisfactorily this admitted discrepancy ...

4. That from the evidence taken before the Committee, the Committee believe, that from the formation of the Union until last Autumn, the general Dietary of the Workhouse was, in quantity at least, too low, and more particularly that the allowances of bread was insufficient; and they find that this dietary was often further diminished by the dishonesty of the Master. Some of the inmates of the Workhouse were in the habit of eating raw potatoes and grain and refuse food which had been thrown to the hogs and fowls.

5. That it has also been proved that instances occurred in which inmates of the Workhouse, employed in Bone-crushing, ate the gristle and marrow of the bones which they were set to break.

6. That . . . by a very irregular and improper practice, the produce of the labour of the paupers in bone-crushing at the Workhouse is stated to have been disposed of among the Guardians, by the Chairman putting up the same at a sort of mock auction in the Board-room.

7. That this employment – or in fact any labour which can justly be considered of a penal or disgusting character – should not be adopted by Boards of Guardians, as such a course must tend to prevent the really destitute poor from entering the Union House, and is not consistent with a mild and considerate administration of the law.

2.3.4 Workhouse Reality

George Lansbury (1859–1940), MP 1910–12 and 1922–40, and Leader of the Labour Party 1931–5, spent most of his life in Bow and was known as the 'John Bull of Poplar'. A man of deep sympathy and strong religious principles, he became a guardian in 1892 and later wrote in his memoirs an account of his first visit to a workhouse. In 1905 he was appointed to the Royal Commission on the Poor Law, and he was one of the signatories of the Minority Report. His policy as a guardian was 'decent treatment and hang the rates', denounced by others for its costliness as 'Poplarism'. Though written late in life, his memoirs hardly reflect 'emotion recollected in tranquility', but this account represents the strength of feeling aroused by workhouse conditions, not all of which were by any means as unsatisfactory as those of Poplar.

From George Lansbury, My Life *(1928), pp. 135–6*
My first visit to a workhouse was a memorable one. Going down a narrow lane, ringing the bell, waiting while an official with a not

too pleasant face looked through a grating to see who was there, and hearing his unpleasant voice – of course, he did not know me – made it easy for me to understand why the poor dreaded and hated these places, and made me in a flash realise how all these prison or bastille sort of surroundings were organised for the purpose of making self-respecting, decent people endure any suffering rather than enter. It was not necessary to write up the words 'abandon hope all ye who enter here'. Officials, receiving ward, hard forms, whitewashed walls, keys dangling at the waist of those who spoke to you, huge books for names, history, etc., searching, and then being stripped and bathed in a communal tub, and the final crowning indignity of being dressed in clothes which had been worn by lots of other people, hideous to look at, ill-fitting and coarse – everything possible was done to inflict mental and moral degradation. The place was clean: brass knobs and floors were polished, but of goodwill, kindliness, there was none. There is a little improvement in the ordinary workhouses of today, but not much. Most of them are still quite inhuman, though infirmaries, hospitals, and schools are all vastly improved. But 30 years ago the mixed workhouse at Poplar was for me Dante's *inferno*. Sick and aged, mentally deficient, lunatics, babies and children, able-bodied and tramps all herded together in one huge range of buildings. Officers, both men and women, looked upon these people as a nuisance, and treated them accordingly. Food was mainly skilly, bread, margarine, cheese and hard, tough meats and vegetables, and occasionally doses of salted, dried fish. Clothing was of the usual workhouse type, plenty of corduroy and blue cloth. No under garments for either men or women, no sanitary clothes of any sort or kind for women of any age, boots were worn until they fell off. The paupers, as they were officially styled, were allowed out once a month and could be visited once a month. Able-bodied men were put to stone-breaking or oakum-picking. No effort was made to find work for men or women.

3 Public Health in the Nineteenth Century

3.1 THE BEGINNINGS OF ACTION

3.1.1 Reports on the State of Large Towns, etc., 1844-5

The Royal Commission appointed by Sir Robert Peel in 1843 presented two reports in 1844 and 1845. Evidence was given by many witnesses, including Dr Southwood Smith and Dr Duncan, who was soon to become the country's first Medical Officer of Health. Dr Lyon Playfair, who provided statistical evidence on conditions in Lancashire, was a notable scientist and, later, MP.

From the First Report of the Commissioners of Inquiry into the State of Large Towns and Populous Districts, 1844
We, the undersigned Commissioners appointed by Your Majesty to inquire into the present state of large towns and populous districts in England and Wales, with reference to the matters hereunder specified:–

'The causes of disease among the inhabitants.

'The best means of promoting and securing the public health, under the operation of the laws and regulations now in force, and the usages at present prevailing. . . .'

We desire, in the first place, to express the sense which we entertain of the importance of the subject committed to us, not only as involving general benefit to the public, but especially a gradual improvement in the moral and physical condition of large numbers of Your Majesty's poorer subjects. . . .

Having obtained the information, respecting the operation of the laws now in force, which had been collected under previous inquiries . . . we proceeded to examine before the Board such persons as were prepared from long experience or observation to give their testimony upon the general subject. . . .

We then extended our investigations, and for that purpose we prepared a letter . . . to the municipal and other public officers in fifty towns where the rate of mortality appeared by the return of the registers of deaths . . . to be the highest. . . .

Each of these towns was afterwards visited by one of the Commissioners . . .

We have great satisfaction in representing to Your Majesty that in these local inquiries a lively and cordial interest was taken by the inhabitants; . . .

In addition to these our investigations, we promoted renewed inquiries by others into the sanatory state of several towns and populous districts, more especially of those places where the growth of the population has been attended by a high rate of mortality. . . .

As an example, of a town chiefly commercial, the Report relating to Liverpool, by Dr Duncan, physician to the Liverpool Dispensary, shows the great extent of mortality, of which the local authorities and the principal inhabitants appear to have been, up to a recent period, unaware, but which has been fully established by the returns in the registers of deaths. Competent witnesses concur in ascribing such an extent of mortality to the general want of drainage and cleansing, ill-conditioned dwellings, defective ventilation, scanty supplies of water, and to other causes capable of remedy. . . .

The returns obtained from . . . Sheffield, exhibits the different rates of mortality prevalent among artisans of similar occupations, when resident in the closer parts of the town, or in the more open suburbs. . . .

In consequence of facts . . . connecting personal and household uncleanliness, a low state of health, and extensive disease, with the deficiency and impurity of the supplies of water in the districts inhabited by the poorer classes, we directed our special inquiries to those existing arrangements, to which these defects were attributed.

We find that the laws in force, and the usages at present prevailing with regard to the supply of water to the great majority of towns and districts investigated, provide only for carrying the mains through the principal streets . . . it appears that they all stop short of a most important point, namely, measures for carrying supplies under an economical and properly regulated system, into the habitations of the poorer consumers. In a large proportion of the poorer districts the inhabitants have only out-door supplies by means of stand-pipes or common tanks or wells. In many instances they are obliged to fetch water from considerable distances from their dwellings, at much inconvenience, delay, labour, and expense; in many towns they are dependent for supplies either on collections of rainwater, or on water taken from adjacent streams, or pumped from springs, frequently liable to be polluted.

Upon the examination of the statements and answers from the towns to which our inquiries have been directed, it appears that only in six instances could the arrangements and the supplies be deemed in any comprehensive sense good; while in thirteen they appear to be indifferent, and in thirty-one so deficient as to be pronounced bad.

MINUTES OF EVIDENCE: DR SOUTHWOOD SMITH

I wish particularly to draw attention to the importance of having a certain number of rooms in the dwelling houses of the poor, though I am aware of the difficulty of legislating on this matter, and of the still greater difficulty of carrying out practically what the legislature may declare to be its intention and will. Still it is right that the attention of the public and of the legislature should be called to the physical deterioration, and the moral degradation, which result from the want of proper room in the dwelling-houses of the poor ... it is one of the influences which, for want of a better term, may be called unhumanizing, because it tends to weaken and destroy the feelings and affections which are distinctive of the human being, and which raise him above the level of the brute. ... In the filthy and crowded streets in our large towns and cities you see human faces retrograding, sinking down to the level of brute tribes, and you find manners appropriate to the degradation. Can any one wonder that there is among these classes of the people so little intelligence, so slight an approach to humanity, so total an absence of domestic affection, and of moral and religious feeling? ... if from early infancy, you allow human beings to live like brutes, you can degrade them down to their level.

From the Second Report of the Commissioners of Inquiry into the State of Large Towns and Populous Districts, 1845
Until the publication of the reports made to the Poor Law Commissioners in 1839, upon the condition of the poorer classes of

Your Majesty's subjects in certain parts of the Metropolis, followed by the Report of a Select Committee of the House of Commons in the year 1840, 'on the Health of Large Towns and Populous Districts', the extensive injury to the public health, now proved to arise from causes capable of removal, appears to have escaped general observation, while the means of remedying the evils by improvements in drainage, or by other structural arrangements, as have been carried into operation, have been executed more with a view to the appearance of the town, or the comfort of a portion of its inhabitants, than directed to maintain the health of the whole community. . . .

REGULATIONS FOR BUILDINGS

XXII. The Legislature has hitherto sanctioned but few local Acts, containing provisions for regulating the disposition of land as regards the width of streets, and the space to be allotted for houses, and restrictions are rarely placed upon the mode of constructing houses to provide the occupants with those comforts and conveniences, which are now considered necessary parts of every dwelling. . . .

We recommend that, subject to proper control, the local administrative body be empowered to raise money for the purchase of property for the purpose of opening thoroughfares, and widening streets, courts, and alleys, so as to improve the ventilation of the densely crowded districts of towns, as well as to increase the general convenience of traffic. . . .

XXIII. In the course of our investigations our attention has been frequently drawn to the propriety of recommending the adoption of regulations to prevent the erection of houses back to back so as to obstruct their due ventilation. We have taken every opportunity of ascertaining the opinions of practical men upon this subject, and we have endeavoured to trace any particular evil effects upon the health of inhabitants of houses so situated. The results of our inquiries do not convince us that the evils arising from such a mode of constructing houses are so marked as to call for any special enactment, and the testimony of builders, while they confirm this opinion tends to the conclusion that means may be provided for their efficient ventilation. The mere provision that an open space shall be left at the back, as well as the front of a house, affords little security for a due supply of fresh air in the interior. . . .

With the view therefore of ensuring better external ventilation, we recommend that courts and alleys be not built of a less width than twenty feet, and that they have an opening of not less than ten feet from the ground upwards at each end; the width of the court being in proportion to the height of the houses.

XXIV. The extent to which the practice of living in cellars prevails in some large towns has caused the enactment of local laws for their regulation. . . .

Local Acts have already been passed for Liverpool, Leeds, and London, prohibiting the use of cellars as dwellings, unless they are so constructed as to provide protection against the existence of evils.

We recommend that such provisions be made general, and that after a limited period the use of cellars as dwellings be prohibited, unless the rooms are of certain dimensions, are provided with a fire-place and window, of sufficient size, and made to open, and have an open space in front; and that the foundations be properly drained.

SECOND REPORT, APPENDIX, PART 2
Large towns in Lancashire: Report on their sanitary condition by Dr Lyon Playfair

. . . There are every year in Lancashire 14,000 deaths and 398,000 cases of sickness which might be prevented, and . . . 11,000 of the deaths consist of adults engaged in productive labour . . . every individual in Lancashire loses 19 years, or nearly one-half of the proper term of his life, and . . . every adult loses more than 10 years of life, and, from premature old age and sickness, much more than that period of working ability. Without taking into consideration the diminution of the physical and mental energies of the survivors from sickness, and other depressing causes; without estimating the loss from the substitution of young and inexperienced labour for that which is skilful and productive; without including the heavy burdens incident to the large amount of preventible widowhood and orphanage; without calculating the cost of the maintenance of an infantile population, nearly one-half of which is swept off before it attains two years of age, and about 59 per cent of which never become adult productive labourers; I estimate the actual pecuniary burdens borne by the community in the support of removable disease and death in Lancashire alone at the annual sum of five millions of sterling.

3.1.2 The Commons Debate on the Health of Towns Bill, 1847

These brief quotations from the debate on Lord Morpeth's abortive Health of Towns Bill of 1847 illustrate the arguments used on both sides.

Morpeth (1802–64) succeeded to the earldom of Carlisle in 1848. From 1846 to 1850, he was First Commissioner of Woods and Forests in Lord John Russell's first administration, and from 1848 to 1850 President of the General Board of Health set up under the Public Health Act of 1848.

Charles Newdegate (1816–87) was a leading Conservative, and MP for North Warwickshire, 1843–85.

From the House of Commons Debates, 18 June–1 July 1847

(18 June): Mr Newdegate . . . objected to the Bill on the ground that it usurped the powers which were now placed – and which ought to continue to be placed – in the hands of the municipal authorities. Instead of this, a new authority was proposed to be introduced totally foreign to every principle of the English Constitution . . . he regarded it as a departure from the free principles of the British Constitution, and a gradual usurpation, behind the backs of Parliament, of the power which ought to belong to the representatives of the people, and one step more towards the adoption of the continental system of centralisation, to which he was decidedly opposed. . . .

In a later debate (8 July) Newdegate said that he was anxious to have a comprehensive system of sanitary reform, but would be no party to a social revolution.

(1 July): Viscount Morpeth said . . . It was asked, why did they not let the towns petition for the extension of this measure? But his conviction was, that if such a regulation were adopted, the localities most in need of improvement, would be the very towns from which the invitations to interfere would not proceed. As to the word 'centralisation' there was nothing in it so very formidable in his ears. He believed the word was formidable to those only whose deeds merited punishment. Centralisation was either a very good or a very bad thing, according to the object to which it was applied, and the mode in which it operated. There was, he thought, no case in which it was more likely to be attended with good

results than that to which the Bill before the Committee applied. The proper sewerage of towns, the cleansing and lighting of streets, and the abundant supply of water, were the very matters in which the interference of an impartial and scientific superintendent authority would be most useful, and which were more likely to be effectually carried out under such superintendence, than under the struggling or desultory efforts of particular localities. That superintendence it was the object of the Bill to supply; but it would do no more. However useful the authority of the Commissioners might be, he, for one, should object to it, if it were to have the effect of superseding or paralysing local efforts. Their business would be to give advice, and to stimulate, if necessary, local efforts . . . If defective at all, he believed the Bill contained too little of stringent or compulsory power to effect what was desirable to have done. . . .

3.1.3 The First Public Health Act, 1848

After his failure in 1847 Morpeth carried a more modest measure in the following year, though the exclusion from its provisions of the City of London, due to the strength of the Corporation and the complexity of London's problems, raised a storm of protest. London was eventually dealt with in 1855 by the creation of the Metropolitan Board of Works, replaced in 1888, after some unsavoury revelations of corrupt practices, by the newly-constituted London County Council.

From the Public Health Act, 1848

I. Whereas further and more effectual Provision ought to be made for improving the sanitary Condition of Towns and populous Places in England and Wales, and it is expedient that the Supply of Water to such Towns and Places, and the Sewerage, Drainage, cleansing, and paving thereof, should, as far as practicable, be placed under one and the same local Management and Control . . . this Act may from Time to Time be applied . . . to any Part of England and Wales, except . . . the City of London. . . .

IV. The First Commissioner for the Time being of Her Majesty's Woods and Forests, Land Revenues, Works, and Buildings, together with such Two other Persons as Her Majesty may be pleased to appoint, shall be and constitute a Board for superintending the Execution of this Act, and shall be called 'The General Board of Health' . . . and the said First Commissioner shall be the President of the said Board; ... Provided always, that the said General Board of Health shall be continued only for Five Years ...

VI. The General Board of Health may from Time to Time appoint proper Persons to be Superintending Inspectors for the Purposes of this Act ...

VIII. From Time to Time after the passing of this Act, upon the Petition of not less than One Tenth of the Inhabitants rated to the Relief of the Poor of any City, Town, Borough, Parish, or Place, or where it shall appear from the last Return made up by the Registrar General that the Number of Deaths annually in any City, Town, Borough, Parish, or Place have on an Average exceeded the Proportion of Twenty-three to a Thousand, the General Board of Health may direct a Superintending Inspector to visit such Place, and to make public Inquiry, as to the Sewerage, Drainage, and Supply of Water, etc. ...

X. If after such Inquiry or further Inquiry aforesaid it appear to the said General Board of Health to be expedient that this Act should be applied to the Place with respect to which Inquiry has been made ... they shall report to Her Majesty accordingly; and it shall be lawful for Her Majesty, to order that this Act shall be put in full Force and Operation within such City, Town, Borough, Parish, or Place; ...

XII. In every District exclusively consisting of the whole or Part of One Corporate Borough the Mayor, Aldermen, and Burgesses of such Borough shall be the Local Board of Health under this Act ...

XXXVII. The Local Board of Health shall from Time to Time appoint fit and proper Persons to be Surveyor, Inspector of Nuisances, Clerk, and Treasurer for the Purposes of this Act ...

XL. The Local Board of Health may from Time to Time, if they shall think fit, appoint a fit and proper Person, being a legally qualified Medical Practitioner or a Member of the Medical Profession, to be and be called the Officer of Health, who shall be removable by the said Local Board, and shall perform such Duties as the said General Board shall direct; ...

XLIX. It shall not be lawful newly to erect any House, or to rebuild any House unless and until a covered Drain or Drains be constructed, of such Size and Materials, and at such Level, and with such Fall as upon the Report of the Surveyor shall appear to be necessary ...

LI. It shall not be lawful newly to erect any House, or to rebuild any House, without a sufficient Watercloset or Privy and an Ashpit, furnished with proper Doors and Coverings; . . .

LV. And be it enacted, That the Local Board of Health shall provide that all Streets within their District, including the Foot Pavements thereof, are properly swept, cleansed, and watered, and that all Dust, Ashes, Rubbish, Filth, Dung, and Soil thereon are collected and removed . . .

LXVII. It shall not be lawful to let or occupy as a Dwelling any Vault, Cellar, or underground Room built or rebuilt after the passing of this Act, or which shall not have been so let or occupied before the passing of this Act; and it shall not be lawful to let or continue to let, or to occupy or suffer to be occupied, separately as a Dwelling, any Vault, Cellar, or underground Room, whatsoever, unless the same be in every Part thereof at least Seven Feet in Height . . .

3.2 THE WORK OF DR (SIR) JOHN SIMON

Simon (1816–1904) was of French extraction (and therefore insisted on having his name stressed on the second syllable). He had considerable organising ability, and gathered round him a team of able young doctors who carried out investigations throughout the country. Unlike Chadwick he was not personally well-known outside official circles, but his series of reports, first for the City of London, and then for the Privy Council, attracted attention and proved influential, while his *English Sanitary Institutions*, written after his premature retirement, is a classic of its kind.

Only short quotations are given here, but they illustrate his concern for the poor and helpless. His seventh report to the Privy Council (1864) helped to bring about the transfer of financial responsibility from parishes to unions in 1865, and his eighth exercised a similar influence on the overcrowding clause of the Sanitary Act of 1866.

3.2.1 The Social Condition of the Poor in London, 1849

This extract from Simon's first report as MOH of the City of London inevitably reminds one of the 'coal in the bath' stories told of councilhouse tenants in the 1920s.

From the First Annual Report of the Medical Officer of Health to the City of London, 1849

THE SOCIAL CONDITION OF THE POOR

Not least, among the influences prejudicial to health in the City of London, as elsewhere, must be reckoned the social condition of the lower classes; and I refer to this the more especially, because often, in discussion of sanitary subjects before your Hon. Court, the filthy, or slovenly, or improvident, or destructive, or intemperate, or dishonest habits of these classes, are cited as an explanation of the inefficiency of measures designed for their advantage. It is constantly urged, that to bring improved domestic arrangements within the reach of such persons is a waste and a folly; that if you give them a coal-scuttle, a washing-basin, and a watercloset, these several utensils will be applied indifferently to the purposes of each other, or one to the purposes of all; and that meanwhile the objects of your charitable solicitude will remain in the same unredeemed lowness and misery as before. Now it is unquestionable, and I admit it – that in houses containing all the sanitary evils which I have enumerated – undrained, and waterless, and unventilated – there do dwell whole hordes of persons, who struggle so little in self-defence against that which surrounds them, that they may be considered almost indifferent to its existence, or almost acclimated to endure its continuance. It is too true that, among these classes, there are swarms of men and women, who have yet to learn that human beings should dwell differently from cattle; swarms, to whom personal cleanliness is utterly unknown; swarms, by whom delicacy and decency in their social relations are quite unconceived. Men and women, boys and girls, in scores of each, using jointly one single common privy; grown persons of both sexes sleeping in common with their married parents; a woman suffering travail in the midst of the males and females of three several families of fellow-lodgers in a single room; an adult son sharing his mother's bed during her confinement; – such are instances recently within my knowledge (and I might easily adduce others) of the degree and of the manner in which a people may relapse into the habits of savage life, when their domestic condition is neglected, and when they are suffered to habituate themselves to the uttermost depths of physical obscenity and degradation. . . .

I am far from insinuating, or suspecting, that the majority of the poorer population of the city has fallen to that extreme debasement which I have just illustrated as affecting some portion (perhaps not an inconsiderable portion) of the poorest; but I dare not suppress my knowledge that such instances exist, nor can I refrain from stating my belief, that ignorance and poverty will soon contribute to increase them, if sanitary and social improvement do not co-operate against their continuance.

Contemplating such cases, I feel the deepest conviction that no sanitary system can be adequate to the requirements of the time, or can cure those radical evils which infest the under-framework of society, unless the importance be distinctly recognised, and the duty manfully undertaken, of improving the social condition of the poor.

3.2.2 Disease Investigated for the Privy Council, 1858–71
These are extracts from the annual reports written by Simon as Medical Officer of the Privy Council committee on health matters.

From the Seventh Annual Report of the Medical Officer of the Committee of Council on Health, 1864 (1865)

HOUSE ACCOMMODATION OF RURAL LABORERS
In further pursuit of an object which had been proposed in 1863 ... my Lords during 1864 caused to be made throughout England an inquiry as to the House-Accommodation had by the agricultural and other laborers of rural districts. The inspector employed on this important inquiry was Dr Hunter. He, in making it, examined in the different counties of England as many as 5,375 occupied houses, and investigated, in each place that he visited, what local circumstances were in operation to affect the quality of the dwellings of the poor. . . .

To the insufficient quantity and miserable quality of the house-accommodation generally had by our agricultural laborers, almost every page of Dr Hunter's report bears testimony. And gradually for many years past the state of the laborer in these respects has been deteriorating. Especially within the last twenty or thirty years the evil has been in very rapid increase, and the household circumstances of the laborer are now in the highest degree deplorable. Except in so far as they whom his labor enriches see fit to treat him with a kind of pitiful indulgence, he is quite peculiarly help-less in the matter. Whether he shall find house-room on the land which he contributes to till, whether the house-room which he gets shall be human or swinish, whether he shall have the little space of garden that so vastly lessens the pressure of his poverty – all this does not depend on his willingness and ability to pay reasonable rent for the decent accommodation he requires, but depends on the use which others may see fit to make of their 'right to do as they will with their own' . . . Yet were this the whole hardship, his case would be less desperate than it is. . . . But an extraneous element weights the balance heavily against him, and he loses those fair chances of free trade. The element to which I refer is the influence of the Poor Law in its provision concerning settlement and chargeability. Under this influence, each parish has a pecu-niary interest in reducing to a minimum the number of its resident laborers:– for, unhappily, agricultural labor, instead of implying a safe and permanent independence for the hard-working laborer and his family, implies for the most part only a longer or shorter circuit to eventual pauperism . . . and thus all residence of agricul-tural population in a parish is glaringly an addition to its poor-rates. . . . But large proprietors feel the burthen very definitely and considerably, and, while feeling it, cannot but know that they have facilities, which are deemed not to be illegal, for shifting it away from themselves. They have but to resolve that there shall be no laborers' dwellings on their estates, and their estates will thence-forth be virtually free from half their responsibility for the poor. . . . As regards the extent of the evil, it may suffice to advert to the evidence which Dr Hunter has compiled from the last Census, that destruction of houses . . . had, during the last ten years, been in progress in 821 separate parishes or townships in England. . . .

It would however, be unjust to suppose that the relations between the large landowner and the laboring population are universally such as I have described. . . . There are some of the very largest land-properties in the country, where for generations there has been the tradition of a better treatment . . . judgment must not be blinded to the fact that they, in proportion to the mass of observed cases, are altogether exceptional and rare, and that, while our Poor Law continues unaltered in its provisions concerning settle-ment and chargeability, such instances must tend to become still rarer.

From the Eighth Annual Report of the Medical Officer of the Committee of Council on Health, 1865 (1866)

THE DISTRIBUTION OF DISEASE IN ENGLAND, AND THE CIRCUMSTANCES BY WHICH IT IS REGULATED

In pursuance of the systematic study which my Lords have for several years had in progress in this department, as to the distribution of disease in England, and as to the circumstances by which the distribution is regulated, their Lordships in 1865 ordered some additional inquiries, generally of the same kind as heretofore, to be undertaken, and also, in one respect, opened a new line of investigation.

Of these inquiries, the largest related to the Housing of the Poorer Population in Towns. In general intention this inquiry harmonised with one which had just before been made into the housing of the Rural Poor. Both were undertaken with reference to projected amendments of the Public Health Law, and had for their chief object to ascertain how far that law in its present state enables local authorities to prevent dangerous degrees of overcrowding in dwellings, and the use of dwellings unfit for human habitation. . . .

The broad results may be told in these very few words – that, neither against degrees of crowding which conduce immensely to the multiplication of disease, as well as to obvious moral evils, nor against the use of dwellings which are permanently unfit for human habitation, can local authorities in towns, except to a certain extent in some privileged places, exercise any effectual control . . . even in small country towns and villages, where the evil least admits of excuse, overcrowding is often in glaring excess. And thus, speaking generally, it may be said that the evils are uncontrolled in England.

No one, I apprehend, can doubt but that this state of things contravenes the intentions of the Legislature. . . . And the fact that the evils do nevertheless continue . . . constitutes an evident and urgent claim for such new legislation as will amend the present technical insufficiencies of the law.

3.2.3 English Sanitary Institutions

In this work Simon surveyed the history of English sanitary policy up to the Act of 1866, which he regarded with pride as his most important achievement.

From Dr John Simon, English Sanitary Institutions (*1890*), *p. 444*

THE POLITICS OF POVERTY

Be done what may under the Sanitary Acts to banish from the dwellings of the poor all worst degrees of uncleanliness and over-crowding, the condition remains, that scanty earnings can buy but scantily of the necessaries and comforts of life; and that, where the sternest frugality has to be exercised with regard to necessary food and clothing, where indeed but too often severe privation in those respects has to be endured, only very humble purchase of dwelling-space, and still humbler provision of means of comfort and cleanliness within the space, can be afforded. Question, how the house-accommodation of the poor labouring classes may be rendered such as humane persons would wish it to be, is therefore necessarily in great part question, how far poverty can be turned into non-poverty, how far the poor can be made less poor.

3.3 THE CLIMAX OF LEGISLATION

3.3.1 The 'Imperative Mood', 1866

This title is taken from Simon's comment on the 1866 Act in his book: that 'the grammar of common sanitary legislation' had at last acquired 'the novel virtue of an imperative mood'.

From the Sanitary Act, 1866

19. The Word 'Nuisances' under the Nuisance Removal Act shall include,

Any House or Part of a House so overcrowded as to be dangerous or prejudicial to the Health of the Inmates.

Any Factory, Workshop, or Workplace not kept in a cleanly State, or not ventilated in such a manner as to render harmless as far as practicable any Gases, Dust, or other Impurities generated in the course of the work carried on therein that are a Nuisance or injurious or dangerous to Health, or so over-crowded while work is carried on as to be dangerous or preju-dicial to the Health of those employed therein: ...

Any Chimney (not being the Chimney of a private Dwelling House), sending forth Black Smoke in such Quantity as to be a Nuisance: ...

20. It shall be the Duty of the Nuisance Authority to make from

Time to Time, either by itself or its Officers, Inspection of the district, with a view to ascertain what Nuisances exist calling for action under the Powers of the Nuisance Removal Acts, and to enforce the Provisions of the said Acts in order to cause the Abatement thereof. . . .

35. On Application to One of Her Majesty's Principal Secretaries of State by a Nuisance Authority . . . the Secretary of State may, as he may think fit, declare the following Enactment to be in force in the District of such Nuisance Authority, and the Nuisance Authority shall be empowered to make Regulations for the following Matters; . . .

1. For fixing the Number of Persons who may occupy a House or Part of a House which is let to Lodgings or occupied by Members of more than One Family:

2. For the Registration of Houses thus let or occupied in Lodgings:

3. For the Inspection of such Houses, and the keeping the same in a cleanly and wholesome State:

4. For enforcing therein the Provision of Privy Accommodation and other Appliances and Means of Cleanliness in proportion to the Number of Lodgings and Occupiers, and the cleansing and ventilation of the common Passages and Staircases:

5. For the cleansing and lime-whiting at stated Times of such Premises: . . .

37. The Nuisance Authority may provide for the Use of the Inhabitants within its District Hospitals or temporary Places for the Reception of the Sick.

3.3.2 Completion of the Environmental Services, 1875

A small selection of significant clauses is quoted from the Public Health Act of 1875. The whole Act Simon described, justly, as 'the *end* of a great argument'. It was to a large extent a tribute to his work that it stood for sixty years.

From the Public Health Act, 1875

PROHIBITION OF OCCUPYING CELLAR DWELLINGS

71. It shall not be lawful to let or occupy or suffer to be occupied separately as a dwelling any cellar (including for the purposes of this Act in that expression any vault or underground room) built

or rebuilt after the passing of this Act, or which is not lawfully so let or occupied at the time of the passing of this Act.

Existing Cellar Dwellings only to be let or occupied on certain Conditions. . . .

POWER OF LOCAL AUTHORITIES TO PROVIDE HOSPITALS

131. Any local authority may provide for the use of the inhabitants of their district hospitals or temporary places for the reception of the sick, and for that purpose may –

Themselves build such hospitals or places of reception;

Contract for the use of any such hospital or part of a hospital or place of reception;

Enter into any agreement with any person having the management of any hospital, for the reception of the sick inhabitants of their district, on payment of such annual or other sum as may be agreed on.

Two or more local authorities may combine in providing a common hospital. . . .

Officers of local authorities; appointment of officers of urban authority

189. Every urban authority shall from time to time appoint fit and proper persons to be medical officer of health, surveyor, inspector of nuisances, clerk, and treasurer. . . . Every urban authority shall also appoint or employ such assistants, collectors and other officers and servants as may be necessary and proper for the efficient execution of this Act, and may make regulations with respect to the duties and conduct of the officers and servants so appointed or employed.

A similar clause was added for rural authorities.

3.3.3 Public Hospitals, 1867

An outcry against conditions in the sick wards of workhouses led to the appointment of the first medical officer to the Poor Law Board, and to the declaration by Gathorne Hardy (afterwards Lord Cranbrook), President of the Board, that a deterrent poor law policy should not be applied to the sick, a sentiment with which Chadwick and the other reformers of 1834 would have agreed. Unions were encouraged to form Sick Asylum Districts for the establishment of hospitals, and in London to pool their resources in a Common Poor Fund, with a

Metropolitan Asylums Board to manage hospitals and out-patient dispensaries.

From the Metropolitan Poor Act, 1867

7. Asylums to be supported and managed according to the provision of this Act may be provided under this Act for reception and relief of the sick, insane, or infirm, or other class or classes of the poor chargeable in unions and parishes in the metropolis. . . .

LXIX. Expenses incurred for the following purposes shall be repaid out of the common poor fund, that is to say, –

(1) For the maintenance of lunatics in asylums . . .

(2) For the maintenance of patients in any asylum specially provided under this Act for patients suffering from fever or small-pox: . . .

(3) For all medicine and medical and surgical appliances supplied to the poor in receipt of relief . . .

From the Public Health (London) Act, 1891

LXXX. (1) The metropolitan asylum managers, subject to such regulations and restrictions as the Local Government Board prescribe, may admit any person, who is not a pauper and is reasonably believed to be suffering from fever or smallpox or diphtheria, into a hospital provided by the managers.

(2) The expenses incurred by the managers for the maintenance of any such person shall be paid by the board of guardians of the poor law union from which he is received. . . .

(4) The admission of a person suffering from an infectious disease into any hospital provided by the metropolitan asylum managers, or the maintenance of any such person therein, shall not be considered to be parochial relief, alms, or charitable allowance to any person, or to the parent or husband of any person; nor shall any person or his or her parent or husband be by reason hereof deprived of any right or privilege, or be subjected to any disability or disqualification.

3.4 VACCINATION

3.4.1 'A Victorian National Health Service'[1]

The first Act, in 1840, had not made it clear that the vaccination service could be charged to the poor rates, and was exempt from the franchise disqualification: hence this amendment. The 1867 Act saw the completion of a comprehensive and compulsory service, and was strengthened in 1871, at the time of the country's worst epidemic, which killed 44,000 people.

Compulsory vaccination was not strictly enforced in later years, but was not formally abandoned until 1946 (National Health Service Act) though conscientious objection was permitted in 1898.

From the Vaccination (Amendment) Act, 1841
I. Whereas an Act was passed in the Fourth Year of the Reign of Her present Majesty, intituled An Act to extend the Practice of Vaccination; but no express Provision was thereby made for defraying the Expences of carrying the same into execution. . . . I shall be and be deemed to have been lawful for the Guardians of every Parish or Union by whom the Contracts for Vaccination may respectively be or have been made under the Provisions of the Said Act, to defray the Expences incident to the Execution of the Said Act out of any Rates or Monies which may come or may have come into their Hands respectively for the Relief of the Poor.
II. The Vaccination, or Surgical or Medical Assistance incident to the Vaccination, of any Person resident in any Union or Parish, or of any of his Family, under the said Act, shall not be considered to be Parochial Relief, Alms, or charitable Allowance to such Person, and no such Person shall by reason of such Vaccination or Assistance be deprived of any Right or Privilege, or be subject to any Disability or Disqualification whatsoever.

From the Vaccination Act, 1867
XVI. The parent of every child born in England shall within three months after the birth of such child . . . take it or cause it to be taken to the public vaccinator of the vaccination district in which it shall be then resident, according to the provisions of this or any other Act, to be vaccinated, or shall within such period as aforesaid cause it to be vaccinated by some medical practitioner. . . .

[1] R. Lambert, 'A Victorian National Health Service: State Vaccination 1855–71', *Historical Journal*, 1962.

XVII. Upon the same day in the following week when the operation shall have been performed by the public vaccinator such parent . . . shall again take the child or cause it to be taken to him or to his deputy that he may inspect it, and ascertain the result of the operation . . .

XXI. Every public vaccinator who shall have performed the operation of vaccination upon any child, and have ascertained that the same has been successful, shall, within twenty-one days after the performance of the operation, transmit by post or otherwise a certificate certifying that the said child has . . . been successfully vaccinated, to the registrar of births and deaths in the district within which the birth was registered . . . and upon request shall deliver a duplicate thereof to the parent . . .

XXVI. It is hereby declared, that the vaccination, or the surgical or medical assistance incident to the vaccination, of any person in a union or parish, heretofore or hereafter performed or rendered by a public vaccinator, shall not be considered to be parochial relief, alms, or charitable allowance to such person or his parent, and no such person or his parent shall by reason thereof be deprived of any right or privilege, or be subject to any disability of disqualification.

4 Housing in the Nineteenth Century

4.1 THE FIRST LEGISLATION

4.1.1 Back-to-Back in Manchester, 1844

Much early legislation for the improvement of towns was put through by authorities in Local Acts. Manchester had had a succession of these since the late eighteenth century, though they did little to improve the slums. A Manchester Police Act of 1844 did, however, succeed in checking back-to-back building. As will be seen in this extract, it was also concerned with many other aspects of urban life, including the display of female legs for the delectation of the prurient.

From the Manchester Police Act, 1844

65. The Owner of every house to which no sufficient privy or ash-pit is attached shall provide such fit and proper privy to the same and also such fit and sufficient ashpit, and in such situation, as the council shall consider requisite.

66. No house shall hereafter be built without there being constructed to the satisfaction of the council, either in such house, or in a yard attached to such house, a privy with proper doors and coverings, and also an ashpit, provided that in the case of houses in courts a privy and ashpit, or two or more privies and ashpits, may, with the approbation of the council, be used in common by the inmates and occupiers of such houses. . . .

75. Every furnace employed or to be employed in the working of engines by steam . . . shall, in all cases where the same shall be practicable, be constructed so as to consume or burn the smoke arising from such furnace. . . .

103. [Certain offences were listed as liable to incur a fine of 40s including:]

Every female who shall stand on the outside of any window the sill whereof shall be more than six feet in height from the level of the street, for the purpose of cleaning the same, or for any other purpose whatsoever.

From the Royal Sanitary Commission, First Report, 1869

MINUTES OF EVIDENCE: THE EVIDENCE OF MR J. HERON, TOWN CLERK OF MANCHESTER

144. In Manchester, under our Act of 1844, a privy and ashpit in such a situation as satisfies the corporation is required to every house. The corporation have required the existence of a yard behind each house in which the privy and ashpit will be placed. The consequence of that legislation has been that in Manchester, since 1844, the building of back-to-back houses, which is one of the most crying nuisances that can be imagined, has been illegal. The clauses of the act have necessitated behind each house a yard, and then between the yards of those cottages and the cottages bordering into the other street there is necessarily a passage, so that the nuisances created by and the evils arising from back-to-back houses and cottages being erected have not been allowed to exist.

4.1.2 The First Working Class Housing Act, 1851

True to his evangelical creed, Lord Ashley, who sponsored this measure, had in mind the moral improvement of the working classes. Until their domiciliary condition was Christianised, he declared, 'all hope of moral or social improvement was utterly vain'. Unfortunately the Act was completely disregarded by authorities.

From an Act to Encourage the Establishment of Lodging Houses for the Labouring Classes, 1851

I. Whereas it is desirable, for the Health, Comfort, and Welfare of the Inhabitants of Towns and populous Districts, to encourage the Establishment therein of well-ordered Lodging Houses for the Labouring Classes . . .

XXXV. In any Borough, the Council . . . may from Time to Time appropriate for the Purposes of this Act in the Borough any Lands vested in the Mayor, Aldermen, and Burgesses . . .

XXXVI. The Council . . . may from Time to Time, on any Lands so appropriated . . . erect any Buildings suitable for Lodging

Houses for the Labouring Classes, and convert any Buildings into Lodging Houses for the Labouring Classes, and may from Time to Time alter, enlarge, repair, and improve the same respectively, and fit up, furnish, and supply the same respectively with all requisite Furniture, Fittings, and Conveniences.

4.1.3 Loans to Local Authorities for Housing, 1866

This supplement to the Act of 1851 was used by only one authority, Liverpool. Otherwise only charitable housing trusts and private individuals took advantage of it, some of the latter, indeed, making substantial profits out of it by charging higher interest rates than they paid to the Loan Commissioners.

From the Labouring Classes' Dwelling Houses Act, 1886: An Act to Enable the Public Works Loan Commissioners to Make Advances Towards the Erection of Dwellings for the Labouring Classes

1. Whereas by 'The Labouring Classes Lodging Houses Act, 1851', Powers were vested in certain Local Authorities for the Purpose of facilitating the Erection of Lodging Houses for the Labouring Classes:

And whereas it is desirable that further Provision should be made for facilitating and encouraging the Erection of Dwellings for the Labouring Classes in populous Places . . . .

2. This Act shall be deemed to be incorporated with and shall be taken as Part of 'The Labouring Classes Lodging Houses Act, 1851' . . .

4. The Public Works Loan Commissioners may out of the Funds for the Time being at their Disposal from Time to Time advance on Loan to any Local Authority . . . such Money as may be required for the Purpose of assisting in the Purchase of Land and Buildings, or in the Erection, Alteration, and Adaptation of Buildings to be used as Dwellings for the Labouring Classes.

4.2 THE TORRENS AND CROSS ACTS

4.2.1 Clearing Single Houses, 1868

This was the first attempt to grapple with the problem of insanitary houses. It was strenuously resisted, a clause enabling local authorities to replace bad houses being struck out in debate, and it had little effect hough it did at least establish the principle that house-owners were esponsible for keeping their property in decent condition.

W. T. M. Torrens, who introduced the measure, was MP for Finsbury, 1865–85, and was much concerned with social reform.

rom the Artisans' and Labourers' Dwellings Act, 1868

. Whereas it is expedient to make Provision for taking down or mproving Dwellings occupied by Working Men and their Families vhich are unfit for Human Habitation, and for the building and Maintenance of better Dwellings for such Persons . . .

. If in any Place to which this Act applies the Officer of Health nd that any Premises therein are in a Condition or State dangerous o Health so as to be unfit for Human Habitation, he shall report he same to the Local Authority.

. The Local Authority shall refer such Report to a Surveyor or Engineer, who shall thereupon consider the Report, and report to he Local Authority what is the Cause of the Evil . . . and the Remedy thereof . . .

. Upon Receipt of the Report of the Surveyor and Engineer the Local Authority . . . shall make an Order . . . which shall be subect to Appeal . . . and if such Objections are overruled, the Local Authority . . . shall cause to be prepared a Plan and Specification f the Works . . . and an Estimate of the Cost of such Works, equired to be executed . . .

8. The Owner on whom the Local Authority shall have imposed he Duty of executing the Work shall, within Two Calendar Months thereafter, commence the Works as shown on the Plan . . and shall diligently proceed with and complete the same . . . nd if such Owner shall fail therein . . . the Local Authority shall, s the Case may seem to them to require, either order the Premises o be shut up or to be demolished, or may themselves execute he required Works.

4.2.2 Clearing Whole Areas, 1875

Disraeli's Home Secretary, Sir Richard Cross (1823–1914) in 1875 carried this well-intentioned and well-known 'Cross Act', which, though t went further than the Torrens Act, bears a reputation higher than its ctual achievement warrants. Powers for clearing insanitary areas were f limited value without powers to replace the houses destroyed, while he compensation paid was almost invariably excessive.

From the Artisans' and Labourers' Dwellings Improvement Act, 187

UNHEALTHY AREAS
1. Scheme by local authority

3. Where an official representation . . . is made to the local authorit
that any houses, courts, or alleys within a certain area under th
jurisdiction of the local authority are unfit for human habitatio
. . . and that the evils connected with such houses, courts, o
alleys, and the sanitary defects in such area, cannot be effectuall
remedied otherwise than by an improvement scheme for the re
arrangement and reconstruction of the streets and houses withi
such area . . . the local authority shall take such representatio
into their consideration, and if satisfied of the truth thereof, an
of the sufficiency of their resources, shall pass a resolution to th
effect that such area is an unhealthy area, and that an improvemen
scheme ought be made in respect of such area, and after passin
such resolution they shall forthwith proceed to make a scheme fo
the improvement of such area. . . .

4. An official representation shall mean . . . a representation mad
to the local authority by the medical officer of health of sucl
authority . . .

5. The improvement scheme . . . shall provide for the accommoda
tion of at the least as many persons of the working class as may b
displaced in the area with respect to which the scheme is pro
posed, in suitable dwellings, which, unless there are any specia
reasons to the contrary, shall be situate within the limits of th
same area, or in the vicinity thereof; . . .

3. Execution of scheme by local authority

9. When the confirming Act authorising any improvement schem
of a local authority under this Act has been passed by Parliament
it shall be the duty of that authority to take steps for purchasin
the lands required for the scheme, and otherwise for carrying th
scheme into execution as soon as practicable. They may sell o
let all or any part of the area . . . to any purchasers or lessees . .
under the condition that such purchasers or lessees will . . . carr
the scheme into execution; and in particular they may insert i
any grant or lease of any part of the area provisions binding th
grantee or lessee to build thereon . . . and to maintain and repai
the buildings . . . but the local authority shall not themselves

without the express approval of the confirming authority, under-take the rebuilding of the houses or the execution of any part of the scheme, except that they may take down any or all of the buildings upon the area, and clear the whole or any part thereof, and may lay out, form, pave, sewer, and complete all such streets upon the land purchased by them as they may think fit. . . .

Provided that in any grant or lease of any part of the area which may be appropriated by the scheme for the erection of dwellings for the working classes, the local authority shall impose suitable conditions and restrictions as to the elevation, size, and design of the houses, and the extent of the accommodation to be afforded thereby, and shall make due provision for the maintenance of proper sanitary arrangements. . . .

19. (2) Whenever the compensation payable in respect of any lands proposed to be taken compulsorily requires to be assessed, the estimate of the value of such lands shall be based upon the fair market value . . . due regard being had to the nature and con-dition of the property . . . and to the state of repair thereof, and all circumstances affecting such value, without any additional allowance in respect of the compulsory purchase of an area.

4.2.3 Report on the Working of the Acts, 1882
Concern at the difficulties encountered in the application of the Torrens and Cross Acts led to the appointment of a Select Committee, chaired by Cross himself. Some slight amendments followed in a new Artisan's Dwellings Act, 1822.

From the Report of the Select Committee on the Artisans' and Labourers' Dwellings Improvement Acts, 1882

(A) – AS TO THE ACTS OF 1875–1879 (SIR R.A. CROSS'S ACTS)
Owing to the obligations imposed by the Acts of 1875, of providing accommodation for *at least as many* persons of the working classes as may be displaced, it has been possible to reserve but a small portion of the areas thus cleared for commercial purposes. . . .

The estimated amount to be received for recoupment by sale of land is about £370,000, which would leave the net loss to the Metropolitan Board from the whole transaction at £1,211,336, being about 76 per cent of the gross cost. . . . A large proportion of the difference between the cost and the recoupment, which may be fairly estimated at not less than £560,000, is due to the obligation to rebuild labourers' dwellings, instead of selling the sites for ordinary purposes.

The areas dealt with were in almost every case cleared, and the persons living in any individual area were dispossessed with such compensation as was awarded to them before any rebuilding commenced. It is stated that very few, if any, of the families thus dispossessed returned for the purpose of occupying the new buildings; and in one case where a block built by the Peabody Trustees on an adjoining site was available for the persons dispossessed, and holdings were offered to them, very few accepted them. The buildings of the Peabody Trustees appear to be somewhat beyond the means, and unsuited to the wants and special callings, of the poorer class of persons occupying areas with which it has been found necessary to deal. . . .

Your Committee would call attention to the importance of favouring in every way facilities of transit between the great centres of industry and the outlying districts, and especially between the metropolis and its suburbs. Owing to economic causes land in the central parts of London is, generally speaking, becoming too valuable to be easily made use of as sites for dwellings for the working classes, and property of this kind, including areas scheduled under these Acts, is being constantly bought up and converted to other purposes.

4.2.4 Workmen's Fares, 1883

This Act followed a recommendation of the 1882 committee and extended a practice already required of the Metropolitan Railway in London since 1861.

From the Cheap Trains Act, 1883

3. (1) If at any time the Board of Trade have reason to believe –
   (*a*) that upon any railway or part of a railway . . . a due and sufficient proportion of the accommodation provided by such company or companies is not provided for passengers at fares not exceeding the rate of one penny a mile; or
   (*b*) that upon any railway carrying passengers proper and sufficient workmen's trains are not provided for workmen going to and returning from their work at such fares and at such times between six o'clock in the evening and eight

o'clock in morning as appear to the Board of Trade to be
reasonable, . . .
then and in either case the Board of Trade may . . .

(2) . . . order the company to provide such accommodation or
workmen's trains at such fares as, having regard to the circumstances, may appear to the said Board or the Commissioners to be
reasonable.

4.3 THE COMING OF LOCAL AUTHORITY HOUSING

4.3.1 Birmingham and the Cross Act

The most striking application of the Cross Act took place in Birmingham. Joseph Chamberlain had taken office as Mayor in 1873, and been
shocked, as the speech quoted shows, at the conditions he found in the
town's centre. He took advantage of the Act to carry out a programme
of 'sagacious audacity', clearing a squalid area (at an outlay of £1,500,000)
and creating a fine new road, Corporation Street, and a business quarter.
Not until the 1890s, however, was the success of the scheme assured,
and it was only in 1937–8 that any profit could be shown.[1]

From J. L. Garvin, The Life of Joseph Chamberlain, *Vol. I (1932)
pp. 195–6, 198–9*

Chamberlain: 'We bring up a population in the dank dreary, filthy
courts and alleys . . . we surround them with noxious influences of
every kind, and place them under conditions in which the obser-
vance of even ordinary decency is impossible; and what is the
result? . . . Their fault! Yes, it is legally their fault, and when
they steal we send them to gaol and when they commit murder we
hang them. But if the members of the Council had been placed
under similar conditions – if from infancy we had grown up in the
same way – does any one of us believe that he should have run no
risk of the gaol or the hangman? For my part I have not sufficient
confidence in my own inherent goodness to believe that anything
can make headway against such frightful conditions as those I have
described. It is no more the fault of these people that they are
vicious and intemperate than it is their fault that they are stunted,
deformed, debilitated and diseased.'

Where the jumble of slums had stood Corporation Street rose

[1] Asa Briggs, *History of Birmingham*, II, 81. (For a further note on housing
in Birmingham see 4.3.9.)

into being. ... Good lighting, pure water, fresher air, cleansed streets, more space within and without, sanitary measures of strict vigilance – all these benefits were brought into the reconstructed quarter. Figures like the following statistics are beyond eloquence in their silent tribute to this short but intense part of Chamberlain's career:

Average death-rate per 1000 for 1873–75: 53.2
Average death-rate per 1000 for 1879–81: 21.3

4.3.2 'How the Poor Live', 1883

Andrew Mearns's *Bitter Cry of Outcast London* being too long to include, a brief quotation is given from one of the articles preceding it which G. R. Sims wrote and on which Mearns drew. Sims was a prolific writer, journalist and playwright, long remembered for his tear-jerking ballad *Christmas Day in the Workhouse*. The references are to the Zulu War (1879) and the involvement in Egypt (1882).

From an article by G. R. Sims

Is it too much to ask that in the intervals of civilizing the Zulu and improving the conditions of the Egyptian fellah the Government should turn its attention to the poor of London and see if it cannot remedy this terrible state of things?

4.3.3 The Royal Commission of 1884–5

As mentioned in the introduction, it was Lord Salisbury who called for a Royal Commission on the Housing of the Working Classes, though he also had the support of Joseph Chamberlain, who was critical of Parliament's timid respect for property rights. The Commission was set up under the chairmanship of the President of the Local Government Board, Sir Charles Dilke, and included among its members the Prince of Wales, Salisbury himself, Cross and the notable Roman Catholic, Cardinal Manning, while Lord Shaftesbury and Chadwick, both now over eighty, gave evidence.

The Commission's report is too long and involved to quote at length: a summary is therefore given, with short quotations.

From the Report of the Royal Commission on the Housing of the Working Classes, 1884–5: Summary

As soon as it started its enquiries the Commission found that although much housing legislation had been passed some of it had proved 'a dead letter'. This was particularly true of Lord Shaftesbury's Act of 1851. When Shaftesbury himself, then eighty-three, appeared before the Commission, he deplored the fact that so little use had been made of the Act, which could have met most of the needs that the thirty years since its passing had revealed. 'At the time when that Act was passed,' he commented, 'there was no feeling in the country on the matter at all, and therefore it passed unnoticed.'

On the more recent legislation the Commission itself took the view that it was far too complex and elaborate: 'if efforts have been made in Parliament to improve the dwellings of the poor, the result has been to make knowledge as to the remedies for the evils attainable only by very difficult and elaborate study'. Local authorities, in any case too much under the control of property owners, had therefore been doubly reluctant to move, and had proved 'supine', and resistant to Government pressure: 'in some localities', the Commission noted, 'anything that savours of centralisation is at once condemned without a trial'.

Moreover, the legislation passed had been mainly concerned with sanitary conditions, not with houses themselves, and although there had been 'enormous' progress, the poverty of many people had left them at the mercy of bad landlords. Jerry-building was rife: 'the old houses are rotten from age and neglect. The new houses often commence where the old ones leave off, and are rotten from the first. It is quite certain that the working classes are largely housed in dwellings which would be unsuitable even if they were not overcrowded'.

Overcrowding was in part the result of sanitary clearance, which left the dispossessed nowhere to go. 'The pulling down of buildings inhabited by the very poor, whether undertaken for philanthropic, sanitary or commercial purposes, does cause overcrowding into the neighbouring slums, with the further consequence of keeping up the high rents. Even if the classes so disturbed could afford to pay for better accommodation, they have not the faculty to seek it. When notice is given they never seem to appreciate the fact that their homes are about to be destroyed until the workmen come to pull the roof from over their heads. Lord Shaftesbury described how the inhabitants had been seen like people in a besieged town, running to and fro, and not knowing where to turn. The evidence of the inability of the poor to protect themselves in this and in other particulars is conclusive.'

Railway construction had also added seriously to the difficulties, and railway companies had shown complete disregard for the people they had turned out to build stations etc. The building of St Pancras Station in the 1860s, for instance, had led to the destruction of five hundred homes. Parts of St Pancras, therefore, had not become more overcrowded simply because they were already so full that they could not crowd in more. A case of eleven families in eleven rooms was noted, and another, from Newcastle, of 140 families in thirty-four houses. Old houses were divided into tenements and as the doors were never closed many people (known in Southwark as ''appy dossers') regularly slept on the stairs and in the passages.

The Peabody Trust and other organisations had done valuable work, but their tenements were in the main too expensive: 'model dwellings do not reach the class whose need is greatest'.

The failure to achieve more improvement was administrative, however, rather than legislative. Far too many Medical Officers of Health were non-resident, and inspectors of nuisances were both unskilled and uncommon. The Commission recommended that inspectors should be properly trained and that authorities should be advised to appoint full-time medical officers, who should be compelled to live in the area for which they were responsible.

In a special section the Commission also recommended that the population should be encouraged to spread itself. Many people had to live near their work, but might be encouraged to move into areas of lower rent if there were cheap fares on the railways. Already 'the State has interfered in this matter in the public interest, rather with reference to what the working classes can afford than to what will pay the railway companies', and the Board of Trade should make more use of its powers to compel the railways to offer cheap fares.

One comforting conclusion that the commission did reach was that the standard of morality in the overcrowded areas was 'higher than might have been expected', and Mearns when giving evidence was forced to modify the charges of immorality which he had made in his *Bitter Cry*.

To stir the local authorities into action without imposing centralised control on them, the Commission proposed that they should have the power to make their own by-laws. Details apart, however, in the last resort it placed its reliance for improvement on the pressure of public opinion as a force providing 'some motive power' for action. It was hardly a strong lead.

4.3.4 Local Authority Powers, 1890

Like the Public Health Act of 1895, the Housing Act of 1890 consolidated existing legislation, though it also added to it by permitting the building of single houses and the inclusion of gardens. Local authority provision was still thought of, however, essentially in terms of the clearance of insanitary areas.

From the Housing of the Working Classes Act, 1890

REQUISITES OF IMPROVEMENT SCHEME AS TO ACCOMMODA-
TION OF WORKING CLASSES

11. (1) Subject as hereinafter mentioned, every scheme comprising an area in the county or city of London shall provide for the accommodation of at the least as many persons of the working class as may be displaced in the area comprised therein, in suitable dwellings, which, unless there are any special reasons to the contrary, shall be situate within the limits of the same area, or in the vicinity thereof.

Provided that

(a) Where it is proved to the satisfaction of the confirming authority on an application to authorise a scheme that equally convenient accommodation can be provided for any persons of the working classes displaced by the scheme at some place other than within the area or the immediate vicinity of the area comprised in the scheme, and that the required accommodation has been or is about to be forthwith provided, either by the local authority or by any other person or body of persons, the confirming authority may authorise such scheme, and the requirements of this section with respect to providing accommodation for persons of the working class shall be deemed to have been complied with to the extent to which accommodation is so provided; and

(b) Where the local authority apply for a dispensation under this section, and the officer conducting the local inquiry directed by the confirming authority reports that it is expedient, having regard to the special circumstances of the locality and to the number of artisans and others belonging to the working class dwelling within the area, and being employed within a mile thereof, that a modification should be made, the confirming authority, without prejudice to any other powers conferred on it by this part of this Act, may in the Provisional Order authorising the scheme, dispense altogether with the obligation of the local authority to provide for the accommodation of the persons of the working class who may be displaced by the scheme to such extent as the confirming authority may think expedient, having regard to such special circumstances as aforesaid, but not exceeding one half of the persons so displaced. . . .

PART III: WORKING-CLASS LODGING-HOUSES
Definition of purposes of labouring classes lodging-houses Acts
53. (1) The expression 'lodging-houses for the working classes' when used in this part of this Act shall include separate houses or cottages for the working classes, whether containing one or several tenements, and the purposes of this part of this Act shall include the provision of such houses and cottages.

(2) The expression 'cottage' in this part of this Act may include a garden of not more than half an acre, provided that the estimated annual value of such garden shall not exceed three pounds. . . .
59. The local authority may, on any land acquired or appropriated by them, erect any buildings suitable for lodging-houses for the working classes, and convert any buildings into lodging-houses for the working classes, and may alter, enlarge, repair, and improve the same respectively, and fit up, furnish, and supply the same respectively with all requisite furniture, fittings, and conveniences.

MANAGEMENT OF LODGING-HOUSES
Management to be vested in local authority
61. (1) The general management, regulation, and control of the lodging-houses established or acquired by a local authority under this part of this Act shall be vested in and exercised by the local authority.

(2) The local authority may make such reasonable charges for the tenancy or occupation of the lodging-houses provided under this part of this Act as they may determine by regulations.

4.3.5 Housing Estates, 1900

An amending Act of 1900 met a need by enabling authorities where necessary to build outside their own areas, where land was usually cheaper. The LCC developed 'estates' at Tooting, Norbury and Tottenham.

From The Housing of the Working Classes Act, 1900

EXERCISE OF POWERS OUTSIDE DISTRICT

1. Where any council have adopted Part III of the Housing of the Working Classes Act, 1890 ... they may, for supplying the needs of their district, establish or acquire lodging-houses for the working classes under that Part outside their district.

4.3.6 Health and Housing, 1909

This Act is notable for its tardy prohibition on back-to-back housing, its introduction of town-planning and its extension of the medical functions of county authorities, which enhanced the professional status of the MOH.

Neither Parliament nor the LGB, of course, could wave a magic wand and abolish back-to-back houses, and it was not until the 1930s that the problem began to be seriously tackled, while houses of this kind are still waiting to be pulled down in the early 1970s.

From the Housing and Town Planning Act, 1909

PART I: HOUSING OF THE WORKING CLASSES

1. Part III of the Housing of the Working Classes Act, 1890, shall take effect in every urban or rural district, or other place for which it has not been adopted, as if it had been so adopted. . . .

PROHIBITION OF BACK-TO-BACK HOUSES

43. Notwithstanding anything in any local Act or by-law in force in any borough or district, it shall not be lawful to erect any back-to-back houses intended to be used as dwellings for the working classes, and any such house commenced to be erected after the passing of this Act shall be deemed to be unfit for human habitation for the purposes of the provisions of the Housing Acts. . . .

PART II: TOWN PLANNING

54. (1) A town planning scheme may be made as respects any land which is in course of development or appears likely to be

E

used for building purposes, with the general object of securing proper sanitary conditions, amenity, and convenience in connexion with the laying out and use of the land. . . .

PART III: COUNTY MEDICAL OFFICERS, COUNTY PUBLIC HEALTH AND HOUSING COMMITTEE, ETC.

68 (1) Every county council shall appoint a medical officer of health under section seventeen of the Local Government Act, 1888.

(2) The duties of a medical officer of health of a county shall be such duties as may be prescribed by general order of the Local Government Board and such other duties as may be assigned to him by the county council. . . .

(5) A medical officer of health of a county shall be removable by the county council with the consent of the Local Government Board and not otherwise.

(6) A medical officer of health of a county shall not be appointed for a limited period only. . . .

(7) A medical officer of health appointed after the passing of this Act under the said section as amended by this section shall not engage in private practice. . . .

71. (1) Every county council shall establish a public health and housing committee, and all matters relating to the exercise and performance by the council of their powers and duties as respects public health and the housing of the working classes shall stand referred to the public health and housing committee.

4.3.7 The End of Back-to-Back, 1910
The quotation is from the introduction by Dr (afterwards Sir) Arthur Newsholme, Medical Officer of the LGB, to a special report by Dr Darra Mair to the Local Government Board on the health hazards of back-to-back housing.

From a Report to the Local Government Board, 1910
. . . The problem has been studied, as in previous inquiries on the same subject, by instituting comparisons between death-rates in back-to-back and in through houses of similar class. In some or all of the following important particulars, however, Dr Darra Mair's study differs from previous studies of the subject. Thus the comparison between back-to-back and through houses has not been limited to one town, but has extended to thirteen industrial towns in the West Riding of Yorkshire. In the next place, the comparison of the two types of houses has been limited to houses in good

structural condition situated in healthy areas, in order that, so far as practicable, the issue might not be confused by influences other than that of through ventilation. Thirdly, in order to avoid accidental statistical error, the vital statistics have been taken for a period extending over ten years. Lastly, and most important of all, the death-rates in this report have been corrected for variations in the age and sex constitution of populations. . . .

The statistical results thus obtained confirm, on the whole, the results of previous less complete inquiries. They show that even relatively good types of back-to-back houses, when compared with through houses, have a death-rate from all causes taken together which is fifteen to twenty per cent. in excess of the death-rate in through houses; although this excess is not evident in back-to-back houses built in blocks of four, possessing some degree of cross ventilation, unlike those built in continuous rows.

It is noteworthy, however, that in back-to-back houses there is excessive mortality from certain important groups of diseases, whether these houses are built in blocks of four or in continuous rows. The groups of diseases thus showing excess are diseases of the chest, like bronchitis and pneumonia, and diseases especially associated with defective growth and development of the young child. . . .

The statistics also show that the excessive mortality associated with back-to-back houses falls chiefly on childhood and old age.

4.3.8 The LGB and Housing, 1915

From the Forty-Second Annual Report of the Local Government Board, 1912–13, Part II, p. xxxiv

We recognise that in England and Wales private enterprise has always been, and, so far as can be foreseen, will continue to be the main source of the provision of houses for the working classes. It is only in those places where private enterprise has failed to provide such houses that the local authority is required to step in.

Loans sanctioned outside London under Part I of the Housing Act, 1890 between 1891 and 1913 totalled £2,700,000. By 1913 some 15,000 houses had been erected by local authorities under Part III of the Act.

4.3.9 Birmingham after Chamberlain

J. S. Nettlefold, of the firm in which Joseph Chamberlain had made his fortune, was a cousin and disciple of Chamberlain, who stayed in local politics when Chamberlain himself went to Westminster. He was active in municipal affairs, with a particular interest in housing, and a pioneer of town-planning. The corporation's reluctance to build houses is, however, very evident in this extract.

Neville Chamberlain (1869–1940), soon to be Lord Mayor of Birmingham, and later, Minister of Health, Chancellor of the Exchequer and Prime Minister, was Joseph Chamberlain's second son.

From Asa Briggs, History of Birmingham, Borough and City, 1865–1938 *(1952), pp. 85–6*

By thirty-two votes to thirty the Council decided [in 1901] to set up a new Housing Committee, which would take over from the Estates and Health Committee all powers exercised under the Housing Acts, and such powers under the Public Health Acts as might be thought desirable. With men like Nettlefold to direct it, the committee worked with great determination. It refused to recommend a large-scale programme of municipal building on the grounds that such a scheme would check private enterprise and require a means test to make it work fairly. Council policy remained unchanged down to 1914, when a Special Housing Committee still reported that 'it is doubtful whether a public body could build as cheaply as a private individual, whose whole life has been devoted to a study of his business, and who in his own interest would be sure to watch every detail with a view to keeping down the cost'. Municipal building was only a measure of last resort. 'In the last resort, if private enterprise failed, the Corporation must step in, but they feel very strongly that the public money can be used to much greater advantage than in building houses.' Nor was large-scale demolition suggested. The Council pinned its faith on private building in the suburbs, along with a cheap transport policy. . . .

The housing policy of the Council down to 1914 had by no means solved Birmingham's housing problems. The Special Committee, set up in July 1913, with Neville Chamberlain as chairman reported bluntly that 'a large proportion of the poor in Birmingham are living under conditions of housing detrimental to both health and morals'. Two hundred thousand people were still housed in 43,366 dwellings of a back-to-back type, when there were only 2,881 of this type in Liverpool and none in Manchester.

5 The Local Government Board at Work

5.1 'A NEW POOR LAW'

5.1.1 The Over-Sixties in the Workhouse, 1847-1930

One of the most distressing aspects of workhouse life was the separation of families. Old people, in particular, felt this keenly (5.1.3), and although Chadwick's regulations permitted exceptions (2.2.1, XI) they were rarely made. The matter therefore became one for legislation, but it was not until 1885, when – significantly enough – the franchise had been extended to rural workers, that the LGB pressed the matter on the attention of guardians (5.1.4). The relevant clauses were repeated in the last Poor Law Act.

From the Poor Law Board Act, 1847

XXIII. When any two persons, being husband and wife, both of whom shall be above the age of sixty years, shall be received into any workhouse . . . such two persons shall not be compelled to live separate and apart from each other in such workhouse.

From the Divided Parishes and Poor Law Amendment Act, 1876

POOR LAW AMENDMENTS

X. When any two persons, being husband and wife, shall be admitted into any workhouse, and either of them shall be infirm, sick, or disabled by any injury, or above the age of sixty years, it shall be lawful for the guardians of the union or parish to which such workhouse shall belong to permit in their discretion such husband and wife to live together, and every such case shall be reported forthwith to the Local Government Board.

From the Poor Law Act, 1930

PART II: RELIEF OF THE POOR

28. (1) Where a husband and wife, both being above the age of sixty years, are received into a workhouse, they shall not whilst in the workhouse be compelled to live apart from one another.

(2) Where a husband and wife are admitted into a workhouse, and either of them is infirm, sick or disabled by any injury, or above the age of sixty years, the council of the county or county borough may permit them to live together, but any such case shall be reported forthwith to the Minister.

5.1.2 Old People in the Workhouse

The recollections by Flora Thompson (1877–1947) of her early life in a poor rural area of north-east Oxfordshire in the last decades of the nineteenth century were first published in 1939 as *Lark Rise*, which was followed by *Over to Candleford* and *Candleford Green*. 'Lark Rise' was her home village of Juniper Hill, 'Candleford' being Buckingham in the next county. (A quotation from *Lark Rise* is at 7.3.3.)

From Flora Thompson, Candleford Green *(1943), p. 52*

For many who had worked hard all their lives and had preserved their self-respect, so far, the only refuge in old age was the Work-house. There old couples were separated, the men going to the men's side and the women to that of the women, and the effect of this separation on some faithful old hearts can be imagined. With the help of a few shillings a week, parish relief, and the still fewer shillings their children – mostly poor like themselves – could spare, some old couples contrived to keep their own roof over their heads. Laura knew several such old couples well. The old man, bent nearly double upon his stick, but clean and tidy, would appear at the Post Office periodically to cash some postal order for a tiny amount sent by a daughter in service or a married son. 'Thank God we've got good children', he would say, with pride as well as gratitude in his tone.

5.1.3 Circular on Elderly Couples, 1885

From the Fifteenth Annual Report of the Local Government Board, 1885, p. 23

AGED MARRIED COUPLES IN WORKHOUSES
Circular to guardians

Local Government Board,
3 November 1885

I am directed by the local government board to state that their attention has been drawn to complaints, in connection with the enforcement of the workhouse test by boards of guardians, that aged married couples on their admission to the workhouse are separated and required to live apart. The Board therefore deem it desirable to bring under the special attention of the guardians the statutory provisions with reference to the non-separation in the workhouse of husband and wife in certain cases.

[The Circular then cites the relevant clauses of the acts of 1847 and 1876.]

Hugh Owen,
Secretary

5.1.4 Workhouse Indulgences, 1892 and 1894

The report of 1834 had been mainly concerned with the able-bodied and the need for a 'workhouse test'. It had suggested separate institutions for the various types of pauper (such as are listed in 2.2.1), so that the old, for instance, 'might enjoy their indulgences'. In practice, however, the old had had to put up with deterrent conditions. From the 1880s there was increasing concern at the condition of so many old people, and a growing realisation of the number who had no refuge but the poor law. A campaign for old age pensions began, stimulated by Germany's adoption of pensions in 1889, and representations were made to the LGB, which from 1892 began to permit indulgences.

From the Twenty-Second Annual Report of the Local Government Board, 1892–3

APPENDIX A: ALLOWANCE OF TOBACCO OR SNUFF TO WORK HOUSE INMATES, CIRCULAR LETTER TO THE BOARD OF GUARDIANS

Local Government Board,
9 November 1892

I am directed by the Local Government Board to state that during some few years past they have received applications from the boards of guardians of various unions and parishes for orders authorising them to allow tobacco or snuff to certain classes of the inmates of the workhouse, and these applications have been complied with.

Applications of the kind referred to have recently become very numerous, and . . . the Board have now issued a General Order.

It will be seen that it empowers the guardians to allow tobacco or snuff to such of the workhouse inmates who are not able-bodied, or who are employed upon work of a specially disagreeable character, as the guardians may consider should be supplied with the same. . . .

The Order empowers the guardians to determine in what rooms and at what times smoking shall be allowed . . .

Hugh Owen,
Secretary

From the Twenty-Fourth Annual Report of the Local Government Board, 1894–5

APPENDIX A: ALLOWANCE OF TEA, ETC., TO FEMALE INMATES OF THE WORKHOUSE, CIRCULAR LETTER TO THE BOARD OF GUARDIANS

Local Government Board,
10 March, 1894

I am directed by the Local Government Board to state that they have received several proposals from boards of guardians that they should be authorised to make allowances of dry tea, with sugar and milk, to certain classes of inmates of workhouses, and that the Board have deemed it desirable to issue a general order on the subject.

It will be seen that the Order enables the Guardians, if they think fit, to cause dry tea, with sugar and milk, to be supplied to such of the female inmates of the workhouse as they may consider should be so supplied.

The allowances authorised by the guardians under the provisions of the Order will of course be in addition to the tea prescribed by the dietary in force at the workhouse.

Hugh Owen,
Secretary

5.1.5 Out-Relief and Friendly Societies, 1894

Although it had been assumed that workers would save through friendly societies during their active life, in order to keep themselves out of the workhouse in old age, until 1894 there was no positive encouragement to do so. The concession was made mandatory upon guardians in 1904, the instruction being that 5s of friendly society payments should be disregarded.

From the Outdoor Relief (Friendly Societies) Act, 1894

1. Notwithstanding any orders or regulations of the Poor Law Commissioners or the Local Government Board under and by virtue of the Poor Law Amendment Act, 1834, or of Act amending the said Act, it shall be lawful for any board of guardians, if they think fit, to grant relief out of the poor rates to any person otherwise entitled to such relief, notwithstanding that the said person shall, by reason of his membership of a friendly society, be in receipt of any sum, and that estimating the amount of the relief that shall be granted to such person being a member of a friendly society as aforesaid it shall be at the discretion of the board of guardians whether they will or will not take into consideration the amount which may be received by him from such friendly society.

5.1.6 The New Guardians, 1895

The reform of county government in 1888 was followed six years later by the establishment of urban and rural district councils and by changes in the election of guardians, which abolished property qualifications and *ex officio* appointments. Women could now be elected, and by the time of the report of the Royal Commission in 1909, 1,300 were serving as guardians.

James Stewart Davy, whose report is quoted here, eventually became Assistant Secretary of the Poor Law Division of the LGB, and was partly responsible for the appointment of the Royal Commission, to which he gave evidence. As this report shows, and his evidence to the Commission was to confirm, he was rigid in his adherence to a narrow interpretation of the principles of 1834.

From the Twenty-Fifth Annual Report of the Local Government Board, 1895-6

APPENDIX B: REPORT OF MR J. S. DAVY, INSPECTOR FOR THE DISTRICT COMPRISING THE COUNTIES OF SUSSEX, KENT, AND PART OF SURREY

Out of the 1,000 guardians who administer the poor law in this district, nearly half were elected for the first time, and this fact makes the year an eventful one. Under the old system of election many guardians filled the office, not because they took any particular interest in the subject, but because they have been elected as being the only available men in the parish or from some other accidental reason. This class has been largely replaced by others who either hoped to gain some municipal or political advantage or who felt a genuine interest in poor law or other local administration, and among these last were many ladies. A large proportion of the new members were convinced that large and easy reforms of the poor law administration lay ready to their hands, and as might have been expected many questions which were either new or dormant were warmly discussed and anxiously considered, while the visiting committees of the workhouses, recruited by many ladies, have been exceptionally active. The newspaper press has teemed with criticisms both of the law and of its administration, and in fact the whole fabric of the poor law has been subjected to a keen and in many cases to a hostile scrutiny.

It is beyond question that historically speaking the reform of the poor law in 1834 has been an entirely successful piece of social legislation, but the question in the minds of many thinking men was whether that reform had not done its work in such a way as to make it possible to start afresh on other lines. The press was full of suggestions as to what those other lines should be. . . .

It has been most interesting to observe how soon the new boards, as they become acquainted with the actual facts, realised the difficulty and danger of upsetting in any material particular the policy of administration which has been tested by long experience. In the result while many sound and beneficial reforms of a minor character have been introduced, the instances where there has been any abrupt departure from the principles which have up to now guided the administration have been extremely rare. . . . So far as out-door relief is concerned the changes have been somewhat greater. . . . Partly this has been due to a reasoned conviction of the mischief which results from the grant of inadequate doles, while in some few cases it can be traced either to definite socialistic opinions or to inexperience.

5.1.7 A New Policy for the Aged, 1900

The agitation for old age pensions led to the appointment in 1893 of a Royal Commission on the Aged Poor, which reported in 1895. Its recommendations were meagre, but led to significant instructions from the LGB, which in 1896 discouraged the forcing of old people into the workhouse, and in 1900 required that they should normally be relieved in their own homes. It was this step which caused an inflexible adherent of deterrence to complain that 'this instruction is a new poor law'.[1] There is in fact little evidence that guardians paid any heed to the instruction.

From the Thirtieth Annual Report of the Local Government Board, 1900–1, pp. 18–19

A CIRCULAR LETTER TO BOARDS OF GUARDIANS, 4 AUGUST 1900

With regard to the treatment of the aged deserving poor, it has been felt that persons who have habitually led decent and deserving lives should, if they require relief in their old age, receive different treatment from those whose previous habits and character have been unsatisfactory, and who have failed to exercise thrift in the bringing up of their families or otherwise. The Board consider that aged deserving persons should not be urged to enter the workhouse at all unless there is some cause, which renders such a course necessary but that they should be relieved by having adequate out-door relief granted to them. Such relief should when granted be always adequate.

When, however, it is necessary that such persons should receive indoor relief, the Board consider that they might be granted certain privileges which could not be accorded to every inmate of the workhouse.

The Board had intended to issue an Order dealing with this matter, but have been unable to do so at present. It may be convenient, however, if they indicate the heads of the regulations which they had in contemplation.

[1] S. and B. Webb, *English Poor Law History*, Part 2, *The Last Hundred Years*, I, p. 354.

1. That the guardians should form a special class of inmates of 65 years of age and upwards . . . who by reason of their moral character or behaviour or previous habits are sufficiently deserving to be members of the class.

2. That for such inmates extra day-rooms should be provided . . . in which they would have the opportunity of separation from disreputable inmates, and in which their meals, other than dinner, might be served. . . .

3. That sleeping accommodation in separate cubicles should be provided for them.

4. That privileges should be given them as regards the hours of going to bed and rising.

5. That considerable increased liberty should be granted to them, and greater facilities for being visited by their friends.

6. That for each inmate of this class a locker should be provided. . . .

7. That as regards the inmates of this class the provisions in the Orders relating to the supply of tobacco, dry tea and sugar should be made compulsory.

5.2 CHILDREN UNDER THE POOR LAW

5.2.1 Poor Law Recidivism?

The growing concern for the aged was matched by an increase of consideration for pauper children, many of whom were still in barrack-like District Schools, though boarding-out in various forms had been increasingly resorted to since the late 1860s. As pauperism was regarded as principally a moral evil, it was feared that children brought up on poor relief might tend to rely on it throughout life (in fact, of course, the reverse was usually the case, for understandable human reasons). Hence the inquiry of 1896, the results of which were evidently received with relief.

From the Twenty-Sixth Annual Report of the Local Government Board, 1896–7, p. xcii

In pursuance of an Order of the House of Commons we obtained and presented to Parliament a return of the number of male and female inmates of Metropolitan Separate or District Poor Law Schools during the preceding thirty years. It appeared that the total number of inmates of these Workhouses and Infirmaries on the 1st June 1896 who had been educated in these poor law schools within the period referred to was 435, of whom 229 were males and 206 females. Of this number 131 males and 101 females had been chargeable through sickness or permanent mental or bodily infirmity, leaving only 98 males and 105 females who had become chargeable from other causes. As the total number of the inmates of these institutions on the 30th May 1896 was, according to the weekly returns of pauperism, 37,969, the proportion of the inmates who had been in the poor law schools at any time during the preceding thirty years was only one in 87, or taking the number who were chargeable through some cause other than sickness or permanent mental or bodily infirmity, the proportion who had been in the poor law schools within that period was only one in 187. The average daily number of children attending Metropolitan Separate or District Poor Law Schools was, during the years ending at Lady-day 1875, 1885, and 1895, 8,383, 11,004, and 11,747 respectively. The facts as shown by the return, cannot but be regarded as satisfactory.

5.2.2 Getting Children Out of the Workhouse, 1900

Following a parliamentary report in 1896 the LGB urged guardians to remove children from the workhouse, and, after the Royal Commission on the Poor Law had made the same recommendation, issued an order in 1913 that no child over three should be kept in from 1915. Nevertheless, the new Ministry of Health found that there were still recalcitrant guardians in 1920.

From the Thirtieth Annual Report of the Local Government Board, 1900–1, p. 18

A CIRCULAR LETTER TO BOARDS OF GUARDIANS, 4 AUGUST 1900

The removal of children from workhouses has been urged upon the Board . . . and I am directed to urge upon Boards of Guardians to let no opportunity pass of carrying such an arrangement into effect. The opportunity will frequently arise when there is a question of enlarging the infirmary wards of the workhouse, or of increasing the accommodation in some other respect, and when it may be felt that the wisest course would be to provide the extra accommodation needed by removing the children altogether from the workhouse by the provision of cottage homes, by the hire of scattered homes, by boarding out and emigration, ample means are afforded by which children may be entirely removed from association with the workhouse and workhouse surroundings.

6 The Rising Tide of Social Concern

6.1 NEW IDEOLOGIES

6.1.1 Idealist Philosophy

The slow progress of political and social reform, and the continued evidence of poverty and misery, led in the 1870s and 1880s to much searching of conscience, especially at Oxford during Jowett's famous Mastership of Balliol (1870–93). T. H. Green (1836–82) was a Fellow of Balliol under Jowett, and from 1878 Professor of Moral Philosophy, exercising considerable influence, and numbering among his students such men as Arnold Toynbee, who took a lively interest in working-class affairs and was a pioneer of economic history; H. H. Asquith and Herbert Samuel, both of whom became notable political figures; and two leading exponents of private charity, Bernard Bosanquet (who also became a leading philosopher) and Charles Loch.

Green came to be regarded as a collectivist, but his interest in social reform was largely limited to individual improvement, and he sought for a moral basis for political and social action. He concerned himself with practical issues, becoming, for instance, the first Fellow to be elected to Oxford town council.

From Lecture on Liberal Legislation and Freedom of Contract, Works of Thomas Hill Green, *Vol. III (1880) p. 375*
Our modern legislation . . . with reference to labour, and education, and health, involving as it does manifold interference with freedom of contract, is justified on the ground that it is the business of the state, not indeed directly to promote moral goodness . . . but to maintain the conditions without which a free exercise of the human faculties is impossible . . . we shall probably all agree that a society in which the public health was duly protected, and necessary education duly provided for, by the spontaneous action of individuals, was in a higher condition than one in which the

compulsion of law was needed to secure these ends. But we must take men as we find them.

Until such a condition of society is reached, it is the business of the state to take the best security it can for the young citizens' growing up in such health and so much knowledge as is necessary for their real freedom. In so doing it need not at all interfere with the independence and self reliance of those whom it requires to do what they would otherwise do for themselves. . . . It was not their case that the laws we are considering were specially meant to meet. It was the over-worked women, the ill-housed and untaught families, for whose benefit they were intended. And the question is whether without these laws the suffering classes could have been delivered quickly or slowly from the condition they were in. . . . No-one considering the facts can have any doubt as to the answer to this question.

6.1.2 The Fabians on the Poor Law

The Fabian Society, founded in 1884 as part of the Socialist stirrings of the 1880s, had G. B. Shaw and Sidney Webb among its earliest and most influential members. It was a cautious, practical organisation (hence its name), opposed to the Marxist Social Democratic Federation of H. M. Hyndman, and seeing its role as mainly educational, carried out in meetings and lectures and in the publication of pamphlets and tracts, all of which still continue.

J. F. Oakeshott was a civil servant and statistician, utopian in outlook, and for some years a member of the Fabian executive.

From J. F. Oakeshott, The Humanizing of the Poor Law, Fabian Tract No. 54 (1894, 3rd edn. 1905)

THE HATRED OF THE WORKHOUSE

The growth of humanitarian feeling has had its influence on Poor Law Administration, and the inhumanity of the early part of the nineteenth century would not be tolerated by public opinion to-day. At the same time the administration of the law is still wanting in humanity . . . many men and women every year deliberately prefer death by starvation outside the workhouse to accepting relief from the rates with its deprivation of the privileges of citizenship and its dishonorable stigma of pauperism on aged and young, infirm and able-bodied, deserving and undeserving alike. . . . A Return ordered by the House of Commons (C–279) shows that in London alone, in 1902, no less than thirty-four persons, of whom twenty-four were fifty years old and upwards, were certified by the verdicts of coroner's juries to have died of starvation and privation. In no case could any recent application for relief be traced; and they were never discovered to be *in extremis* by the Relieving Officers, or by any charitable society or individual. Who can say how many times thirty-four would have to be multiplied, if a similar return were made for the whole country, and if we included all those whose deaths were accelerated by starvation, but which were declared by juries to have been due to 'natural causes'? And even then there must be added that host of similar deaths which never come before the coroner at all. . . .

OUTDOOR RELIEF

The influence of the Local Government Board has always been directed towards the abolition of out-door relief, but with some three or four exceptions, out of 646 unions, the Board of Guardians have not bowed to the official pressure, and have been supported in their resistance by the general public opinion. When we analyse the statistics, we see that public opinion is right, for nearly one half of the adult recipients of out-door relief consists of the aged, the sick and widows. But then this question forces itself upon us: are all the remainder undeserving, and, if not, can the deserving amongst them be best assisted outside or inside the workhouse? The number of able-bodied persons to whom out-door relief was given on the 1st January, 1904 in England and Wales was 14,483 men, and 52,013 women. As many as 12,898 of the men were relieved on account of sudden or urgent necessity, sickness, accident or infirmity of their own or of a member of their family, or for funeral expenses; of the women, 34,261 were widows, 10,233 were wives of able-bodied paupers, and the remainder was made up of single women, mothers of illegitimate children, wives with husbands in gaol, wives of soldiers, sailors and sundry others. . . .

CONCLUSION

The Local Government Act of 1894 abolished property qualification, plural voting and ex-officio Guardianship, and thus made the Boards democratic bodies, so far as mere machinery goes. The working classes, who make up four-fifths of the people, can control the elections if they will, and by their ignorance or inaction are mainly responsible for the persistence of the present state of things. The possibility of a humane administration of the law depends on the creation of an enlightened public opinion which will sweep away the gentlemen of no occupation and the retired publicans, who, up to the present, have so often been elected to protect the rates and grind the poor, and the election of administrators, of whatever class or sex, on the ground of their knowledge and capacity.

The expense of relieving the poor, who are not wilfully improvident, is part of the ransom that Property has to pay to Labor; and it is a ransom which is not begged as a charity but demanded as an instalment of justice. With the growth of enlightenment and the spread of humane ideas amongst all classes, and consequently greater intelligence amongst the mass of voters in the use of their political power, we shall have better laws better administered. The worn-out, deserving worker will be maintained in self-respect in his old age; the temporarily disabled will be helped without pauperisation; the children will be started in life without stigma; the professional shirker will be forced to earn his own living; the vicious and criminal will be put under restraint. Pauperism will be blotted out; Poverty will be a social disease; and Idleness will be a social crime. This may be to-day a fantastic dream, but the dreams of to-day will be the facts of to-morrow.

6.2 THE PROBLEM OF OLD AGE

6.2.1 Booth on Old Age, 1894

Charles Booth (1840–1916), member of a Liverpool business family, made himself a wealthy manufacturer and shipowner, and developed in middle life an interest in social problems and a flair for statistical investigation. He was startled in 1885 by a claim from Hyndman that no less than a quarter of London's working-class was living in extreme poverty, and set out to disprove it. The ultimate result was the seventeen-volume *Life and Labour of the People in London*, not completed until 1902, the first two volumes of which, published in 1889 and 1891, showed that Hyndman had even underestimated the problem.

Before going further Booth turned his attention to what his investigations had shown to be the largest single cause of pauperism, old age. A first limited enquiry in 1892 was extended to unions throughout the country, and the results were presented in 1894 in *The Aged Poor in* *ngland and Wales*, while he returned to the subject in 1902 in the last *olume of *Life and Labour of the People in London* [6.2.2].

*rom Charles Booth, The Aged Poor in England and Wales *(1894)*, *. 43, 53, 54, 330–1*

Jumbers of Paupers at each age:

	65–	70–	75–	80–
ndoor Total	39,017	36,539	23,173	15,415
Outdoor Total	71,451	86,841	63,221	40,770
Medical Total	7,078	7,311	5,643	5,445
otal Paupers	117,540	130,691	92,037	61,630
Ion-Paupers				
otal	454,402	287,223	141,296	87,777

'he 5 years from 70 to 75 are on the whole the most prolific of aupers, there being in all 130,000 of those ages as against 117,000 or 65–70, and 101,000 for 60–65. . . .

I have compared the amount of existing old-age pauperism with ıe volume and rate of decrease of general pauperism in various roups. The result is to show that very little connection exists, and ve cannot assume that the undoubted and satisfactory improve-ıent which has taken place in pauperism generally has any appli-ation to the condition of the old.

To sum up – the official figures show beyond dispute that nearly ıne-third of the old in England and Wales receive parish relief. . . .

Old age stands out plainly as the prevailing cause of pauperism fter 65, and increasing age of increasing pauperism . . . on the ʾhole people are poor because they are old, and poorer in some laces than in others because the whole community there is less rosperous.

There are a few parishes where out relief is considered a dis-race, but in most places no stigma attaches to its acceptance by ıe old. It is regarded as a matter of course, and often claimed very ıuch as a right. . . .

As regards entering the workhouse, it is the one point on which ıo difference of opinion exists among the poor. The aversion to ıe 'House' is absolutely universal, and almost any amount of ıffering and privation will be endured by the people rather than

go into it. Loss of liberty is the most general reason assigned fo
this aversion, but the dislike of decent people to be compelled t
mix with those whose past life and present habits are the reverse o
respectable is also strongly felt. There is no doubt, too, that ther
is a widespread dread of the separation of man and wife. This i
not easily accounted for, as such separation, unless at the desire o
the old people themselves, is illegal. There seems, however, n
doubt that in effect they are separated. It may be, however, tha
married quarters are not often demanded, and that where none ar
provided it would hardly occur to an old couple, probably ignorar
of the law, to make such an application. . . . The main explanatio
is to be found in the fact that the objection to the workhouse is
sentiment. The poor neither know nor want to know anythin
about it or its regulations.

6.2.2 Pensions at Seventy

From Charles Booth, Life and Labour of the People in Londo
Vol. XVII (1902), pp. 144, 145, 146, 148

THE ORGANISATION OF CHARITY

As my plan [for Old-Age Pensions] bears closely on the admini
tration both of the Poor Law and of private charity, I will ventu
to recapitulate it. I would make seventy the age at which a fr
and honourable pension should be granted to everyone who up t
then had not received poor relief (other than medical) and I pi
the amount at seven shillings per week. . . . There would be n
restriction as to earnings (if at seventy any are still possible); n
as to amount of savings; the seven shillings would be in additic
to whatever the recipient had or might earn, but would be draw
weekly by personal application. . . . If on this system any who di
not exactly need the money, should still collect it, so much th
better for maintaining the dignity of the rest; as one may welcon
a bishop or a lord who deigns to travel third class. . . .

At and after seventy most of the difficulties and, I think, all th
dangers of a universal pension system melt away. Its cost is n
longer prohibitive, while the coming of the pension would be
untold value in limiting the liabilities which prolonged life enta
not only on the individual, but on thrift agencies and on charitab
funds, and would lift from very many old hearts the fear of th
workhouse at the last.

It is, however, before seventy, and mainly between sixty and seventy, that the battle of independence has to be fought; and it is to the beneficial effect of a coming pension on the lives of the people, especially during this period, that I attach especial importance. . . .

The motive to save up to the time of the pension and beyond it would be strong; as also, too, would be the motive with those living nearer the line of pauperism, to avoid application to the Poor Law. The effect of looking forward to a pension would be the exact opposite to that of the anticipation of Poor Law relief, any claim to which must rest upon absolute destitution. . . .

It is commonly said that few of the old who are now inmates of workhouses could, if a pension were granted, find any home outside. That may be so, but it hardly affects the question. The object of the pension, actual or prospective, is to *maintain* a home, which is a very different thing from suddenly *finding* one. . . .

The abolition of out-relief is, I think, essential, and at the same time quite possible, if Poor Law and organized private effort will work hand in hand, and if the pension, which becomes in itself a great motive to thrift, is assured in the future.

6.3 THE PROBLEM OF POVERTY

6.3.1 Life and Labour in London

From Charles Booth, Life and Labour of the People in London, *Vol. I (1889), pp. 4–7, 33, 62, 131*

For the district inquiry, resulting in the division of the people into 8 classes, I have relied upon information obtained from the School Board visitors, of whom there are 66 in the East London district. . . .

The School Board visitors perform amongst them a house-to-house visitation; every house in every street is in their books, and details are given of every family with children of school age. . . . No one can go, as I have done, over the description of the inhabitants of street after street in this huge district (East London), taken house by house and family by family – full as it is of picturesque details noted down from the lips of the visitor to whose mind they have been recalled by the open pages of his own schedules – and doubt the genuine character of the information and its truth. . . . The materials for sensational stories lie plentifully in every book of our notes. . . . There is struggling poverty, there is destitution, there is hunger, drunkenness, brutality, and crime; no one doubts that it is so. My object has been to attempt to show the numerical relation which poverty, misery, and depravity bear to regular earnings and comparative comfort, and to describe the general conditions under which each class lives. . . .

If the facts thus stated are of use in helping social reformers to find remedies for the evils which exist, or do anything to prevent the adoption of false remedies, my purpose is answered. It was not my intention to bring forward any suggestions of my own. . . .

With regard to the disadvantages under which the poor labour and the evils of poverty, there is a great sense of helplessness: the wage earners are helpless to regulate their work and cannot obtain a fair equivalent for the labour they are willing to give; the manufacturer or dealer can only work within the limits of competition; the rich are helpless to relieve want without stimulating its sources. To relieve this helplessness a better stating of the problems involved is the first step. . . . In this direction must be sought the utility of my attempt to analyse the population of London. . . .

The 8 classes into which I have divided the people are:

A. The lowest class of occasional labourers, loafers, and semi-criminals.

B. Casual earnings – 'very poor'.

C. Intermittent earnings } together the 'poor'.
D. Small regular earnings }

E. Regular standard earnings – above the line of poverty.

F. Higher class labour.

G. Lower middle class.

H. Upper middle class.

The divisions indicated here by 'poor' and 'very poor' are necessarily arbitrary. By the word 'poor' I mean to describe those who have a sufficiently regular though bare income, such as 18s to 21s per week for a moderate family, and by 'very poor' those who from any cause fall much below this standard. The 'poor' are those whose means may be sufficient, but are barely sufficient, for decent independent life; the 'very poor' those whose means are insufficient for this according to the usual standard of life in this country. My 'poor' may be described as living under a struggle to obtain the necessaries of life and make both ends meet; while the 'very poor' live in a state of chronic want. It may be their own fault that this is so; that is another question; my first business is simply with the numbers who, from whatever cause, do live under conditions of poverty or destitution. . . .

Grouping the classes together, A, B, C, and D are the classes in poverty, or even in want, and add up to 314,000, or 35 per cent of the population; while E, F, G, and H are the classes in comfort, or even in affluence, and add up to 577,000, or 65 per cent of the population. . . .

The Standard of Life. – Omitting Class A, which rather involves the question of disorder, we have in Classes B, C, and D the problem of poverty. In the population under review the 100,000 of 'very poor' (Class B) are at all times more or less 'in want'. They are ill-nourished and poorly clad. But of them only a percentage – and not, I think, a large percentage – would be said by themselves, or by anyone else, to be 'in distress'. From day to day and from hand to mouth they get along; sometimes suffering, sometimes helped, but not always unfortunate, and very ready to enjoy any good luck that may come in their way. They are, very likely, improvident, spending what they make as they make it; but 'the improvidence of the poor has its bright side. Life would indeed be intolerable were they always contemplating the gulf of destitution on whose brink they hang'. ('A Village Tragedy', by Mrs Woods). Some may be semi-paupers, going into the 'house' at certain seasons, and some few receive out-door relief, but on the whole they manage to avoid the workhouse. On the other hand, the 200,000 of 'poor' (Classes C and D), though they would be much the better for more of everything, are not 'in want'. They are neither ill-nourished nor ill-clad, according to any standard that can reasonably be used. Their lives are an unending struggle and lack comfort, but I do not know that they lack happiness. . . .

6.3.2 Poverty in York

An investigation in York in 1899, by Benjamin Seebohm Rowntree (1871–1954), of the philanthropic family of cocoa manufacturers, gave general confirmation of Booth's findings for London, and was notable for the distinction drawn between 'primary' and 'secondary' poverty. In later years he was to follow his first study with *Poverty and Progress* (1941) and *Poverty and the Welfare State* (1951).

From R. Seebohm Rowntree, Poverty. A Study of Town Life
(1901), pp. vii-x, 295-304

INTRODUCTION

My object in undertaking the investigation detailed in this volume
was, if possible, to throw some light upon the conditions which
govern the life of the wage-earning classes in provincial towns, and
especially upon the problem of poverty. . . .

The great value of Mr Charles Booth's classical work on *The
Life and Labour of the People of London* led me to hope that a similar investigation made for a provincial town might be of use, as it
was impossible to judge how far the general conclusions arrived at
by Mr Booth in respect of the metropolis would be found applicable
to smaller urban populations. . . .

As a primary object of my inquiry has been to ascertain not only
the proportion of the population living in poverty, but the nature
of that poverty, I have divided the population so living into two
classes:—

(a) Families whose total earnings are insufficient to obtain the
minimum necessaries for the maintenance of merely physical efficiency. Poverty falling under this head I have
described as 'primary' poverty.

(b) Families whose total earnings would be sufficient for the
maintenance of merely physical efficiency were it not that
some portion of them is absorbed by other expenditure,
either useful or wasteful. Poverty falling under this head is
described as 'secondary' poverty. . . .

CHAPTER 10. SUMMARY AND CONCLUSION

In this chapter it is proposed to briefly summarise the facts set
forth in the preceding pages, and to consider what conclusions
regarding the problem of poverty may be drawn from them.

Method and Scope of Inquiry. – The information regarding the
numbers, occupation, and housing of the working classes was
gained by direct inquiry, which practically covered every working-
class family in York. In some cases direct information was also
obtained regarding earnings, but in the majority of cases these were
estimated, the information at the disposal of the writer enabling
him to do this with considerable accuracy.

The Poverty Line. – Having thus made an estimate, based upon carefully ascertained facts, of the earnings of practically every working-class family in York, the next step was to show the proportion of the total population living in poverty. . . .

To ascertain the total number living in 'primary' poverty it was necessary to ascertain the minimum cost upon which families of various sizes could be maintained in a state of physical efficiency. This question was discussed under three heads, viz. the necessary expenditure for (1) food; (2) rent; and (3) all else. . . .

It was shown that for a family of father, mother, and three children, the minimum weekly expenditure upon which physical efficiency can be maintained in York is 21s. 8d. made up as follows:

	s.	d.
Food	12.	9.
Rent (say)	4.	0.
Clothing, light, fuel, etc.	4.	11.
	21.	8.

. . . This estimate was based upon the assumptions that the diet is selected with a careful regard to the nutritive values of various food stuffs, and that these are all purchased at the lowest current prices. . . . It further assumes that no clothing is purchased which is not absolutely necessary for health. . . .

No expenditure of any kind is allowed for beyond that which is absolutely necessary for the maintenance of merely physical efficiency.

The number of persons whose earnings are so low that they cannot meet the expenditure necessary for the above standard of living, stringent to severity though it is, and bare of all creature comforts, was shown to be no less than 7230, or almost exactly 10 per cent of the total population of the city. . . .

The number of those in 'secondary' poverty was arrived at by ascertaining the total number living in poverty, and subtracting those living in 'primary' poverty. The investigators, in the course of their house-to-house visitation, noted those families who were obviously living in a state of poverty, i.e. in obvious want and squalor. Sometimes they obtained definite information that the bulk of the earnings was spent in drink or otherwise squandered, sometimes the external evidence of poverty in the home was so clear as to make verbal evidence superfluous.

In this way 20,302 persons, or 27.84 per cent of the total population, were returned as living in poverty. Subtracting those whose poverty is 'primary', we arrive at the number living in 'secondary' poverty, viz. 13,072, or 17.93 per cent of the total population. . . .

From the commencement of my inquiry, I have had opportunities of consulting with Mr Booth, and comparing the methods of investigation and the standards of poverty adopted. As a result I feel no hesitation in regarding my estimate of the total poverty in York as comparable with Mr Booth's estimate of the total poverty in London, and in this Mr Booth agrees.

The proportions arrived at for the total population living in poverty in London and York respectively were as under:-

| London | 30.7 per cent |
| York | 27.84 per cent |

. . . We have been accustomed to look upon the poverty in London as exceptional, but when the result of careful investigation shows that the proportion of poverty in London is practically equalled in what may be regarded as a typical provincial town, we are faced by the startling probability that from 25 to 30 per cent of the town populations of the United Kingdom are living in poverty. . . .

The Results of Poverty. – The facts regarding the proportion of poverty are perhaps the most important which have been dealt with in this volume, but the conditions under which the poor live, and the effects of those conditions . . . will have also claimed the serious attention of the reader.

Housing. – It has been shown that in York 4705 persons, or 6.4 per cent of the total population, are living more than two persons to a room, whilst the actual number who are living, and especially sleeping, in rooms which provide inadequate air-space for the maintenance of health is undoubtedly very much greater. . . .

The close relation which exists between over-crowding and poverty is indicated by the fact that 94 per cent of the overcrowded families are in poverty either 'primary' or 'secondary'. . . .

Relation of Poverty to Health. – Turning now to the relation of poverty to health, it has been shown in the preceding pages how low is the standard of health amongst the very poor. . . . It becomes obvious that the widespread existence of poverty in an industrial country like our own must seriously retard its development.

Workmen's Household Budgets. – . . . the labouring class receive upon the average about 25 per cent less food than has been proved by scientific experts to be necessary for the maintenance of physical efficiency. This statement is not intended to imply that labourers and their families are chronically hungry, but that the food which they eat (although on account of its bulk it satisfies the cravings of hunger) does not contain the nutrients necessary for normal physical efficiency. . . .

As the investigation into the conditions of life in this typical provincial town has proceeded, the writer has been increasingly impressed with the gravity of the facts which have unfolded themselves.

That in this land of abounding wealth, during a time of perhaps unexampled prosperity, probably more than one-fourth of the population are living in poverty, is a fact which may well cause great searchings of heart. . . . No civilisation can be sound or stable which has at its base this mass of stunted human life.

6.3.3 Winston Churchill's Hair Stands on End

Churchill entered Parliament as a Conservative in 1900, but broke away in 1904 on the tariff reform issue and joined the Liberals, becoming a junior minister in 1905 and entering the Cabinet, at the age of only thirty-three, in 1908. Rowntree's book stirred an interest in social problems, and from 1903 he was in touch with the Webbs, who later introduced Beveridge to him, and after joining the Liberals he became a close friend of Lloyd George. From all of these he learnt much which shaped the great measures he carried at the Board of Trade from 1908.

From R. S. Churchill, Young Statesman, 1901–14, Winston S. Churchill, *Vol. II (1967), pp. 30–2*

In December, 1901 Churchill was Morley's guest at dinner. . . . Morley commended to Churchill a book recently published, *Poverty: A Study of Town Life* by Seebohm Rowntree. Churchill went out and bought a copy of this classic study of the poor of the city of York, and was greatly moved by it. He set out to bring it to the attention of those whom it might otherwise have passed by, writing an article for a Service journal. There is no record that the review was ever published, but Churchill's manuscript survives. . . .

At Blackpool on 9 January 1902 he said:
'I have been reading a book which has fairly made my hair

stand on end, written by a Mr Rowntree who deals with poverty in the town of York.'

[To a leading Conservative politician in Birmingham Churchill wrote on 23 December 1901]:

I have lately been reading a book by Mr Rowntree called *Poverty*, which has impressed me very much, and which I strongly recommend you to read. It is quite evident from the figures which he adduces that the American labourer is a stronger, larger, healthier, better fed, and consequently more efficient animal than a large proportion of our population, and this is surely a fact which our unbridled Imperialists, who have no thought but to pile up armaments, taxation and territory, should not lose sight of. For my own part, I see little glory in an Empire which can rule the waves, and is unable to flush its sewers.

7 Turning Away from the Poor Law

7.1 THE CHILDREN

7.1.1 The Fear of Physical Deterioration

Rowntree had already made use of statistics on the rejection of Army recruits on account of physical unfitness, and the South African War had revealed how many men, even by wartime standards, were unfit for service. At a time when conscript armies abroad seemed to threaten Britain's position, there were fears of a physical decline of the British race. The Balfour government had little interest in social problems, but an interdepartmental committee was appointed in 1903 to quiet concern, and reported in the following year, though it was left to the Liberals from 1906 to carry out some of the committee's cautious proposals, which included school meals and medical inspection (7.1.2), checks on drinking and a ban on juvenile smoking (7.1.3), and insistence on full-time appointments for Medical Officers of Health (4.3.6).

From the Report of the Interdepartmental Committee on Physical Deterioration, 1904

227. In estimating the causes which contribute to render the poor careless of, or indifferent to, the conditions of proper feeding, it is only fair to remember the extreme narrowness and squalor of their surroundings. Under any aspect of this multiform problem, it is difficult to keep away for long from the housing difficulty, and it enters very largely into the matter immediately under discussion; houses that were originally built for one family have, by the operation of pressure upon limited space and high rents, become occupied by several, but often only one room in the whole house contains a grate of proper service for cooking, with the result that a large number of tenements do not contain the requisite apparatus for the preparation of food, and the culinary art, if practised at all, is reduced to its crudest form of expression. . . .

348. With scarcely an exception, there was a general consensus of opinion that the time has come when the State should realise the necessity of ensuring adequate nourishment to children in attendance at school; it was said to be the height of cruelty to subject half-starved children to the process of education, besides being a short-sighted policy, in that the progress of such children is inadequate and disappointing; and it was, further, the subject of general agreement that, as a rule, no purely voluntary association could successfully cope with the full extent of the evil. Even those witnesses who were inclined to think that its magnitude had been much exaggerated, did not question the advisability of feeding, by some means or other, those children who are underfed, provided it could be done quietly and without impairing parental responsibility. . . .

7.1.2 School Meals and Health Services
From the Education (Provision of Meals) Act, 1906

1. A local education authority . . . may take such steps as they think fit for the provision of meals for children in attendance at any public elementary school in their area, and for that purpose –

   (*a*) may associate with themselves any committee on which the authority are represented, who will undertake to provide food for those children. . . .

   (*b*) may aid that committee by furnishing such land, buildings, furniture, and apparatus, and such officers and servants as may be necessary for the organisation, preparation, and service of such meals;

but the authority shall not incur any expense in respect of the purchase of food to be supplied at such meals.

2. There shall be charged to the parent of every child in respect of every meal furnished to that child under this Act such an amount as may be determined by the local education authority. . . .

3. Where the local education authority resolve that any of the children attending an elementary school within their area are unable by reason of lack of food to take full advantage of the education provided for them, and have ascertained that funds other than public funds are not available or are insufficient in amount to defray the cost of food furnished in meals under this Act, they may

apply to the Board of Education, and that Board may authorise them to spend out of the rates such sum as will meet the cost of the provision of such food, provided that the total amount expended by a local education authority . . . shall not exceed the amount which would be produced by a rate of one halfpenny in the pound. . . .

4. The provision of any meal under this Act to a child and the failure on the part of the parent to pay any amount demanded under this Act in respect of a meal shall not deprive the parent of any franchise, right, or privilege, or subject him to any disability. . . .

5. No teacher seeking employment or employed in a public elementary school shall be required as part of his duties to supervise or assist, or to abstain from supervising or assisting, in the provision of meals, or in the collection of the cost thereof.

From the Education (Administrative Provisions) Act, 1907

13. (1) The powers and duties of a local education authority . . . shall include –

(a) power to provide, for children attending a public elementary school, vacation schools, vacation classes, play-centres, or other means of recreation during their holidays. . . .

(b) the duty to provide for the medical inspection of children immediately before, or at the time of, or as soon as possible after, their admission to a public elementary school, and on such other occasions as the Board of Education direct, and the power to make such arrangements as may be sanctioned by the Board of Education for attending to the health and physical condition of the children educated in public elementary schools.

7.1.3 The First Children Act, 1908

The first general Act for child care was carried by Herbert (later, Lord) Samuel (1870–1963) as under-secretary at the Home Office. It followed a number of the recommendations of the Committee on Physical Deterioration, including the setting-up of juvenile courts, and made negligence an offence. The 'overlaying' of babies, referred to in clause 3, was responsible at this time for some 1600 deaths a year.

The Poor Law Act of 1889 had given the guardians parental powers over children who were orphans or were deserted by their parents. Not until 1948, on the abolition of the poor law, was a special service created for them [10.1.2].

From the Children Act, 1908

PART II: PREVENTION OF CRUELTY TO CHILDREN AND YOUNG PERSONS

12. – (1) If any person over the age of sixteen years, who has the custody, charge, or care of any child or young person, wilfully assaults, ill-treats, neglects, abandons, or exposes such child or young person . . . that person shall be guilty of a misdemeanor . . . and for the purposes of this section a parent or other person legally liable to maintain a child or young person shall be deemed to have neglected him in a manner likely to cause injury to his health if he fails to provide adequate food, clothing, medical aid, or lodging for the child or young person, or if, being unable otherwise to provide such food, clothing, medical aid, or lodging, he fails to take steps to procure the same to be provided under the Acts relating to the relief of the poor. . . .

13. Where it is proved that the death of an infant under three years of age was caused by suffocation . . . whilst the infant was in bed with some other person over sixteen years of age, and that that other person was at the time of going to bed under the influence of drink that other person shall be deemed to have neglected the infant in a manner likely to cause injury to its health within the meaning of this Act.

Other offences in relation to children and young persons

14. If any person causes or procures any child or young person, or allows that child or young person, to be in any street, premises, or place for the purpose of begging or receiving alms, or of inducing the giving of alms, whether or not there is any pretence of singing playing, performing, offering anything for sale or otherwise, that person shall, on summary conviction, be liable to a fine not exceeding twenty-five pounds, or to imprisonment with or without hard labour, for any term not exceeding three months. . . .

15. If any person over the age of sixteen years who has the custody charge or care of any child under the age of seven years allows that child to be in any room containing an open fire grate not sufficiently protected to guard against the risk of the child being burnt or scalded, and by reason thereof the child is killed or suffers serious

injury, he shall on summary conviction be liable to a fine not exceeding ten pounds. . . .

37. Nothing in this Act shall be construed to take away or affect the right of any parent, teacher, or other person having the lawful control or charge of a child or young person to administer punishment to such child or young person.

PART III: JUVENILE SMOKING

39. If any person sells to a person apparently under the age of sixteen years any cigarettes or cigarette papers, whether for his own use or not, he shall be liable, on summary conviction, in the case of a first offence to a fine not exceeding two pounds. . . .

40. It shall be the duty of a constable and of a park keeper, being in uniform, to seize any cigarettes or cigarette papers in the possession of any person apparently under the age of sixteen whom he finds smoking in any street or public place. . . .

119. If any person gives, or causes to be given, to any child under the age of five any intoxicating liquor, except upon the order of a duly qualified medical practitioner, or in case of sickness, or apprehended sickness, or other urgent cause, he shall, on summary conviction, be liable to a fine not exceeding three pounds.

120. – (1) The holder of the licence of any licenced premises shall not allow a child to be at any time in the bar of the licensed premises, except during the hours of closing.

7.2 THE UNEMPLOYED

7.2.1 The Chamberlain Circular, 1886

This circular, which introduced the principle of 'tiding over' the unemployed during a period of depression, without recourse to the poor law, followed the distress of the severe winter of 1885–6, and probably owed something to the shock administered by the unemployed riots in London in February 1886.

Chamberlain was President of the LGB in Gladstone's third cabinet in 1886, from February to April, when he broke with Gladstone over Home Rule.

From the Sixteenth Annual Report of the Local Government Board, 1886–7

Local Government Board, Whitehall, S.W.,
15 March 1886

The inquiries which have been recently undertaken by the Local Government Board unfortunately confirm the prevailing impression as to the existence of exceptional distress amongst the working classes. This distress is partial as to its locality, and is no doubt due in some measure to the long continued severity of the weather.

The returns of pauperism show an increase, but it is not yet considerable; and the numbers of persons in receipt of relief are greatly below those of previous periods of exceptional distress.

The Local Government Board have, however, thought it their duty to go beyond the returns of actual pauperism which are all that come under their notice in ordinary times, and they have made some investigation into the condition of the working classes generally.

They are convinced that in the ranks of those who do not ordinarily seek poor law relief there is evidence of much and increasing privation, and if the depression in trade continues it is to be feared that large numbers of persons usually in regular employment will be reduced to the greatest straits.

Such a condition of things is a subject for deep regret and very serious consideration.

The spirit of independence which leads so many of the working classes to make great personal sacrifices rather than incur the stigma of pauperism, is one which deserves the greatest sympathy and respect, and which it is the duty and interest of the community to maintain by all the means at its disposal. . . .

It is not desirable that the working classes should be familiarised with poor law relief, and if once the honourable sentiment which now leads them to avoid it is broken down, it is probable that recourse will be had to this provision on the slightest occasion.

The Local Government Board have no doubt that the powers which the guardians possess are fully sufficient to enable them to deal with ordinary pauperism, and to meet the demand for relief from the classes who usually seek it. . . .

But these provisions do not in all cases meet the emergency. The labour test is usually stone breaking or oakum picking. This work, which is selected as offering the least competition with other labour, presses hardly upon the skilled artisans, and, in some cases, their proficiency in their special trades may be prejudiced by such employment. Spade husbandry is less open to objection, and when facilities offer for adopting work of this character as a labour test, the Board will be glad to assist the guardians by authorising the hiring of land for the purpose, when this is necessary. In any case, however, the receipt of relief from the guardians, although accompanied by a task of work, entails the disqualification which by statute attaches to pauperism.

What is required in the endeavour to relieve artisans and others who have hitherto avoided poor law assistance, and who are temporarily deprived of employment is –

1. Work which will not involve the stigma of pauperism;
2. Work which all can perform, whatever may have been their previous avocations;
3. Work which does not compete with that of other labourers at present in employment;

   And, lastly, work which is not likely to interfere with the resumption of regular employment in their own trades by those who seek it.

The Board have no power to enforce the adoption of any particular proposals, and the object of this circular is to bring the subject generally under the notice of guardians and other local authorities.

In districts in which exceptional distress prevails, the Board recommend that the guardians should confer with the local authorities, and endeavour to arrange with the latter for the execution of works on which unskilled labour may be immediately employed. . . .

In all cases in which special works are undertaken to meet exceptional distress it would appear to be necessary, 1st, that the men employed should be engaged on the recommendation of the guardians as persons whom, owing to previous condition and circumstances, it is undesirable to send to the workhouse, or to treat as subjects for pauper relief, and 2nd, that the wages paid should be something less than the wages ordinarily paid for similar work, in order to prevent imposture, and to leave the strongest temptations to those who avail themselves of this opportunity to return as soon as possible to their previous occupations. . . .

I shall be much obliged if you will keep me informed of the state of affairs in your district, and if it should be found necessary to make any exceptional provision, I shall be glad to know at once the nature of such provision, and the extent to which those for whom it is intended avail themselves of it.

(Signed) J. Chamberlain.

7.2.2 The Political Quandary, 1905

The Unemployed Workmen Act was the last attempt to grapple with unemployment by temporary relief on a local basis. The winter of 1904–5 had seen much unemployment, with demonstrations and 'hunger marches', which alarmed many in view of the growing strength of Labour. The Act permitted authorities to use rate-funds to aid the administrative costs of 'distress committees' specially set up to provide relief raised from charities, and an appeal by Queen Alexandra for funds produced £153,000.

Walter Long (1854–1924) was a paternalistic Conservative land-owner who was President of the LGB from 1900 to 1905 and prepared the Bill which his successor, the Prime Minister's brother, Gerald Balfour, actually introduced.

Lloyd George recognised that the government was in a quandary and that the measure was useless unless it went further. In 1906, indeed, the new Liberal government replaced the Queen's appeal by a Treasury grant of £200,000, but although the Act continued in force until the war Beveridge showed that it had hardly touched the men it was intended to assist.

From the House of Commons Debate, 20 June 1905: The Unemployed Workmen Bill, Second Reading
Mr Gerald Balfour [President of the Local Government Board]: The present Bill did not pretend to deal with the whole of the vast and complicated problem known as the 'unemployed question'. . . . The object throughout was to assist only a limited class of the unemployed . . . respectable workmen settled in a locality, hitherto accustomed to regular work, but temporarily out of employment through circumstances beyond their control, capable workmen with hope of return to regular work after tiding over a period of temporary distress. His meaning would be made more clear by reference to Mr Charles Booth's classification of the inhabitants

of the poorer districts of London. . . . The unemployed specially contemplated in the Bill were those who would be classed under D and E.

The feeling that respectable persons who were out of employment through no fault of their own . . . should have some prospect before them other than the workhouse or the guardians' relief yard was one that must be reckoned with. Moreover, it was a growing feeling, and (if resisted) the effect would very probably be a reaction which would carry us very much further . . . than the modest proposals of the Bill.

Mr Walter Long said that if a man, who had been maintaining his wife and family, was through no fault of his own unable to find employment, there was no alternative under the present system except starvation on the one hand, or refuge in the Poor Law on the other. He asked those who had been connected with Poor Law administration how many men and women had they known who, once having gone on the Poor Law and entered the workhouse, had been raised from that condition and again become self-supporting citizens? How could guardians help a man to become self-supporting again? . . . How could they provide work without competing with local industry? The result was that they had to fall back on stone-yards and similar expedients. Many a man had told him that when he entered on his career of destitution the fact that he had been put to polish the same brass knob, or to clean the same window which half-a-dozen had cleaned before, degraded him.

From the House of Commons Debate, 17 August 1905: The Unemployed Workmen Bill, Third Reading

Mr David Lloyd George: Having gone through the Bill he was amazed that so much fuss had been made about a Bill which would do very little good, except that it had recognised a very important principle – a principle he should have thought the Government's supporters would have been the last to recognise. Did they realise what they were giving statutory recognition to? . . . The Bill contained the germs of a revolution, and whichever Party might be in power in the future could not stop there. It recognised the right of a man to call upon the State to provide him with work. The State replied by recognising the right but would not provide the work. The Bill was like a motor-car without petrol or only such petrol as it could beg on the road.

Privately, Lloyd George expressed himself still more strongly. The Act, he wrote to his brother William, 'is one of the most revolutionary departures of modern times. The Tories don't realise what they have let themselves in for.' – W. George, *My Brother and I* (1958), p. 173.

7.2.3 Beveridge on the Unemployed Workmen Act, 1907

From the Report of the Royal Commission on the Poor Laws and the Relief of Distress (Appendix vol. viii), p. 15: Minutes of Evidence

EVIDENCE OF W. H. BEVERIDGE

For the purpose of a general conclusion as to its value, the Unemployed Workmen Act is best considered as a final effort to meet by the provision of temporary relief work the difficulty occasioned by exceptional trade depression. ... It has been felt that during a passing depression of trade men hitherto industrious and competent, finding it impossible to obtain employment, may so deteriorate through idleness and privation as to become unfit for employment. ... It has been argued, therefore, that to provide temporary work in such cases may do permanent good by preventing deterioration. ... A bridge of relief work might be constructed to carry men over the depression. ...

The Act failed and was foredoomed to failure, simply because it was founded on a misconception of the problem. The class of men contemplated by the Act, men temporarily unable to obtain employment through exceptional causes beyond their control, has not been forthcoming in numbers sufficient to fill even the 3000 to 4000 vacancies provided. An altogether different class of men, the normally under-employed, has flooded the registers ten times over.

7.3 OLD AGE PENSIONS

7.3.1 Asquith's Promise and Performance, 1908

Asquith succeeded Campbell-Bannerman as Prime Minister in 1908, but presented his budget, leaving the actual Bill to Lloyd George. His estimate of the possible number of pensioners proved too low by some 80,000, evidence, as Lloyd George pointed out later, that there had been many who had been unwilling to apply to the poor law.

Britain's aged poor benefited greatly from the pensions, but Ireland's did even better, for by 1911 some 200,000 were drawing pensions, though the census of that year showed only 190,000 over 70 in all, eligible and ineligible alike.[1]

[1] B. B. Gilbert, *The Evolution of National Insurance*, p. 228.

From the House of Commons Debate, 7 May 1908

Mr Asquith: . . . Last year, in introducing the Budget, I said that this Parliament and this Government had come here pledged to social reform; and I pointed to two figures in our modern society that make an especially strong and, indeed, an irresistible appeal. . . . One is the figure of the child. . . . The other figure is the figure of old age, still unprovided for except by casual and unorganised effort, or, by what is worse, invidious dependence upon Poor Law relief. I said then that we hoped and intended this year to lay firm the foundations of a wiser and a humaner policy. With that view, as the Committee may remember, I set aside £1,500,000 which was temporarily applied to the reduction of debt, and I anticipated that other £750,000 which, through the activity of the Inland Revenue, has been swept into the old Sinking Fund of last year, would also be available. I propose now to show how we intend to redeem the promises which I then made. I need not remind the Committee that this question in one shape or another has been before the country now for the best part of thirty years. . . . But up to this moment nothing has been done, nothing at all. In the meantime other countries have been making experiments. The German system, which is one of compulsory State-aided assurance, has been in existence since 1889. . . . More instruction, I think, for our purposes is to be derived from the legislation initiated in Denmark in 1891, in New Zealand in 1898, and subsequently in New South Wales and Victoria. . . .

There is one governing consideration which in framing our proposals we have kept steadily in view. The problem of making better provision for the aged is only one of a group of questions the settlement of which should as far as possible be harmonious and self-consistent. A Royal Commission has now been at work for some time investigating the administration of the Poor Law, and we understand that its Report may be expected before many months. . . . It appears to the Government to be a preliminary specially necessary in itself – and reasonably certain not to clash with any wider proposal which the Commissioners may make – to take the care of the aged and place it once for all outside both the machinery and the associations of our Poor Law system. . . .

The first conclusion at which we arrived, and as to which I do not think there will be any really serious difference of opinion in this House, was that all so-called contributory schemes must be ruled out. They do not meet the necessities of the case. If the contribution which is to be the condition of a pension were left to the option of the would-be pensioner, the assistance of the State might be confined to a comparatively small class, and that not by any means necessarily the most necessitous or the most deserving class. On the other hand, if it were sought to make the contribution compulsory with no practical machinery in this country by which it could be worked, you would certainly have to face the hostility of many other competing bodies like the trade unions, friendly societies, insurance companies, and a host of others. Moreover . . . none of its benefits would come into actual enjoyment until after the lapse of twenty or more years. . . . The next, what is called the universal scheme, associated with the name of Mr Charles Booth, is also out of the range of practical politics. The actual working cost of such a scheme is problematical, because no one can tell in advance how many of the people legally entitled would fail or decline to claim their pensions. . . .

The possible cost, as distinguished from the actual, might vary according as seventy or sixty-five was selected as the qualifying age, from £16,000,000 to something over £27,000,000 – figures which are obviously prohibitive. . . . A further point is that in our view the obligation to provide the pension must, as between the State and the pensioner, rest on the Treasury and not on the local authority. . . . To make the charge a local burden would first of all lead to every inequality and make large differences between place and place as the proportion of the aged poor to the whole population varied. It would reintroduce the terrible evils of the old laws of settlement and bear most heavily on the most necessitous districts. . . .

It follows from these considerations that any practical scheme must be based on some kind of discrimination – by which I mean upon the ability of the claimant to comply with certain qualifying conditions. Those conditions resolve themselves into four distinct categories – age, means, status, and character. . . .

A serious question is how far the status of pauper is to be regarded as a disqualification for a pension. In Denmark, the receipt of Poor Law relief within ten years disqualifies for pension. . . . Most of the Bills which have been introduced have made similar suggestions. I may say at once that the Government do not take that view. It is a very hard thing and a very unnecessary thing to make the mere fact of receipt of Poor Law relief an absolute disqualification. We propose, therefore, and this is provisional, for the whole thing is necessarily experimental in the first year and subject to revision as experience is gained, to exclude in the first year actual paupers, and not to go back. We do not go back on the past.

As to character, I think the less you go into that question, short of actual conviction for crime, the better. All those suggested tests which look so well on paper, thrift, prudence, good repute, etc., when you put them into a concrete shape, are not only extremely difficult to apply, but in their application produce cases of unwarrantable hardship. ... Having run through these heads, take the case of persons over sixty-five years and persons over seventy years. Persons over sixty-five years number 2,116,000. If you deduct those with incomes over 10s. a week, the number is 778,000; aliens, criminals, and lunatics, 33,000; and paupers, 368,000, or a reduction to a total of 1,179,000, leaving the total of pensionable persons at 937,000. The number of persons over seventy being taken at 1,254,286, and making similar deductions, you get a total of pensionable persons of 572,000. That is the best estimate that we can make, and we must not be held too closely to it, if experience shows different results. ...

As regards the amount of the pension, it has been generally agreed in this country that 5s a week, or £13 a year, should be the sum. Let me assume that the maximum of £13 a year ... was to be awarded in all cases, and to make no allowance, as you must do, for the differential treatment of married couples. The annual cost of providing pensions for the total number of pensionables – and I hope I shall be forgiven for that barbarous word – would work out as follows. For persons over sixty-five the cost would be £12,180,000; and for persons over seventy the cost would be £7,440,000.

7.3.2 The Old Age Pensions Act, 1908
The lingering relics of moral conditions for benefits should be noted. They were rarely applied, and were abolished in 1919.

From the Old Age Pensions Act, 1908

1. (1) Every person in whose case the conditions laid down by this Act for the receipt of an old age pension are fulfilled, shall be entitled to receive such a pension. ...

(4) The receipt of an old age pension under this Act shall not deprive the pensioner of any franchise, right, or privilege, or subject him to any disability.

2. The statutory conditions for the receipt of an old age pension by any person are –

(1) The person must have attained the age of seventy:

(2) The person must satisfy the pension authorities that for at least twenty years up to the date of the receipt of any sum on account of a pension he has been a British subject, and has had his residence in the United Kingdom:

(3) The person must satisfy the pension authorities that his yearly means as calculated under this Act do not exceed thirty-one pounds ten shillings.

3. (1) A person shall be disqualified for receiving an old age pension

(a) While he is in receipt of any poor relief and, until the thirty-first day of December nineteen hundred and ten, if he has at any time since the first day of January nineteen hundred and eight received, or hereafter receives, any such relief . . .

(b) If, before he becomes entitled to a pension, he has habitually failed to work according to his ability, opportunity, and need, for the maintenance or benefit of himself and those legally dependent upon him:

Provided that a person shall not be disqualified under this paragraph if he has continuously for ten years up to attaining the age of sixty, by means of payments to friendly, provident, or other societies, or trade unions, or other approved steps, made such provision against old age, sickness, infirmity, or want or loss of employment as may be recognised as proper provision for the purpose . . .

(c) While he is detained in any asylum . . .

(d) During the continuance of any period of disqualification arising or imposed in consequence of conviction for an offence.

(2) Where a person has been convicted of any offence and ordered to be imprisoned, he shall be disqualified for receiving an old age pension while he is detained in prison and for a further period of ten years after the date on which he is released from prison. . . .

7.3.3 Pensions in the Village

During the debates on the pensions Bill critics suggested that the pensions would be recognised by recipients as merely out-relief under another name, a specious argument which is refuted by this extract from Flora Thompson's autobiographical study. Mrs Thompson herself was a post-office worker when the pensions were introduced.

From Flora Thompson, Lark Rise *(1939), p. 100*

There were one or two poorer couples, just holding on to their homes, but in daily fear of the workhouse. The Poor Law authorities allowed old people past work a small weekly sum as outdoor relief; but it was not sufficient to live upon, and, unless they had more than usually prosperous children to help support them, there came a time when the home had to be broken up. When, twenty years later, the Old Age Pensions began, life was transformed for such aged cottagers. They were relieved of anxiety. They were suddenly rich. Independent for life! At first when they went to the Post Office to draw it, tears of gratitude would run down the cheeks of some, and they would say as they picked up their money 'God bless that Lord George! (for they could not believe one so powerful and munificent could be a plain 'Mr') and God bless *you*, miss!' and there were flowers from their gardens and apples from their trees for the girl who merely handed them the money.

7.4 THE LEADING SPIRITS

7.4.1 Speeches by Lloyd George

Something of the radical passion of Lloyd George's spell-binding oratory is seen in these extracts. The budget speech of 1909 introduced the 'People's Budget', which raised a storm of controversy and led to two elections and the limiting of the powers of the Lords by the Parliament Act, 1911.

Lloyd George had visited Germany in 1908 to see something at first hand of its social insurance system. Both he and Churchill were strongly influenced by German experience.

From Better Times *(A Collection of Speeches) (1910)*

THE BUDGET SPEECH, HOUSE OF COMMONS, 29 APRIL 1909
. . . We are pledged, definitely pledged, by speeches from the Prime Minister given both in the House and outside, to

supplementing our Old Age Pensions proposals. How is that to be done?

It has been suggested that we should reduce the age limit. . . .

A reduction of the age limit to 65 would cost an additional fifteen to twenty millions a year to the Exchequer. I will not say that is beyond the resources of a rich country like this, but it is much the most wasteful way of dealing with the question, for whilst it would afford relief to many thousands and hundreds of thousands probably who neither need nor desire it, and whose strength is probably more happily and profitably employed in labour, it would leave out of account altogether, far and away the most distressing and the most deserving cases of poverty.

What are the dominating causes of poverty amongst the industrial classes? . . . Old age, premature breakdown in health and strength, the death of the breadwinner, and unemployment due either to the decay of industries and seasonable demands, or to the fluctuations or depressions in trade. The distress caused by any or either of these causes is much more deserving of immediate attention than the case of a healthy and vigorous man of 65 years of age, who is able to pursue his daily avocation, and to earn without undue strain an income which is quite considerable enough to provide him and his wife with a comfortable subsistence.

When Bismarck was strengthening the foundations of the new German Empire one of the very first tasks he undertook was the organisation of a scheme which insured the German workmen and their families against the worst evils arising from these common accidents of life. And a superb scheme it is. It has saved an incalculable amount of human misery to hundreds of thousands and possibly millions of people.

Wherever I went in Germany, north or south, and whomever I met, whether it was an employer or a workman, a Conservative or a Liberal, a Socialist or a Trade Union leader – men of all ranks, sections and creeds, with one accord joined in lauding the benefits which have been conferred upon Germany by this beneficent policy. . . .

I know it is always suggested that any approval of the German scheme necessarily involves a condemnation of the Act of last year. That is not so. The Act of last year constitutes the necessary basis upon which to found any scheme based on German lines. It would be quite impossible to work any measure which would involve a contribution from men who are either already 70 years of age or approaching the confines of that age as a condition precedent to their receiving any benefits. It was therefore essential that people who had attained this great age should be placed in a totally different category. But that is not a reason why the young and vigorous who are in full employment should not be called upon to contribute towards some proposals for making provision for those accidents to which we are all liable, and always liable.

At the present moment there is a network of powerful organisations in this country, most of them managed with infinite skill and capacity, which have succeeded in inducing millions of workman in this country to make something like systematic provision for the troubles of life. But in spite of all the ability which has been expended upon them, in spite of the confidence they generally and deservedly inspire, unfortunately there is a margin of people in this country amounting in the aggregate to several millions who either cannot be persuaded or perhaps cannot afford to bear the expense of the systematic contributions which alone make membership effective in these great institutions. And the experience of this and of every other country is that no plan or variety of plans short of an universal compulsory system can ever hope to succeed in coping adequately with the problem. . . .

All I am in a position now to say is that, at any rate, in any scheme which we may finally adopt we shall be guided by these leading principles or considerations. The first is that no plan can hope to be really comprehensive or conclusive which does not include an element of compulsion. The second is that for financial as well as for other reasons, which I do not wish to enter into now, success is unattainable in the near future, except on the basis of a direct contribution from the classes more immediately concerned. The third is that there must be a State contribution substantial enough to enable those whose means are too limited and precarious to sustain adequate premiums to overcome that difficulty without throwing undue risks on other contributors. The fourth, and by no means the least important, is that in this country, where benefit and provident societies represent such a triumph of organisation, of patience and self-government, as probably no other country has ever witnessed, no scheme would be profitable, no scheme would be tolerable, which would do the least damage to those highly beneficient organisations. On the contrary, it must be the aim of every well-considered plan to encourage, and, if practicable, as I believe it is, to work through them. . . . We have already provided for the aged over 70. We have made pretty complete provision for accidents. All we have now left to do in order to put ourselves on a level with Germany – I hope our competition with Germany will not be in armaments alone – is to make some further provision for the sick, for the invalided, for widows and orphans. . . .

The Government are also pledged to deal on a comprehensive scale with the problem of unemployment. . . .

This is a War Budget. It is for raising money to wage implacable warfare against poverty and squalidness. I cannot help hoping and believing that before this generation has passed away we shall have advanced a great step towards that good time when poverty, and the wretchedness and human degradation which always follow in its camp will be as remote to the people of this country as the wolves which once infested its forests.

CAERNARVON, 9 DECEMBER 1909

Yesterday I visited the old village where I was brought up. I wandered through the woods familiar to my boyhood. There I saw a child gathering sticks for firewood, and I thought of the hours which I spent in the same pleasant and profitable occupation, for I also have been something of a 'backwoodsman'. And there was one experience taught me then which is of some profit to me today. I learnt as a child that it was little use going into the woods after a period of calm and fine weather, for I generally returned empty-handed; but after a great storm I always came back with an armful. We are in for rough weather. We may be even in for a winter of storms which will rock the forest, break many a withered branch, and leave many a rotten tree torn up by the roots. But when the weather clears you may depend upon it that there will be something brought within the reach of the people that will give warmth and glow to their grey lives, something that will help to dispel the hunger, the despair, and oppression, and the wrong which now chill so many of their hearths.

7.4.2 Speeches by Churchill

Churchill had claimed in 1906 that Liberalism was 'the cause of the left-out millions', a characteristically happy choice of phrase which was to be unconsciously echoed by President Roosevelt in similar conditions of social concern in America in the 1930s.

The two extracts given here are from a collection of Churchill's speeches.

From Liberalism and the Social Problem, *Speeches by Winston S. Churchill (1909)*

MANCHESTER, MAY 1909

If I had to sum up the immediate future of democratic politics in a single word I should say 'Insurance' – Insurance against dangers from abroad, Insurance against dangers scarcely less grave and much more near and constant which threaten us at home. . . . If I had my way I would write the word 'Insure' over the door of every cottage and upon the blotting-pad of every public man, because I am convinced that by sacrifices which are inconceivably small . . . families can be secured against catastrophes which otherwise would smash them up for ever. I think it is our duty to use the strength and the resources of the State to arrest the ghastly waste not merely of human happiness but of national health and strength which follows when a working man's home, which has taken him years to get together, is broken up and scattered through a long spell of unemployment.

LEICESTER, SEPTEMBER 1909

The social conditions of the British people in the early years of the twentieth century cannot be contemplated without deep anxiety. . . .

[On the 1909 Budget]: a far-reaching plan of social organisation designed to give a greater measure of security to all classes but particularly to the labouring classes. . . . We ought to be able to set up a complete ladder, an unbroken bridge or causeway, as it were, along which the whole body of the people may move with a certain assured measure of security and safety against hazards and misfortunes.

7.4.3 Churchill's Tribute to Lloyd George, 1945

Lloyd George, lately created Earl Lloyd-George of Dwyfor, died in March 1945. As Prime Minister, Churchill paid tribute to him in the Commons on 28 March, and recalled the years when together they had seemed to be devising a new Liberalism.

From the House of Commons Debate, 28 March 1945

Mr Speaker, shortly after David Lloyd George first took Cabinet office as President of the Board of Trade, the Liberals who had been in eclipse for 20 years obtained in January, 1906, an over-whelming majority over all other parties. . . . But this moment of political triumph occurred in a period when the aspirations of nineteenth century Liberalism had been largely achieved. . . . Some new and potent conception had to be found by those who were called into power.

It was Lloyd George who launched the Liberal and Radical forces of this country effectively into the broad stream of social betterment and social security along which all modern parties now steer. There was no man so gifted, so eloquent, so forceful, who knew the life of the people so well. . . . When I first became Lloyd George's friend and active associate, now more than forty years ago, this deep love of the people, the profound knowledge of their lives and of the undue and needless pressures under which they lived, impressed itself indelibly upon my mind. . . .

In his prime, Sir, his power, his influence, his initiative were unequalled in the land. He was the champion of the weak and the poor. These were great days. Nearly two generations have passed. Most people are unconscious of how much their lives have been shaped by the laws for which Lloyd George was responsible. Health insurance and old age pensions were the first large-scale State-conscious efforts to set a balustrade along the crowded cause-way of the people's life and, without pulling down the structures of society, to fasten a lid over the abyss into which vast numbers used to fall. . . . Now we move forward confidently into larger and more far-reaching applications of these ideas. I was his lieutenant in those bygone days, and shared in a minor way in the work. I have lived to see long strides taken, and being taken, and going to be taken, on this path of insurance by which the vultures of utter ruin are driven from the dwellings of the nations. The stamps we lick, the roads we travel, the system of progressive taxation, the principal remedies that have yet been used against unemployment – all these to a very great extent were part not only of the mission but of the actual achievement of Lloyd George.

7.5 THE POOR LAW REPORT, 1909

The Royal Commission appointed in December 1905 reported in February 1909 with two reports, a majority and a minority, the latter largely the work of the Webbs. Brief extracts from both are given, and illustrate the reactions of the members of the Commission to the social realities they had uncovered. There was much common ground between the two reports, especially as to the replacement of the guardians by the local authorities, and they differed mainly in the desire of the majority to retain the concept of a poor law, which the minority wished rather to tackle through its component problems. The differences seemed more serious then than they appear now.

The main recommendations of both are briefly compared in 7.5.2.

7.5.1 The Reports

From the Majority Report, p. 248

'Land of Hope and Glory' is a popular and patriotic lyric sung each year with rapture by thousands of voices. The enthusiasm is partly evoked by the beauty of the idea itself, but more by the belief that Great Britain does, above other countries, merit this eulogium, and that the conditions in existence here are such that the fulfilment of hope and the achievement of glory are more open to the individual than in other and less favoured lands. To certain classes of the community into whose moral and material condition it has been our duty to enquire, these words are a mockery and a falsehood. To many of them, possibly from their own failure and faults, there is in this life but little hope, and to many more 'glory' or its realisation is an unknown ideal. Our investigations prove the existence in our midst of a class whose condition and environment are a discredit, and a peril to the whole community. . . . No country, however rich, can permanently hold its own in the race of international competition, if hampered by an increasing load of this dead weight, or can successfully perform the role of sovereignty beyond the seas, if a portion of its own folk at home are sinking below the civilisation and aspirations of its subject races abroad. . . .

From the Minority Report, p. 684

'UTOPIAN?'

[Our] elaborate scheme of national organisation for dealing with the grave social evil of Unemployment, with its resultant Able-bodied Destitution, and its deterioration of hundreds of thousands of working class families, will seem to many persons Utopian. Experience proves, however, that this may mean no more than that it will take a little time to accustom people to the proposals, and to get them carried into operation. The first step is to make the whole community realise that the evil exists. At present, it is not too much to say that the average citizen of the middle or upper class takes for granted the constantly recurring destitution among wage-earning families due to Unemployment as part of the natural order of things, and as no more to be combated than the east wind. . . . Fifty years hence we shall be looking back with amazement at the helpless and ignorant acquiescence of the governing classes of the United Kingdom, at the opening of the twentieth century, in the constant debasement of character and physique, not to mention the perpetual draining away of the nation's wealth that idleness combined with starvation plainly causes. . . .

We have to report that, in our judgment, it is now administratively possible, if it is sincerely wished to do so, to remedy most of the evils of Unemployment. . . . Less than a century ago the problem of dealing with the sewage of London seemed insoluble. . . . In the same way, a century ago, no one knew how to administer a fever hospital. . . . And, to take a more recent problem, less than half a century ago, when millions of children in the land were growing up untaught, undisciplined, and uncared for, it would have sounded wildly visionary to have suggested that the remedy was elaborate organisation on a carefully thought-out plan. Could there have been anything more 'Utopian' in 1860 than a picture of what today we take as a matter of course, the 7,000,000 children emerging every morning washed and brushed, from 5,000,000 or 6,000,000 homes in every part of the Kingdom, traversing street and road and lonely woodland, going o'er fell and moor, to present themselves at a given hour at their 30,000 schools, where each of the 7,000,000 finds his or her own individual place, with books and blackboard and teacher provided? What has been effected in the organisation of Public Health and Public Education can be effected, if we wish it, in the Public Organisation of the Labour Market.

7.5.2 The Reports Compared
From the Majority and Minority Reports: A Summary

Subject	The Majority Report	The Minority Report
Organisation	The guardians to be replaced by a Public Assistance Authority of the local councils.	The guardians to go and the poor law broken up, to be replaced by specialist committees of the local councils, whose work was to be co-ordinated by a Registrar of Public Assistance. The specialist committees would be concerned with: 1. children of school age; 2. the sick, the aged needing institutional care, etc.; 3. the mentally defective; 4. the aged receiving pensions.
Indoor Relief	The general workhouse to be abolished and replaced by classified institutions.	Separate institutions under the special committees.
Out-Relief	'Home Assistance', applied on a case paper system in cooperation with Voluntary Aid Committees. One uniform order for out-relief.	'Home Aliment', controlled by the Registrar of Public Assistance on the advice of the specialist committees.
Children	To be taken out of the workhouse and boarded out. The provision of meals under the 1906 Act to	The responsibility of the Education Committee.

Subject	The Majority Report	The Minority Report
	be reconsidered and to be supplied either from voluntary sources or by Public Assistance.	
The Aged	Classified Public Assistance institutions, according to physical condition, record, behaviour, etc., with small homes where possible. Public Assistance 'Home Assistance' in other cases, to be adequate and applied under regular supervision.	The responsibility of the Pension Committee.
Medical Relief	Public Assistance Committee coordinating voluntary and statutory provision, with Provident Dispensaries.	Medical Services under the Health Committee, with the Registrar recovering cost where necessary and possible.
Employment and Unemployment	Labour Exchanges. Better industrial training for the young, with a raising of the school leaving age. Facilities for retraining for older workers. Unemployment insurance conducted by the trade unions with some state assistance.	A National Authority, th Ministry of Labour, to organise the national labour market so as to prevent or minimise unemployment. Labour Exchanges. Trade union unemployment insurance with state help. Training and retraining. Part-time further education for the young.
Settlements	Modification and simplification of the law.	Repeal.

7.6 EMPLOYMENT AND UNEMPLOYMENT

7.6.1 The Beveridge Analysis

William Beveridge (1874–1964) first studied unemployment when sub-warden of Toynbee Hall, 1903–5. One of the problems of unemployment was the difficulty men had of learning of vacancies. Labour Exchanges had been developed in Germany, and some had been established in Britain, especially under the Unemployed Workmen Act. Beveridge saw their wider potentialities as a means of relieving the unemployed worker of the unhappy choice, between searching for work himself or turning to a deterrent poor law. The Exchange could either find work or safely provide relief when none was available.

Churchill met Beveridge through the Webbs in 1908, and took him with him into the Board of Trade later that year. The following extracts are taken from his *Unemployment: A Problem of Industry*, published in 1909, when the Labour Exchanges Act was passed. In the following year Beveridge became Director of the new service. A substantial second part, on developments since 1909, was added to *Unemployment* for a second edition in 1930 [8.2.6].

From W. H. Beveridge, Unemployment, A Problem of Industry *(1909), pp. 2, 3, 4, 193, 215–16*

THE PROBLEM AND ITS LIMITS

There has been a steady, if gradual, growth of the sense of public responsibility for the case of the unemployed. If this sense of responsibility is to issue in further action, it is before all things necessary that that case should be fully understood.

The inquiry must be essentially an economic one. . . . The problem must be approached not from the standpoint of the Poor Law or of charitable administration, but from that of industry. The first question must be, not what is to be done with the unemployed individual, but why he is thus unemployed. . . .

The inquiry must be one into unemployment rather than into the unemployed. It will appear at once . . . that any one unemployed individual may represent, and commonly does represent, the concurrence of many different forces, some industrial, some personal. A riverside labourer in Wapping during February, 1908, might be suffering at one and the same time from chronic irregularity of employment, from seasonal depression of his trade, from exceptional or cyclical depression of trade generally, from the permanent shifting of work lower down the river, and from his own deficiencies of character or education. His distress could not be attributed to any one of these factors alone. Classification of men according to the causes of their unemployment is, strictly speaking, an impossibility. The only possible course is to classify the causes or types of unemployment themselves. The problem of unemployment is the problem of the adjustment of the supply of labour and the demand for labour. The supply of labour in a country is, in the widest sense, the supply of population. It is at any moment, apart from the possibilities of emigration and immigration, a fairly fixed quantity. Moreover, it is fixed for each moment, not by anything then happening, but by the habits and actions of millions of disconnected households a generation back. The demand for labour, on the other hand, is an aggregate of thousands or tens of thousands of separate demands in the present. It fluctuates with the fortunes and the calculations of the host of rival employers.

Discrepancy between two things so distinct in immediate origin is obviously possible. The problem has merely to be stated in order to shatter the simple faith that at all times any man who really wants work can obtain it. There is nothing in the existing industrial order to secure this miraculously perfect adjustment. The question is rather as to what there is to secure any sort of adjustment at all, and to keep the demand for labour even within measurable distance of the supply. . . .

I. PRINCIPLES OF FUTURE POLICY
The organised fluidity of labour

Unemployment is a question not of the scale of industry but of its organisation, not of the volume of demand for labour but of its changes and fluctuations. . . . To meet these fluctuations – cyclical seasonal and casual – there are required reserves of labour power Unemployment arises as the idleness of these reserves between the epochs when they are called into action. The solution of the problem of unemployment must consist, therefore, partly in smoothing industrial transitions, partly in diminishing the extent of the reserves required for fluctuation or their intervals of idleness partly, when this plan can go no further, in seeing that the men of the reserve are properly maintained both in action and out of it The problem is essentially one of business organisation, of meeting

without distress the changes and fluctuations without which
industry is not and probably could not be carried on. . . .

An aspect of labour market organisation has to be mentioned,
lying perhaps a little part . . . but of fundamental importance. This
is the function of an efficient Labour Exchange in affording a
direct test of unemployment. The central problem of the Poor
Law is to relieve without relieving unnecessarily. The only principle on which it has hitherto attempted to secure this is the
principle of deterrence. . . .

Deterrence is, in fact, in regard to the able-bodied, an indirect
test of unemployment; unless they are really unable to obtain work
they will not accept relief under harsh conditions. To deterrence
the Labour Exchange offers an alternative and a supplement. If all
the jobs offering in a trade or a district are registered at a single
office, then it is clear that any man who cannot get work through
that office is unemployed against his will. He may be relieved
without deterrence, yet without any fear that he is being relieved
when he could get work, or is being drawn needlessly from industry to pauperism. . . . The Labour Exchange thus opens a way
of 'dispauperisation' more humane, less costly and more effective
than that of the 'workhouse test' – the way of making the finding
of work easy instead of merely making relief hard.

7.6.2 Churchill and Unemployment Insurance, 1909

Churchill presented his plans for labour exchanges to the Commons in
1909, during the debate on the Poor Law Report, and went on to
describe his proposals for unemployment insurance, which, after delays
due to the budget crisis, eventually appeared as part II of the National
Insurance Act, 1911.

'A good Labour night' was a trade union MP's comment on this
speech of 1909.

From the House of Commons Debate, 19 May 1909

Mr Churchill: . . . So I come to unemployment insurance. It is
not practicable at the present time to establish a universal system
of unemployment insurance. It would be risking the policy to cast
one's net so wide. We therefore, have to choose at the very outset
of this subject between insuring some workmen in all trades and
insuring all workmen in some trades. That is the first parting of
the ways upon unemployment insurance. In the first case we can
have a voluntary and in the second case a compulsory system. If

you adopt a voluntary system of unemployment insurance, you are always exposed to this difficulty. The risk of unemployment varies so much between man and man, according to their qualities, character, circumstances, temperament, demeanour towards their superiors – these are all factors; and the risk varies so much between man and man that a voluntary system of unemployment insurance which the State subsidises always attracts those workers who are most likely to be unemployed. That is why all voluntary systems have broken down when they have been tried, because they accumulate a preponderance of bad risks against the insurance office, which is fatal to its financial stability. On the other hand, a compulsory system of insurance, which did not add to the contribution of the worker a substantial contribution from outside has also broken down, because of the refusal of the higher class of worker to assume unsupported a share of the burden of the weaker members of the community. We have decided to avoid these difficulties. Our insurance scheme will present four main features. It will involve contributions from the workpeople and from the employers; those contributions will be aided by a substantial subvention from the State; it will be insurance by trades, following the suggestion of the Royal Commission; and it will be compulsory within those trades upon all, unionist and non-unionist, skilled and unskilled, workmen and employers alike. The hon. Member for Leicester [Mr Ramsay Macdonald] with great force showed that to confine a scheme of unemployment insurance merely to trade unionists would be trifling with the subject. I would only be aiding those who have been most able to aid themselves, without at the same time assisting those who hitherto under existing conditions have not been able to make any effective provision.

To what trades ought we, as a beginning, to apply our system of compulsory contributory unemployment insurance? There is a group of trades well marked out for this class of treatment. They are trades in which unemployment is not only high, but chronic, for even in the best of times it persists; where it is not only high and chronic, but marked by seasonal and cyclical fluctuations, and wherever and howsoever it occurs it takes the form not of short time or of any of those devices for spreading wages and equalising or averaging risks, but of a total, absolute, periodical discharge of a certain proportion of the workers. These are the trades to which in the first instance, we think the system of unemployment insurance ought to be applied. The group of trades which we contemplate to be the subject of our scheme are these: house-building and works of construction, engineering, machine and tool making, ship and boat building, vehicles, sawyers, and general labourers working at these trades.

That is a very considerable group of industries. They comprise, according to the last Census Returns, $2\frac{1}{4}$ millions of adult workers. Two and a quarter millions of adult workers are, roughly speaking, one-third of the adult population of these three kingdoms engaged in purely industrial work; that is to say, excluding commercial, professional, agricultural, and domestic occupations. Of the remaining two-thirds of the adult industrial population, nearly one-half are employed in the textile trades, in mining, on the railways, in the merchant marine, and in other trades, which either do not present the same features of unemployment which we see in the precarious trades, or which, by the adoption of short time or other arrangements, avoid the total discharge of a proportion of workmen from time to time. So that this group of trades to which we propose to apply the system of unemployment insurance, roughly speaking, covers very nearly half the whole field of unemployment. That half, on the whole, is perhaps the worst half. The financial and actuarial basis of the scheme has been very carefully studied by the light of all available information. The report of the actuarial authorities whom I have consulted leaves me no doubt that . . . a financially sound scheme can be evolved which, in return for moderate contributions, will yield adequate benefits. . . . they will be benefits which will afford substantial weekly payments for a period which will cover by far the greater part of the period of unemployment of all unemployed persons in this great group of insured trades. In order to enable such a scale of benefits to be paid it is necessary that we should raise something between 5d and 6d – rather nearer 6d than 5d – per man per week. That sum, we propose, should be made up by contributions, not necessarily equal, between the workman, the employer and the State. . . .

We propose to follow the German example, of insurance cards or books, to which stamps will be affixed every week. As soon as a man in an insured trade is without employment, if he has kept to the rules of the system, all he will have to do is to take his card to the nearest Labour Exchange, which will be responsible, in conjunction with the insurance office, either for finding him a job or for paying him his benefits. I am very glad . . . to submit this not inconsiderable proposal in general outline, so that the Bill for Labour Exchanges which I will introduce tomorrow may not be misjudged as if it stood by itself, and was not part of a considered, co-ordinated, and connected scheme to grapple with this hideous crushing evil which has oppressed for so long the mind of every one who cares about social reform.

7.7 NATIONAL HEALTH INSURANCE

7.7.1 Lloyd George Introduces National Insurance, 1911

Lloyd George had been greatly impressed by what he had seen of the German system of contributory sickness insurance (though Germany had no unemployment insurance) and combined Churchill's interest in unemployment insurance with his own in health insurance in one great National Insurance scheme. He had hoped to work health insurance through the friendly societies, but roused both them and the commercial insurance interests by plans for including 'insurance against death', and after a long struggle had not only to accept defeat on that point but to associate the commercial interests in health insurance through the artificial device of the 'approved society'. He also had to deal with the doctors, and it took all his charm and political skill to get his plans through.

His analysis in this extract of the protection which workers had built up against the accidents of life drove home the need for a wider approach backed by the state.

From the House of Commons Debate, 4 May 1911
The Chancellor of the Exchequer (Mr Lloyd George): I ask leave to introduce a Bill 'To provide for insurance against loss of health, and for the prevention and cure of sickness, and for insurance against unemployment, and for purposes incidental thereto'.

I think it must be a relief to the Members of the House of Commons to turn from controversial questions for a moment to a question which, at any rate, has never been the subject of controversy between the parties in the State. I believe there is a general agreement as to the evil which has to be remedied. . . . In this country . . . 30 per cent of the pauperism is attributable to sickness. A considerable percentage would probably have to be added to that for unemployment. The administration of the Old Age Pensions Act has revealed the fact there is a mass of poverty and destitution in this country which is too proud to wear the badge of pauperism, and which declines to pin that badge to its children. They would rather suffer from deprivation than do so. . . .

The efforts made by the working classes to insure against the troubles of life indicate they are fully alive to the need of some provision being made. There are three contingencies against which they insure – death, sickness, and unemployment. Taking them in the order of urgency which the working classes attach to them, death would come first. There are 42,000,000 industrial policies of insurance against death issued in this country of small amounts where the payments are either weekly, monthly, or occasionally quarterly. The friendly societies, without exception, have funeral benefits, and that accounts for about 6,000,000. The collecting societies are about 7,000,000, and those are also death benefits. Then the great industrial insurance companies have something like 30,000,000 policies. There is hardly a household in this country where there is not a policy of insurance against death. I will not stop to account for it. All that I would say here is we do not propose to deal with insurance against death. It is no part of our scheme at all, partly because the ground has been very thoroughly covered, although not very satisfactorily covered, and also because this, at any rate, is the easiest part of the problem and is a part of the problem which is not beset with the difficulties of vested interests. Fortunately, all the vested interests which deal with sickness and unemployment are of a thoroughly unselfish and beneficent character, and we shall be able, I think, to assist them.

Sickness comes in the next order of urgency in the working-class mind. Between 6,000,000 and 7,000,000 people in this country have made some provision against sickness, not all of it adequate, and a good deal of it defective. Then comes the third class, the insurance against unemployment. Here not a tenth of the working classes have made any provision at all. You have only got 1,400,000 workmen who have insured against unemployment. It is true that perhaps about half of the employment of this country is not affected by the fluctuations of trade. I do not think agricultural labourers or railway servants are affected quite to the same extent. Then there is provision for short time in some of the trades. Taking the precarious trades affected by unemployment, I do not believe more than one-third or one-quarter of the people engaged in them are insured against unemployment. That is the provision which is made at the present moment by the working-classes.

What is the explanation that only a portion of the working-classes have made provision against sickness and against unemployment? Is it they consider it not necessary? Quite the reverse, as I shall prove by figures. In fact, those who stand most in need of it, make up the bulk of the uninsured. Why? Because very few can afford to pay the premiums, and pay them continuously, which enable a man to provide against those three contingencies. As a matter of fact, you could not provide against all those three contingencies anything which would be worth a workman's while, without paying at any rate 1s 6d or 2s per week at the very lowest. There are a multitude of the working classes who cannot spare that, and ought not to be asked to spare it, because it involves the deprivation of children of the necessaries of life. Therefore they are compelled to elect, and the vast majority choose to insure against death alone. Those who can afford to take up two policies insure against death and sickness, and those who can afford to take up all three insure against death, sickness and unemployment, but only in that order. What are the explanations why they do not insure against all three? The first is that their wages are too low. The second difficulty, and it is the greatest of all, is that during a period of sickness or unemployment, when they are earning nothing, they cannot keep up the premiums. They may be able to do it for a fortnight or three weeks, but when times of very bad trade come, when a man is out of work for weeks and weeks at a time, arrears run up with the friendly societies, and when the man gets work, it may be at the end of two or three months, those are not the first arrears which have to be met. . . . What does it mean in the way of lapses? I have inquired of friendly Societies, and, as near as I can get at it, there are 250,000 lapses in a year. That is a very considerable proportion of the 6,000,000 policies. The expectation of life at twenty, is, I think, a little over forty years, and it means that in twenty years' time there are 5,000,000 lapses: that is, people who supported and joined friendly societies, and who have gone on paying the premiums for weeks, months, and even years, struggling along, at last, when a very bad time of unemployment comes, drop out and the premium lapses. . . . I think it necessary to state these facts in order to show that there is a real need for some system which would aid the workmen over these difficulties. I do not think there is any better method, or one more practicable at the present moment, than a system of national insurance which would invoke the aid of the State and the aid of the employer to enable the workman to get over all these difficulties and make provision for himself for sickness, and, as far as the most precarious trades are concerned, against unemployment. . . .

I come to benefits. These will be distributed under three or four different heads. There will be medical relief. There will be the curing side of the benefit, and there will also be allowance for the maintenance of a man and his family during the time of his sickness. . . .

I have now to refer to another branch of medical benefit. We propose to do something to deal with the terrible scourge of consumption. There are, I believe, in this country about four or five hundred thousand persons who are suffering from tubercular disease. From the friendly societies' point of view that is a very serious item, because of the dragging length of the illness. The average illness of patients of the Foresters, I think, was fifty-eight weeks. They received fifty-eight weeks' allowance on an average. Out of the total sick pay of the Foresters about 25 per cent was due to tuberculosis. There are 75,000 deaths every year in Great Britain and Ireland from tuberculosis and, a much more serious matter, if you take the ages between fourteen and fifty-five among males, one out of three dies of tuberculosis between those ages in what should be the very period of greatest strength and vigour and service. . . . It kills as many in this kingdom in a single year as all the zymotic diseases put together, and a very terrible fact in connection with it is that the moment a man is attacked and compromised he becomes a recruit in the destructive army, and proceeds to injure mortally even those to whom he is most attached and to scatter infection and death in his own household. . . .

I do not say that they can cure it, but doctors think they can cure it. . . . But they can only do it if they have the means, and I propose to ask the House to give them. In Germany they have done great things in this respect. They have established a chain of sanatoria all over the country, and the results are amazing. The number of cures that are effected is very large. In this country there are practically only 2,000 beds in sanatoria for tubercular patients. . . . We propose to set aside £1,500,000 of a capital sum for the purpose of aiding local people in building sanatoria throughout the country. . . .

I now come to the machinery of the Bill we have got to work. Collection is the first thing. We shall collect our funds by means of stamps. That is purely the German system. . . . Then comes the question, who is to dispense the benefits? In this country we have fortunately a number of very well-organised, well-managed, well-conducted benefit societies who have a great tradition behind them, and an accumulation of experience which is very valuable when you come to deal with questions like malingering.

We propose, as far as we possibly can, to work through those societies. We propose that all the benefits shall be dispensed through what the Bill would call 'approved societies'. What are the conditions attaching to an approved society? It must be a society with at least 10,000 members; otherwise, it becomes a matter of very great complication which is much more difficult to manage from the actuarial and financial point of view. It must be precluded by its constitution from distributing any of its funds otherwise than by way of benefits. . . . It cannot be a society that allows anybody to make a profit out of this branch of its business. . . . Its affairs must be subject to the absolute control of its own members; it must be self-governing, and its constitution must provide for the election of its committees and representatives and officers. . . .

I will now briefly outline the unemployment insurance. My explanation will be considerably curtailed, owing to the fact that the Home Secretary very fully explained to the House the year before last the principles upon which the Government intended to proceed. The scheme only applies to one-sixth of the industrial population. We propose to apply it only to the precarious trades, which are liable to very considerable fluctuations. The benefit will be of a very simple character; it is purely a weekly allowance. . . . The machinery will be the Labour Exchanges and the existing unions which deal with unemployment. . . .

We have started, first of all, by taking two groups of trades, and we propose to organise them individually – the engineering group and the building group. They include building, construction of works, shipbuilding, mechanical engineering and the construction of vehicles. These are the trades in which you have the most serious fluctuations . . . I ought to say here that you have not the same basis for actuarial calculation, that you have in reference to sickness. ... You cannot say with the almost certainty that you can in sickness that a certain fund will produce such and such benefits. In the case of sickness you have nearly 100 years' experience behind you, and you have the facts with regard to sickness and death. You have not got the facts with regard to unemployment. ...

I have explained as best I could the details of our scheme – the system of contributions and of benefits and the machinery whereby something like 15,000,000 of people will be insured, at any rate against the acute distress which now darkens the homes of the workmen wherever there is sickness and unemployment. I do not pretend that this is a complete remedy ... till the advent of a complete remedy, this scheme does alleviate an immense mass of human suffering.

7.7.2 'The Tide of Social Pity'

Lloyd George's speech on the National Insurance Bill was reprinted, with the text of the Bill itself and a simple explanation, in a cheap pamphlet, *The People's Insurance. Explained by the Rt Hon. David Lloyd George,* MP, as one of a series put out in Lloyd George's name on the controversial issues of the day, the others being *The People's Budget* (1909) and *The People's Will* (on the constitutional crisis, 1910).

From The People's Insurance. Explained by the Rt Hon David Lloyd George, MP *(1911)*

THE ACHIEVEMENT OF A VAST SCHEME
The tide of social pity

I shall require all the enthusiasm of all the progressive and benevolent people in this country to carry through this vast scheme. It is big, but it is simple.

Do not anyone imagine that anything so vast can be achieved easily. It will require the help of everyone. There will inevitably rise certain forces against it, though I am amazed at present to find how few those forces are. In fact, it has struck me that I have had the good fortune to find myself carried forward on a tide of social pity that was only waiting for a chance of expression.

Perhaps it is the accumulation of all the thought and teaching that has been going on in the nation in social matters during the last twenty years. ... It is time that something was done for this nation. We have been talking quite long enough. Now is the time for action, and I ask for the whole nation to join me in my efforts.

7.7.3 'We Have Got L.G. There'

This revealing account of the way in which the commercial insurance interests forced their way into National Insurance, and made their own terms with Lloyd George, was written by W. J. Braithwaite (1875–1938), an able civil servant in Internal Revenue, with an interest in friendly societies and a long connection with Toynbee Hall, who was called in, with others, to help Lloyd George plan and launch National Health Insurance. He collapsed under the strain and, though he had expected to be given charge of the central administration, was passed over in favour of the brilliant administrator, Sir Robert Morant (1863–1920), who had recently been ousted from the Board of Education, where he had framed the 1902 Education Act and developed, among other things, the school medical service.

(Sir) Kingsley Wood (1881–1943), who battled with Lloyd George as the legal adviser of the insurance interests, entered politics in 1918, became a Cabinet Minister in 1933, and was Chancellor of the Exchequer, 1940–3.

The title given to Braithwaite's memoirs is taken from a speech by Lloyd George in which he likened the passage of his Bill through Parliament to driving an ambulance over rough roads.

From Sir Henry N. Bunbury (ed.), Lloyd George's Ambulance Wagon, The Memoirs of William J. Braithwaite, 1911–12 *(1957), pp. 161, 168*

The reception of the bill had been very friendly. There had, however, been one discordant note from ... the spokesman in the House of the Industrial Insurance interest, far the most formidable interest affected by the bill. Interests are very real forces in Parliament. They are alive and active. The public interest which should come before them is inert and dead compared with them, and has no spokesman or representative. ... The history of the bill is how they were bought off, conciliated, and in very few instances over-ruled. ... L. G. made promise after promise, did one dodge after another. ...

... The Industrial storm had already blown up. It was very cleverly worked, and I suppose that Kingsley Wood was at the bottom of it. At any rate he said to me one day when the storm was in full blast, 'We have got L. G. there' (putting his thumb on the desk) 'and shall get our own terms.'

The storm was worked as follows. There were some 80,000 agents, and most houses in the country were called at once a week. Many of these agents had themselves 'bought their books'; all had their jobs at stake. They were induced to think that their whole living was threatened; they, themselves, and friends, poured in a flood of letters upon their MP asking for protection. These small men really thought they were in danger, but their ignorance was colossal. The letters were much of a type. I do not really know whether they were instructed by the Directors to protest, but I have always assumed that they were. Anyhow their protest was effective – very – much the biggest thing I should imagine ever done in the way of pressure on Members, and many MPs were simply terrified as it went on. They looked upon L. G. askance as the author of the evil and L. G. really did 'risk something' when this storm was on. Personally I think that it showed up the representative system at its very worst, and anyhow these men's livings were not at stake.

8 Between the Wars

8.1 THE POST-WAR SETTLEMENT

8.1.1 Reconstruction and the Ministry of Health

In 1917 a Ministry of Reconstruction was formed, under Addison, to prepare for the return of peace, but in the event it exercised little influence on policy. Plans were laid for a Ministry of Health to replace the LGB and reshape the poor law, and after much political wrangling the new Ministry was formed, with Addison as Minister and Morant as Permanent Secretary. Addison's confidence in a general desire for a new world proved over-optimistic, however. There were many who looked rather for a return to pre-war conditions [8.1.6], and financial interests were shocked at the costliness of his policies. Morant's early death in 1920 weakened his position, and in the following year Lloyd George, with characteristic disloyalty, sacrificed him to critical clamour. The Ministry of Health never became what Addison and Morant had intended, and the poor law continued unchanged until 1929.

From Reconstruction Problems, *Speeches by Christopher Addison* (*1918*)

The idea of Reconstruction has passed through more than one phase in the public mind. In the earlier part of the war people looking forward to peace thought of it as a return to pre-war conditions . . . it was assumed that the only thing required was some machinery to enable the country to slide with as little friction as possible into the familiar grooves of July 1914: to go back, as far as was humanely possible to the social and industrial situation as it existed at the outbreak of war . . . but . . . the idea of Reconstruction, of a simple return to pre-war conditions, has gradually been supplanted by a larger and worthier ideal of a better world after the war . . . to give shape and satisfaction to the strong feeling . . that there is very much to be ashamed of when we look back to the conditions of July 1914, and that out of justice to the living and out of reverence to the dead, we are called to rebuild the national life on a better and more enduring foundation.

From the Report of the Ministry of Reconstruction to 31 December 1918 (1919), p. 30

The lines of a great housing programme have been decided on by the government. ... Since the Ministry was first formed, it has been recognised that the provision of adequate house room, and of an effective public health service, are vital parts of any scheme of Reconstruction. The Bill for setting up a Ministry of Health, carrying with it the abolition of the existing system of poor law, has been introduced, and if, as may be hoped, rapid progress is made with an adequate and considered scheme of housing concurrently with the establishment of a Ministry of Health, guarantees will have been given for the future wellbeing of the people which will have no small part in repairing the havoc and wastage of the war.

8.1.2 The Dawson Report, 1920

Before the end of the war Addison had introduced to Lloyd George a notable London physician, Bertrand (afterwards, Lord) Dawson, who had proposed a thorough reorganisation of health services. After the establishment of the Ministry of Health Addison set up a consultative council, with Dawson as its chairman. There followed in 1920 the 'Dawson report', the first sketch of a National Health Service, which came to nothing, however, owing to the mood of economy which was soon to prevail.

Dawson became well-known as King George v's physician, and penned the famous last bulletin on him in 1936.

Ministry of Health Consultative Council on Medical and Allied Services : From the Interim Report on the Future Provision of Medical and Allied Services

To The Right Hon. Christopher Addison, MD, MP, Minister of Health.

Sir,

1. In October last you made the following reference to the Consultative Council on Medical and Allied Services:

'To consider and make recommendations as to the scheme or schemes requisite for the systematised provision of such forms of medical and allied services as should, in the opinion of the Council, be available for the inhabitants of a given area.' . . .

2. In view of the urgency which attaches to the orderly building of a constructive health policy, and the close relationship which exists between medical services and the problems connected with poor law and local government, we think it will promote progress if we set forth the trend of our deliberations and conclusions, and we accordingly have the honour to present an Interim Report.

3. The changes which we advise are rendered necessary because the organisation of medicine has become insufficient, and because it fails to bring the advantages of medical knowledge adequately within reach of the people. . . .

4. The general availability of medical services can only be effected by new and extended organisations, distributed according to the needs of the community. . . . Measures for dealing with health and disease become, with increasing knowledge, more complex and, therefore, less within the power of the individual to provide. . . . As complexity and cost of treatment increase, the number of people who can afford to pay for a full range of services diminishes. Moreover, enlightened public opinion is appreciating the fact that the home does not always offer the best hygienic conditions for dealing with serious illness, which requires special provision in order to give the patient a full chance of recovery. . . .

6. Preventive and curative medicine cannot be separated on any sound principle, and in any scheme of medical services must be brought together in close co-ordination. They must likewise be both brought within the sphere of the general practitioner, whose duties should embrace the work of communal as well as individual medicine. . . .

7. Any scheme of services must be available for all classes of the community. . . . In using the word 'available', we do not mean that the services are to be free; we exclude for the moment the question how they are to be paid for. . . .

8. The services may be classified into – Those which are Domiciliary as distinct from those which are Institutional. Those which are Individual as distinct from those which are Communal.

9. We begin with the home, and the services, preventive and curative, which revolve round it, viz., those of the doctor, dentist, pharmacist, nurse, midwife and health visitor. These we style domiciliary services, and they constitute the periphery of the

scheme, the remainder of which is mainly institutional in character.

A Health Centre is an institution wherein are brought together various medical services, preventive and curative, so as to form one organisation.

Health Centres may be either Primary or Secondary, the former denoting a more simple, and the latter a more specialised service.
10. The domiciliary services of a given district would be based on a *Primary Health Centre* – an institution equipped for services of curative and preventive medicine to be conducted by the general practitioners of that district, in conjunction with an efficient nursing service and with the aid of visiting consultants and specialists. . . .

11. A group of Primary Health Centres should in turn be based on a *Secondary Health Centre*. Here cases of difficulty, or cases requiring special treatment, would be referred from Primary Centres. . . . Patients entering a Secondary Health Centre would pass from the hands of their own doctors under the care of the medical staff of that centre. Whereas a Primary Health Centre would be mainly staffed by general practitioners, a Secondary Health Centre would be mainly staffed by consultants and specialists. . . .

13. Secondary Health Centres should in turn be brought into relation with a *Teaching Hospital* having a Medical School. . . .

In those towns where Teaching Hospitals exist, Secondary Health Centres would sometimes be merged in them.

14. *Supplementary Services* – Certain supplementary services would be a necessary part of the scheme. They would be in relation to both Primary and Secondary Health Centres, would often serve a wide area, and would require special staffs. They would comprise provision for patients suffering from such conditions as tuberculosis, mental diseases, epilepsy, certain infectious diseases, and for those in need of orthopaedic treatment.

5.1.3 Unemployment Insurance Extended, 1920

The Unemployment Insurance Act of 1920, though it was passed during the post-war boom, proved to be only the first of twenty-eight passed between 1920 and 1934 in the difficult conditions of large-scale unemployment which the Act of 1911 had never foreseen. It raised the number of insured workers from four million to twelve million, but by the time it came into effect the boom was ending; unemployment had already reached a million and was very soon to rise to two million. There had been no time to build up reserves, and borrowing was resorted to. It was assumed, however, that employment would recover, and every effort was therefore made to spare workers who might be assumed to have a reasonable chance of soon returning to work from having to apply to the poor law: clauses 7(i), 7(iv) and 44 of the Act, together with 2 and 3 in the second schedule, were legislatively manipulated, and the exact significance of 7(iii) was much debated.

Soldiers returning from the war were given, up to 1921, 'out-of-work donations' to cover them while seeking work. These were the only true 'dole' of the period, as there could be no pretence of insurance cover, but the name 'dole' came to be applied to all unemployment benefit, even to 'standard' benefit fully covered by insurance regulations. As with Service pay, the 'donations' included allowances for dependants. Unemployment benefit did not cover dependants, however, but as unemployment rose rapidly during 1921 it became apparent that benefit was inadequate for the kind of men, accustomed to steady work, who were now being put out of work, and there were fears of serious disorders.[1] In the late autumn of 1921, therefore, it was agreed to add dependants' allowances, which, though at first intended only to cover the winter period, were extended to become a normal part of the unemployment scheme, and were therefore also included in Unemployment Assistance after 1934.

From the Unemployment Insurance Act, 1920

INSURED PERSONS

1. All persons of the age of sixteen and upwards who are engaged in any of the employments specified in Part I of the First Schedule to this Act, not being employments specified in Part II of that schedule (in this Act referred to as 'employed persons'), shall be insured against unemployment.

2. Every person who being insured under this Act is unemployed and in whose case the conditions laid down by this Act (in this Act referred to as 'statutory conditions') are fulfilled shall be entitled to receive payments (in this Act referred to as 'unemployment benefit'), at weekly or other prescribed intervals, at such rates and for such periods as are authorised. . . .

UNEMPLOYMENT BENEFIT

7. – (1) The statutory conditions for the receipt of unemployment benefit by a person insured under this Act (in this Act referred to as 'insured contributor') are –

[1] B. B. Gilbert, *British Social Policy, 1914–1939*, p. 84.

(i) that he proves that no less than twelve contributions have been paid in respect of him under this Act;

(ii) that he has made application for unemployment benefit in the prescribed manner, and proves that since the date of the application he has been continuously unemployed;

(iii) that he is capable of and available for work, but unable to obtain suitable employment;

(iv) that he has not exhausted his right to unemployment benefit;

(v) that, if he has been required by an insurance officer ... to attend at any course of instruction he proves that he duly attended in accordance with the requirement. ...

27. In determining whether outdoor relief shall or shall not be granted to a person in receipt of or entitled to receive unemployment benefit, the authority having power to grant the relief shall not take into account any such benefit except in so far as it exceeds ten shillings a week. ...

44. During the period of twelve months next after the commencement of this Act, every person in respect of whom not less than four contributions have been paid shall, notwithstanding that the first statutory condition may not have been fulfilled in his case, be entitled to receive unemployment benefit for periods not exceeding in the aggregate eight weeks. ...

FIRST SCHEDULE
Part I: Employments within the meaning of the act

(a) Employment in the United Kingdom under any contract of service or apprenticeship ... whether paid by time or by the piece.

(b) Employment under such a contract as master or a member of the crew of any ship registered in the United Kingdom. ...

(c) Employment under any local or other public authority, other than any such employment as may be excluded by a special order.

Part II: Excepted employments

(a) Employment in agriculture, including horticulture and forestry.

(b) Employment in domestic service. ...

(c) Employment in the naval, military, or air service of the Crown. ...

(*d*) Employment –
  (i)   under any local or other public authority; or
  (ii) in a police force; or
  (iii) in the service of any railway company . . .
  (iv) in the service of any public utility company . . .
  (v)   in which the persons employed are entitled to rights in a superannuation fund established by or in pursuance of an Act of Parliament . . . where the Minister certifies . . . that the terms and conditions on which the employed person is engaged make it unnecessary that he should be insured.
(*e*) Employment as a teacher . . . within the meaning of the School Teachers (Superannuation) Act, 1918. . . .
(*h*) Employment otherwise than by way of manual labour and at a rate of remuneration exceeding in value two hundred and fifty pounds a year.

SECOND SCHEDULE
Rates and periods of unemployment benefit

1. Unemployment benefit shall be payable in respect of each week of any continuous period of unemployment after the first three days of unemployment, and shall be at the weekly rate of fifteen shillings for men and twelve shillings for women. . . .

Provided that, in the case of an insured contributor under the age of eighteen unemployment benefit shall only be paid at half the full rate.

2. No person shall receive unemployment benefit for more than fifteen or such other number of weeks as may be prescribed . . . within any insurance year. . . .

3. No person shall receive more unemployment benefit than in the proportion of one week's benefit for every six contributions paid in respect of him.

8.1.4 Rent Restriction, 1915

The shortage of houses, wartime movements of population and 'war profiteering' caused a rise in rents which threatened serious dissatisfaction and led to this Act of 1915. For the first time government had to exercise controls against the owners of property, though they were able to allow for unavoidable expenses. An Act of 1920 continued the policy temporarily, but had to be extended as the scale of the need for working-class housing came to be realised. Not until 1933, in the building boom of the thirties, was it possible to begin removing the controls, and they were still in operation for poorer houses when the Second World War led to their being generally reintroduced.

From the Increase of Rent and Mortgage Interest (War Restrictions) Act, 1915

1. (1) Where the rent of a dwelling-house to which this Act applies, or the rate of interest on a mortgage to which this Act applies, has been, since the commencement of the present war, or is hereafter during the continuance of this Act, increased above the standard rent or the standard rate of interest as hereinafter defined, the amount by which the rent or interest payable exceeds the amount which would have been payable had the increase not been made shall, notwithstanding any agreement to the contrary, be irrecoverable. . . .

(3) No order for the recovery of possession of a dwelling-house to which this Act applies or for the ejectment of a tenant therefrom shall be made so long as the tenant continues to pay rent at the agreed rate . . . and performs the other conditions of the tenancy. . . .

2. (2) This Act shall apply to a house or a part of a house let as a separate dwelling where . . . either the annual amount of the standard rent or the rateable value of the house or part of the house does not exceed –

(a) in the case of a house situate in the metropolitan police district; thirty-five pounds;

(b) in the case of a house situate in Scotland, thirty pounds; and

(c) in the case of a house situate elsewhere, twenty-six pounds.

8.1.5 'Homes for Heroes', 1919

Lloyd George had promised homes for heroes, but there was no realisation of the scale of the need, which a later estimate put at 610,000, in new houses alone. Only the local authorities could cope with the demand, especially as it was mainly for rented accommodation, and Addison encouraged them with the first Treasury subsidy, though he left them to raise the necessary funds themselves, at a time when interest rates were very high. It was the realisation that the subsidy had reached £12 million that brought Addison down in 1921. By that time 170,000 houses were building, with a further 39,000 privately built [8.6.8], but the increase in the number of families wanting homes had increased the shortage by 200,000.

The second Act of 1919 provided help for private building, and unsuccessfully tried to limit non-essential building, much of which was going into cinemas, then coming into popularity.

From the Housing, Town Planning, etc. Act, 1919

PART I: HOUSING OF THE WORKING CLASSES
Schemes under Part III of the Act of 1890

1. – (1) It shall be the duty of every local authority . . . to consider the needs of their area with respect to the provision of houses for the working classes and . . . to prepare and submit to the Local Government Board a scheme for the exercise of their powers. . . .

(3) The Local Government Board may approve any such scheme or any part thereof without modification or subject to such modifications as they may think fit, and the scheme or part thereof when so approved shall be binding on the local authority. . .

FINANCIAL PROVISIONS

7. – (1) If it appears to the Local Government Board that the carrying out by a local authority . . . of any scheme approved under section one of this Act . . . has resulted or is likely to result in a loss, the Board shall . . . pay or undertake to pay to the local authority out of moneys provided by Parliament such part of the loss as may be determined to be so payable under regulations made by the Board with the approval of the Treasury. . . .

(2) Such regulations shall provide that the amount of any annual payment to be made under this section shall – in the case of a scheme carried out by a local authority, be determined on the basis of the estimated annual loss resulting from the carrying out of any scheme subject to the deduction therefrom of a sum not exceeding the estimated annual produce of a rate of one penny in the pound. . . .

From the Housing (Additional Powers) Act, 1919

1. – (1) The Minister of Health may, in accordance with schemes made by him with the approval of the Treasury, make grants out of moneys provided by Parliament to any persons or bodies of persons constructing houses.

(2) Grants under this section shall be made only in respect of houses –

(a) which comply with the conditions prescribed by the Minister and are in material accordance with the conditions as to the number of houses per acre and the standards of structural stability and sanitation approved by the Minister in the case of any scheme submitted by a local authority under section one of the Housing, Town Planning, &c. Act, 1919;

(b) which are certified by the local authority . . . to have been completed in a proper and workmanlike manner;

(c) the construction of which is begun within twelve months after the passing of this Act and which are completed within that period or such further period not exceeding four months as the Minister may in any special case allow . . .

2. – (1) The aggregate amount of the grants to be made for the purposes of the preceding section of this Act shall not exceed fifteen million pounds. . . .

5. – (1) Where it appears to a local authority that the provision of dwelling accommodation for their area is or is likely to be delayed by a deficiency of labour or materials arising out of the employment of labour or material in the construction within their area of any works or buildings (other than works or buildings authorised or required by, under, or in pursuance of any Act of Parliament), and that the construction of those works or buildings is in the circumstances of the case of less public importance for the time being than the provision of dwelling accommodation, the authority may by order prohibit the construction of those works or buildings.

8.1.6 'The Good Old Ways'
A speech by Lord Halifax at Oxford in the very different circumstances of 1940 reveals the mood of 1919 which made reconstruction so difficult.

From a Speech by Lord Halifax at Oxford University, 27 February 1940
The similarity between 1914 and 1939 or 1940 is striking . . . but I should be misleading myself and you if I were to suggest that there is no difference between the position in 1914 and the position as you see it today . . . we in 1914 had been born and grown up in an atmosphere of peace. Those who came up to Oxford with me lived in a world that we then thought was stable and secure. That security was rudely shaken in 1914, but not sufficiently shaken for us to have any serious doubt that it would soon be put right or to think that when the war was over the old life would not return.

You, in the light of what has happened since, may think that we were foolish and shortsighted. Perhaps we were. . . . We were sure . . . that once we had dealt with the matter in hand the world would return to old ways, which, in the main, we thought to be good ways. You are not so sure. [*The Times*, 28 February 1940].

8.2. THE PROBLEM OF UNEMPLOYMENT

8.2.1 'The Dole'
The final paragraph of this Ministry of Labour report sums up the impact of 'the great depression in trade' on the insurance scheme. Problems had been, and were to continue to be, met as they arose.

From a Ministry of Labour Report on National Unemployment Insurance to July 1923
. . . Had the Unemployment Insurance Scheme remained as it was framed in the Act of 1920, the strain thrown upon its resources would have been serious but by no means insupportable, for under the rules, and particularly the rule that periods of benefit are proportionate to contributions paid, the new entrants would have been entitled to little or no benefit and many even of those who had been insured since 1911 or 1916 would have run out of benefit, during the long period of depression, without exhausting the resources of the Unemployment Fund.

Such a position, however, though strictly defensible on insurance principles, would have been a most unsatisfactory one. . . . The remedy adopted was to graft on to the original scheme of what may be called 'covenanted' benefit (i.e. benefit drawn as of right by virtue of contributions) a system of 'uncovenanted' benefit. Uncovenanted benefit was allowed as a discretionary grant to unemployed persons who were normally wage earners in insured trades and were genuinely seeking whole-time employment, but who had exhausted their rights derived from payment of contributions, or who even, in exceptional cases, had paid no contributions at all. The history of the Unemployment Insurance Scheme from 1921 onwards is largely that of the passing of one Act after another granting further extensions of uncovenanted benefit on account of the very large numbers who remained unemployed.

At the same time the 'covenanted' rights of insured persons who had contributions to their credit were strictly preserved and were in some respect considerably enlarged.

UNCOVENANTED BENEFIT

The procedure adopted with regard to uncovenanted benefit has been to create what are called 'Special Periods' of from five to nearly twelve months in duration and to authorise payment of benefit for a specified maximum of weeks in each Special Period; this number of weeks has tended more and more to approximate to the full number of calendar weeks in the Special Period, but has never quite reached this figure (i.e. benefit has never been payable continuously to persons unemployed for very long periods). . . .

INSTITUTION OF DEPENDANTS' GRANTS – NOVEMBER, 1921

In November, 1921, a new feature was introduced into the Unemployment Insurance Scheme in the form of an increased rate of benefit for unemployed persons with dependants. In addition to the ordinary weekly rate of 15s or 12s for men and women respectively, 5s a week was allowed for a wife or invalid husband . . . and 1s for each dependent child under the age of 14 years (or 16 years if in full-time attendance at a day school). A special contribution from employers, employed and the Exchequer was levied in order to pay for these allowances.

Originally these allowances were made for a period of six months only. It was found by experience that, although the amounts were not large, they were a most welcome assistance to married men and widows with children, and in not a few cases they enabled respectable and industrious men and women to avoid having recourse to the Poor Law. Accordingly the allowances were continued after the six months were over, and the special contributions levied in respect of them were added to and amalgamated with those previously payable for unemployment insurance. . . .

FINANCIAL PROVISIONS

The grant of uncovenanted benefit necessarily imposed a great strain on the financial resources of the unemployment insurance scheme. It amounted to paying out very large sums of money which were not provided for in the original finance of the scheme. The balance in hand, which had been £22,200,000 in November, 1920 was reduced to £1,000,000 at the end of June, 1921, at which time the weekly payments of benefit were about £2,000,000 as against a weekly revenue of about £340,000. To deal with this situation various measures were taken. In particular the rates of benefit for men and women, which had been raised to 20s. and 16s. in March, 1921, were restored to the previous figures of 15s. and 12s., a substantial increase was made in the weekly rates of contribution, and power was taken to borrow up to £20,000,000 (a figure which was subsequently raised to £30,000,000). . . .

AMOUNT OF BENEFIT PAID

The total amount of unemployment benefit, covenanted and uncovenanted, and of allowances for dependants paid in the period from November 8th, 1920, to June 30th, 1923, is about £128,304,000. This sum of £128,304,000 has been paid in separate weekly amounts, ranging ordinarily from 12s. to 22s. each, and it is estimated that something like 170 million separate payments have been made. . . .

CONTRIBUTORY PRINCIPLE OF INSURANCE

There appears to be a widespread belief that unemployment benefit, or, at any rate, so much of it as is 'uncovenanted', is provided by the taxpayer – as witness the common use of the question-begging epithet of the 'dole'. In truth – and the fact cannot be too strongly emphasised – one-fourth, and no more, of the sums now being paid in benefit and of the cost of administration falls upon the taxpayer, and this represents at the present time the whole of the Exchequer contribution to the Unemployment Insurance Scheme; three-fourths of the benefit and administrative costs fall upon the insured workpeople and their employers.

The total contributions from employers, employed and the Exchequer from the initiation of the scheme in 1912 to 1 July, 1923, are as follows –

	£
Employers	48,000,000
Employed	44,600,000
Exchequer	31,500,000

PRACTICABILITY OF UNEMPLOYMENT INSURANCE

Experience has shown that compulsory insurance against unemployment is entirely practicable. The extended scheme of insurance has passed successfully through the crucial test imposed by an immense volume of unemployment. ... The Unemployment Fund has provided benefits vastly greater than those originally contemplated. It has done so, it is true, at the expense of largely increased contributions and of a considerable debt; but the debt is not so large that it cannot be paid off in a comparatively short space of time as soon as trade revives, and the financial stability of the scheme is not open to serious question. ...

FUTURE POLICY

It remains to profit by experience in order to fashion a wise policy for the future. The great depression in trade has profoundly affected the whole outlook of the insurance scheme. So long as the depression continues – and unhappily the horizon is still dark – it may not be possible to do more than meet current problems as they arise.

8.2.2 Unemployment and the Poor Law

This report records the pressure placed on the poor law by the heavy unemployment of certain areas, and the poor law response, which continued to be guided by nineteenth-century principles. It would seem that although attention was drawn to the variations in relief no attempt was made to discover the reasons for them.

From the Second Annual Report of the Ministry of Health, 1920–1
The total number of persons in receipt of relief ... which was about 450,000 at the date of the Armistice, had increased to 494,000 at the beginning of the year, a figure which still compared favourably with that at the date of the declaration of war, which was 619,000. ...

During the final months of the year, however, the increase in poor relief from about 568,000 at the end of December to over 653,000 at the end of March, practically restored the pre-war level.

It is noticeable that 93 per cent of the increase in poor relief during the year represents out-relief. ... The increase is attributable not to any reduction in the amount of institutional relief, but to the policy adopted by certain Boards of Guardians, of affording unconditional out-relief on fixed scales to unemployed persons, often persons in receipt of unemployment benefit, without adequate discrimination.

This policy appears to have been based on a false analogy

between Poor Law relief and the various payments, especially unemployment benefit, which are made on a pension basis. The recent extension of payments of this kind should, in fact, have had the effect of reducing the proportion of out-relief, but though no doubt it has enabled an appeal to the Poor Law Authorities to be postponed in some cases ... it cannot be said that there is evidence of any appreciable reduction of the class of persons who find it necessary to have recourse to the Poor Law after even a short period of unemployment. ...

The connection between local unemployment and distress requiring Poor Law relief has still to be discovered. It can only be said that while in some Unions a comparatively small degree of unemployment produces a number of applications to the relieving officers, in others acute unemployment may persist for considerable periods without such applications being made. It appears fanciful to suggest that in the latter class the absence of applications for relief can be entirely due to traditions of thrift and mutual assistance based on the careful administration of the Guardians over a period of years, but it is not an unreasonable view that the tendencies of the Guardians form an appreciable element in the establishment or maintenance of such a tradition.

A circular letter was issued on 29th December, 1920, to thirty-six Boards of Guardians by whom outdoor relief was known to be freely given, impressing upon them the necessity for making special examination into each case in which it was proposed to grant out-relief to an able-bodied applicant on account of unemployment. ... It was indicated that in no circumstances would financial help be afforded by the Government towards the cost of out-relief.

About twenty Boards of Guardians have exercised their power to require the performance of a labour test by applicants for relief. At Gloucester a question was raised as to whether the performance of a labour test as a condition of relief would constitute employment disqualifying the recipient for benefit under the Unemployment Insurance Act, but it was decided on appeal that the benefit should be allowed.

8.2.3 'Genuinely Seeking Work'

When Labour took office for the first time in 1924 the government naturally tried to improve conditions for the unemployed. The first section of their Unemployment Insurance Act practically created a tatutory right to benefit, recognising only two kinds, standard and xtended, to both of which workers were entitled. The Act also amended he conditions laid down in 1920 for eligibility, though the onus of roof for 'genuinely seeking work' rested with applicants, and this aused much bitterness until repealed in 1930.

rom the Unemployment Insurance (No. 2) Act, 1924

. (1) Until the thirtieth day of June, 1926, an insured contriutor who is unemployed shall, if and so long as the statutory conlitions are fulfilled in his case ... for the receipt of unemployment enefit ... be entitled ... to receive such benefit. ...

(3) (If the requirements as to the number of contributions tc. are not fulfilled, benefit can continue if the applicant is ormally employed and is making 'every reasonable effort to btain employment'.) ...

. (1). Section seven of the principal Act ... shall be amended as ollows ...

> (iii) that he is capable of and available for work,
> (iv) that he is genuinely seeking work, but unable to obtain suitable employment.

.2.4 Benefit and Maintenance

Vith dependants' allowances and the fall in the cost of living from 1921, nemployment benefit came to be more of a support than had been tended. An interdepartmental committee restated the official view in 923, however, and though the Labour government of 1924 took a ore generous line, the earlier view was again put forward in 1927, first y the Blanesburgh Report [8.2.5, 67], and then as a statement of overnment policy. For long-term unemployment, with all reserves one, the only recourse before the Act of 1934 was to the poor law.

Tom Shaw (1872–1938), a textile trade union secretary, was MP for reston 1918–31, Minister of Labour 1924 and Secretary of State for Var 1929–31.

Sir Arthur Steel Maitland (1876–1935) was MP 1910–35 and Minister f Labour 1924–9.

he Official View: From the Report of the Interdepartmental Comittee on Public Assistance, 1923

4. Benefits under the (insurance) scheme ... have not been esigned to cover all the responsibilities of the unemployed person a all circumstances, but rather to supplement private effort in itigating distress due to involuntary unemployment.

Labour Policy, 1924. From the House of Commons Debate, 9 Ju$_l$
1924

Mr T. Shaw (Minister of Labour): It is neither economical n$_l$
moral to refuse assistance to those who have suffered the wor$_l$
from unemployment, and it is both sound in principle and soun$_l$
in economy to make certain that the genuine workman who
unemployed through no fault of his own shall at any rate n$_l$
starve.

Conservative Policy, 1927. From the House of Commons Debat
6 December 1927

Sir A. Steel Maitland (Minister of Labour): I have never preter
ded that the rates which are proposed are rates for full maintenanc
. . . Unemployment benefits under a State scheme as und$_l$
trade union schemes have always been intended as a help, and, $_l$
the case of the State scheme, a very material help indeed, f$_l$
people to tide over a period of unemployment. That is all that $_l$
any time is claimed for it.

8.2.5 The Blanesburgh Report, 1927

The Unemployment Act of 1924 was passed for only two years, and
1925 the Baldwin government appointed a committee under a judg
Lord Blanesburgh, to advise it. The committee reported in 1927, a$_l$
being confident that industrial conditions were improving recommend$_l$
the abolition of the distinction between standard and extended benef
all unemployed workers being entitled to benefit, those longest u$_l$
employed receiving 'transitional' benefit. The Unemployment Insuran
Act 1927 largely accepted the committee's proposals.

The situation did not improve, however, and by 1931 the numb$_l$
receiving transitional benefit had risen from 120,000 to more than h$_l$
a million.

The committee's findings on the oft-told allegations of abuse of soc
benefits should be noted (35–40).

From the Report of the Unemployment Insurance Committee, 19
(Blanesburgh Committee)

1. From whatever standpoint it be regarded, the whole subj$_l$
bristles with difficulties and demands careful investigation.
raises problems which affect in greater or less degree the mor$_l$
of the community as a whole as well as the well-being, peace
mind and self-respect of many millions of workers. In deali$_l$

with these problems there is room for acute divergence of opinion, and the principles, the administration, the alleged deficiencies, excesses and ulterior consequences of the present system had, before our enquiry began, become a topic of far-reaching comment and keen criticism. A compromise between opposing views, the system had found little favour with extremists of any school. Many post-war difficulties which its benefits have so far enabled this country to surmount, had been forgotten or underrated by many of the critics of the scheme ... public opinion outside the insured classes had become and, we fear, still is predominantly unfavourable to unemployment insurance. ...

0. The rates of contribution in force from 1921 onwards have been abnormal, but they were necessary in view of the unprecedented situation which the scheme has had to face over a period of six years. ... All through, the larger part of the funds has been provided by employers and workers. Up to the 1st July, 1926, the total sum paid into the fund by them since the beginning of unemployment insurance in 1912 was £202,775,000; that paid by the Exchequer was £70,454,000. In 1925–6 the Exchequer contributed £13,002,000 and the employers and workers jointly £33,867,000. ...

4. Extended Benefit. – It is the development of 'extended benefit' which is by far the most important, as it has been the most controversial, of the modifications made by later legislation in the Act of 1920. ...

6. ... It has not been, except for the period covered by the second Act of 1924, a statutory right of any contributor; it was a privilege to be granted in the discretion of the Minister where he deemed it 'expedient in the public interest' to do so. ...

5. Alleged Abuses of Unemployment Insurance. – Throughout the inquiry we have constantly had brought to our notice the conviction held by many that the system of unemployment insurance is subject to widespread abuses. It has accordingly been one of our principal preoccupations to ascertain how far this belief is justified. ...

6. It is convenient to state at once the conclusion we have reached in this matter. It is true that a certain number out of the $11\frac{3}{4}$ millions of insured persons have received relief to which they had no claim. But it is equally true that these cases are relatively few and that result is, we think, due to the vigilance with which the

Ministry, while dealing fairly with the genuine claimant, guards against abuse. . . .

39. We were confirmed in this favourable conclusion by the result of enquiries made by us in different quarters where it seemed to us likely that abuses, if they existed generally, would be notorious. . .

The Secretary of the Charity Organisation Society very candidly says that he began by thinking the abuses serious, but, on enquiry he had been unable to find them. He observes:

'When this material (i.e. that included in their memorandum was read to our people on Monday afternoon last, they were much disappointed at the general character of almost all of it They had hoped that many more examples would be forth coming illustrating the criticisms passed upon the present work ing of unemployment insurance by almost everybody who discusses the subject. This shows the value of bringing these criticisms to the test of demanding examples, and more than on of our secretaries said that they quite expected to find from ou case-papers numerous examples of abuses, but when they cam to look they found very few. This does not, of course, prove tha their previous impression was not a sound one; on the othe hand, it may quite well prove that unfavourable instances impres themselves upon the memory, while the proper and smoot working of a scheme passes almost unnoticed.'

40. There is, we think, great force in this last observation. W believe that it accounts for very many of what we are convince are current misapprehensions. . . .

63. The Unemployment Fund is, and always has been, and in ou view always should be, self-supporting. Our proposed method c liquidation is a temporary addition to the contribution of each c the three parties of 1d. a week in respect of adult men. . . . Th additional contribution is to be specially earmarked for its purpos it will bring in an income of roughly £5,600,000 a year, a fair rat of repayment, we consider, in all the circumstances. It will, c course, to the relief of all contributors, cease so soon as the burde of the initial debt has been discharged.

We are not without hopes of that point being reached within period that may be measured by months rather than by years. . .

67. Rates of Benefit. – We have accepted the principle advocate on all sides that extended benefit as such shall disappear. Und our proposals there will be only one kind of benefit. To that benef

the contributor, if he complies with the conditions, shall be entitled according to these conditions.

Many suggestions have been made to us as to the rates of benefit. . . . This, it must never be forgotten, is a matter in which only a very limited range of choice is permissible. Ideal benefits must not be more generous than is consistent with the necessary conditions of a good scheme; on the other hand, they should certainly be so substantial that the insured contributor can feel that, if he has the misfortune to need them, then, taken in conjunction with such resources as may reasonably in the generality of cases, be expected to have been built up, they will be sufficient to prevent him from being haunted while at work by the fear of what must happen to him if he is unemployed. Subject to these considerations, the amount of benefit must depend upon the contributions that can fairly be called for. . . .

74. . . . Some automatic test of recent contributions is necessary to ensure that the benefits are limited to contributors, or, in other words, to persons in the insured field. We believe that the arrangement we propose will enable benefit to be paid to all who can fairly be said to be genuinely unemployed, and, in so far as there are persons satisfying this test who are seeking benefit in preference to employment, we rely on their being excluded under the second condition, viz.: that they are not 'genuinely seeking work'.

75. If there are those who consider this proposal too severe, we would draw attention to an important fact about unemployment which is often overlooked. Though the returns of the Ministry have shown, say, a million unemployed week after week, these are not the same million. Most of the unemployed remain out-of-work for quite short periods. It is only a small minority who are continuously unemployed for any great length of time. Thus at the worst our proposals could not shut out many, and they would only be those who had failed to obtain work in an average of 15 weeks out of 52. It will be conceded that in the generality of cases persons with so poor a record of employment could scarcely claim still to be in the insured field; that there is grave doubt as to the genuineness of their search for work; and that the exclusion of such individuals is only fair to the general body of insured contributors.

76. To those who consider the arrangement too lenient we would observe that the second condition will eliminate non-genuine persons, and if it is desired, as we believe it is, to include in an in-

surance scheme the great bulk of genuine unemployment and not to drive to the Poor Law persons who are out of work through no fault on their own part, our proposed scheme should realise that object. . . .

83. In its true conception an Unemployment Insurance Scheme should provide for the great bulk of genuine unemployment in a manner honourable to those whom it benefits. We understand that the Poor Law Acts . . . prohibit . . . the unconditional out-door relief of able-bodied persons, and . . . we think both from the point of view of the parties to the Unemployment Insurance Scheme, and on general grounds, that, in so far as it deals with the able-bodied unemployed, Poor Law relief should retain the deterrent effect which now attaches thereto. . . .

178. The really desirable thing is to get rid of unemployment itself. . . .

The risk of genuine unemployment should be insured. An unemployment insurance scheme, compulsory, and covering at least the persons at present covered by the State scheme, should be a permanent feature of our Code of Social Legislation. . . .

8.2.6 Beveridge on Unemployment, 1930

Beveridge's critical survey of developments since 1909 was a sequel to his previous study [7.6.1].

From W.H.Beveridge, Unemployment: A Problem of Industry, Vol. II (1909 and 1930), pp. 288–9, 292, 294, 418–20

Unemployment insurance as introduced was in two senses contractual. First, it gave the insured person legally enforceable rights without Ministerial discretion and without regard to his other resources or private character. Second, it gave these rights in consideration of contributions by or in respect of the insured person; though the contract was compulsory, elaborate measures were taken to make it something like a fair bargain for each industry and each individual. . . .

During the ten-year chaos from 1918 to 1928 unemployment insurance ceased to be contractual in either sense: donation and extended benefit were discretionary grants and irrespective of contributions by the recipient. Since the Act of 1927 unemployment insurance has become contractual again in the first sense but not in the second; an unlimited benefit claimable as of right has replaced the old combination of standard and extended benefit, but is claimable, not for contributions paid, but by virtue of belonging to the insured classes. Moving from contract to status, the insurance scheme of 1911 has become a general system of out-door relief of the able-bodied, administered by a national in place of a local authority, and financed mainly by a tax on employment. ... The difference between the Blanesburgh Committee and the advocates of unlimited non-contributory insurance is simply a difference as to the modes of taxation: the compulsory contributions have a fiscal significance alone. ...

Relief of unemployment is after all a very bad second best to its prevention; however the giving of money during involuntary idleness be hedged round with safeguards, the idleness itself is demoralising, and becomes swiftly more demoralising the longer it lasts. The arguments advanced in 1909, for insurance rather than artificial work as a means of relieving unemployment, assumed transient depressions, not the chronic under-employment of the casual labourer or the five-year idleness of the derelict coalminer. But once it is admitted in principle, that, either under the guise of insurance or in some other form, genuine unemployment can be relieved indefinitely, by the simple device of giving money from a bottomless purse, prevention is only too likely to go by the board. The thoughts and time of Governments and Parliaments may be absorbed – as they have largely been absorbed during the past ten years – in successive extensions and variations of the relief scheme. ...

A SECOND CONCLUSION

The record of the past twenty years of dealing with unemployment is depressing. Those parts of the policies of 1909 which were aimed at the reduction of unemployment – de-casualisation and the evening out of the demand for labour – have failed most completely of adoption; the Labour Exchanges, indispensable as they have become, have had a limited and inadequate success; the disorganisation of the labour market continues. That part of the policies which was designed mainly, though not wholly, for relief of unemployment has grown portentously and grown always in the direction of becoming relief and nothing else.

Yet the failures of these twenty years must not be taken too hardly. After all, what a twenty years they have been! ...

Some things in Britain's destiny are beyond management by its governments and its leaders; the slow vast forces shaping and re-shaping the economic structure of the world and the swift changes of personal desire that determine future numbers work uncontroll-ably. . . . But unemployment is not one of these. It is no mysterious visitation, but in the main the consequence of our own choices, the measure of how our industry adjusts itself to the changing world. For one great industry the changes have been too catastrophic for adjustment and have left a disaster for which there is no full remedy. The problem of the ruined mining areas stands by itself – an ill to make the best of till time ends it, by moving one by one all who can move, by expenditure in organising such work as is possible for those who cannot move. Apart from this acute but limited problem, we know what to do if we wish to get back to the level of unemployment that ruled before the war; we must either lower our standards of life or bring production up to justify them. We know also what to do if we wish to bring unemployment below that level; carry out the main preventive policy of 1909 and organise completely the labour market, abolishing the hawking of labour and casual under-employment and the anarchic recruiting of trades and the blind choice of careers . . . the post-war situation puts frankly the question, how much unemployment we are prepared to carry in order to avoid surrender of our standards of life once gained.

Solution of the problem of unemployment is thus practicable today as it was twenty years ago. . . . 'The problem of unemploy-ment' – this is a point that cannot be too strongly emphasised – 'is insoluble by any mere expenditure of public money. It represents not a want to be satisfied but a disease to be eradicated. It needs not money so much as thought and organisation.' The repeated lesson of twenty-one years since those words were penned is how much more abundant is money than thought, how much harder it is, for the cure of social ills, to change men's habits and open their minds than to slit their purses.

8.2.7 Relaxing Conditions, 1930

The Act of 1930 followed a recommendation of a committee set up by the second Labour government by abolishing the 'genuinely seeking work' requirement, and leaving the onus of proof on officials. The result was a vast increase in the number qualifying for transitional benefit and a significant fall in the number of unemployed on poor relief.[1] A further 'Anomalies Act' had to be passed to disallow claims from married women, seasonal workers and the like.

The first section refers to the expected raising of the school leaving age, which, though later arranged for 1939, did not in fact take place until after the Second World War.

From the Unemployment Insurance Act, 1930

1. The minimum age for entry into insurance shall, instead of being the age of 16, be the age when a person attains the age at which his parents cease to be under an obligation to cause him to receive efficient elementary instruction or the age of 15, whichever is the higher. ...

4. If on a claim for benefit it is proved by an officer of the Ministry of Labour that the claimant, after a situation in any employment which is suitable in his case has been notified to him by an employment exchange ... as vacant or about to become vacant, has without good cause refused or failed to apply for such situation, or refused to accept such situation when offered to him ... he shall be disqualified for receiving benefit for a period of 6 weeks. ...

6. Condition (iv) in sub-section (1) of section 7 of the principal Act which prescribes a statutory condition for receipt of benefit shall cease to have effect.

8.2.8 The Royal Commission on Unemployment, 1932

The Labour government appointed the Commission in 1930, and its final report appeared in 1932, by which time financial stresses had brought down the Labour government and replaced it by the 'National' coalition.

In its report the Commission drew the distinction that had long been apparent between 'occasional' and 'chronic' unemployment, and proposed that they should be dealt with differently, the one by insurance, the other by relief, administered by the local authorities on the basis of a means test.

From the Royal Commission on Unemployment, Final Report, 1932

276. Under our proposals the Insurance scheme will compel and assist the workers in industries exposed to fluctuations in employment to provide for themselves; when they are doing that there is

[1] B. B. Gilbert, *British Social Policy*, 1914–1939, p. 96.

no need to impose a test of needs. When they have exhausted the provision towards which they have contributed out of their wages, then, if they are still unemployed, they must seek relief from another source; but since they will now be receiving relief from funds to which they have not directly contributed, their needs may properly be brought into account and the relief restricted to meeting them. . . .

280. In our examination of the facts of unemployment we found that it was possible to distinguish between (a) the occasional interruptions of work, due to such causes as the termination of a contract, a seasonal falling off in trade, or general downward fluctuation of industrial activity, and (b) the chronic unemployment, caused by permanent loss of markets, displacement by new processes, or a system of engaging labour that retains an excessive reserve of under-employed labour. Unemployment of the latter kind cannot fully be covered by insurance, since it imposes a strain on the insurance fund which ultimately brings insolvency. It creates a need of relief, and the important part it plays in post-war unemployment is a principal reason for setting-up a general system of relief; but it can be cured only by extensive re-direction of labour into new channels or by a change of conditions in the old employments. The other kind of unemployment is the proper field of insurance. . . .

283. We have, of course, been made aware of many criticisms of the principle of insurance; . . . but most of the objections have arisen from the extension of insurance to cases where it is inapplicable. We should not be misled as to the value of insurance by the fact that the finances of the existing scheme have been in difficulty, or that the scheme does not now carry such a large proportion of unemployed workers as it did before the world-wide trade depression of 1930 set in. We have shown that the main reason for the bankruptcy of the Unemployment Fund has been the burden imposed on it, since 1920, of carrying the chronic unemployment of large numbers of persons, suffering from no personal moral or physical defects, but so distributed geographically and industrially that for many of them the chance of further employment is very doubtful. The insurance scheme, as at present devised, covered 57 per cent of the unemployed insured workers qualified for payments at 26 September 1932. But this would represent the real value of insurance only if unemployment were

static and those who were unemployed on a fixed date were subject to continuous unemployment. In fact, a large proportion of unemployment consists of short spells, and of those who were qualified for insurance benefit on a fixed date many will return to employment while others again will fall out of work and be fully qualified for insurance benefit. The experience of the year 1930 was that out of approximately 12 million insured workers about 5 million made claims for benefit in the course of the year, and of these over 3,500,000 satisfied the thirty contributions condition and were qualified for benefit when they made their claims. An insurance scheme which can cover such a large proportion of workers, even in a time of exceptional unemployment, is in our view fully justified as a practical measure for the relief of ordinary unemployment of limited duration. . . .

ARRANGEMENTS OUTSIDE INSURANCE

530. We have discussed the general principles which should govern the administration of a system of payments, outside the insurance scheme to unemployed industrial workers. . . .

532. . . . the choice is between (a) a centrally administered service operated wholly through the Employment Exchanges; and (b) a service locally administered, but subject to central supervision and direction. We have shown reasons for thinking that, if a test of means or needs is to be seriously applied, the 'discretion' inherent in such a system can be successfully exercised only by a responsible local body. . . . We conclude that only general rules or guiding principles can be laid down by the central authority, the main responsibility for administering the service being left with the local authority. These principles are:

(1) assistance should be subject to proof of need;
(2) the need of the applicant should be judged after an assessment of the resources of the household of which he is a member;
(3) the amount of the payment must be less than wages;
(4) the standards to be established should be those which experience shows to be required to relieve need. . . .

533. The first requirement is a new statute which, on the one hand, will authorise Local Authorities to provide assistance for certain classes of able-bodied unemployed workers on proof of need, and for this purpose to establish a new Committee of itself; and, on the

other hand, will charge the Ministry of Labour with the oversight and general direction of this new service. . . .

573. It is, in our judgment, the duty of the community to provide an able-bodied worker with his primary needs where he has inadequate resources, and the provision must be adequate to maintain the applicant in a fit condition to resume employment. . . . Exceptional needs not due to the fact of unemployment remain to be dealt with by the existing services, (including public assistance), appropriate to them. We are concerned only with need directly attributable to unemployment.

8.2.9 The Unemployment Act, 1934

The National government accepted the Royal Commission's proposals for different treatment of occasional and chronic unemployment, but Neville Chamberlain as Chancellor of the Exchequer preferred to create a central body, the Unemployment Assistance Board, for the long-term unemployed, rather than leave them to the local authorities, as the Royal Commission had advised. A corresponding body, the Unemployment Insurance Statutory Committee, was set up to administer the insurance scheme, and Beveridge was called back from academic life to be its chairman.

Section 38(3) of the Act made a statutory requirement of the household means test, which quickly became notorious and was bitterly resented.

From the Unemployment Act, 1934: An Act to Amend the Unemployment Insurance Acts, and to Make Further Provision for the Training and Assistance of Persons who are Capable of, and Available for, Work but Have No Work

PART I: AMENDMENT OF UNEMPLOYMENT INSURANCE ACTS

Insured persons

1. (1) The minimum age for entry into insurance shall, instead of being the age of sixteen years, be the age (not being less than fourteen years) when a person attains the age at which under the law for the time being in force his parents cease to be under an obligation to cause him to attend school. . . .

6. Subsection (1) of section four of the Unemployment Insurance Act, 1930, shall have effect as if there were inserted therein after the words 'offered to him' the words 'or if it is proved by an officer

of the Ministry of Labour that the claimant has neglected to avail himself of a reasonable opportunity of suitable employment'. . . .

Instruction and training

13. (1) Every education authority shall submit to the Minister proposals for the provision of such courses of instruction as may be necessary for persons in their area between the minimum age for entry into insurance and the age of eighteen years who are capable of and available for work but have no work. . . .

Financial provisions

17. (1) There shall be constituted a committee, to be called 'the Unemployment Insurance Statutory Committee', to give advice and assistance to the Minister in connection with the discharge of his functions under the Unemployment Insurance Acts. . . .

20. The Unemployment Insurance Statutory Committee shall make such proposals as may seem to them practicable for the insurance against unemployment of persons engaged in agriculture.

PART II: UNEMPLOYMENT ASSISTANCE

Constitution and functions of Unemployment Assistance Board

35. (1) For the purposes of this Part of this Act there shall be constituted a Board, to be called 'the Unemployment Assistance Board'. . . .

(2) The functions of the Board shall be the assistance of persons who are in need of work and the promotion of their welfare and, in particular, the making of provision for the improvement and re-establishment of the condition of such persons with a view to their being in all respects fit for entry into or return to regular employment, and the grant and issue to such persons of unemployment allowances (hereinafter referred to as 'allowances'). . . .

(3) For the purpose of securing the advice and assistance of persons having local knowledge and experience in matters affecting the functions of the Board, the Board shall arrange for the establishment of advisory committees throughout Great Britain. . . .

36. (1) This Part of this Act applies to any person in whose case the following qualifications are fulfilled,

  (a) that he has attained the age of sixteen years and has not attained the age of sixty-five years; and
  (b) that he is either –
        (i) a person whose normal occupation is employment in

respect of which contributions are payable under the Widows', Orphans' and Old Age Contributory Pensions Acts,

(ii) a person who, not having normally been engaged in any remunerative occupation since attaining the age of sixteen years, might reasonably have expected that his normal occupation would have been such employment as aforesaid but for the industrial circumstances of the district in which he resides; and

(c) that he is capable of and available for work. . . .

37. In the exercise of the functions of the Unemployment Assistance Board, the Board may

(a) provide and maintain training courses for persons who have attained the age of eighteen years and make contributions in respect of the cost of the provision and maintenance of such courses by the Minister or by any local authority or other body.

Allowances and training

38. (1) An allowance may be granted to any person to whom this Part of this Act applies, if he proves

(a) that he is registered for employment.

(b) that he has no work or only such part-time or intermittent work as not to enable him to earn sufficient for his needs; and

(c) that he is in need of an allowance.

(2) The amount of any allowance to be granted to an applicant shall be determined by reference to his needs, including the needs of any members of the household of which he is a member who are dependent on or ordinarily supported by him. . . .

(3) The need of an applicant shall be determined and his needs assessed in accordance with regulations made under this Part of this Act, and such regulations shall in particular provide that the resources of an applicant taken into account shall include the resources of all members of the household of which he is himself a member (due regard being had also to the personal requirements of those members whose resources are taken into account).

8.2.10 The Household Means Test

From the First Report of the Unemployment Assistance Board, 1935
Under the Act unemployment allowances are based on the 'house-

hold', that is, by reference to the needs of the applicant and the members of his household dependent on him; they are essentially different from unemployment benefit which is an individual and contractual right to a fixed sum. . . .

In considering the 'needs' of the household, it is also necessary to consider what 'means' are available towards those needs. The Act . . . recognises that the members of a household who have resources, particularly wages . . . are entitled to some part of their earnings for the purpose of living their own lives. . . . Thus it does not require a destitution test to be applied to the household.

The Act, however, contains no definition of 'members of the household'. The household does not necessarily correspond with family relationship. . . . The Board instructed its officers that the facts of a particular case might be examined along two broad lines. These are, first, that a person who was a member of the household during childhood should be regarded as a member of that household; and second, that a person who came into the household after reaching the age of employment on terms that made it clear that he was paying a reasonable rate for his board and lodging should be regarded as a 'lodger'. . . . Thus, an adult son in the house of his unemployed father is a member of his father's household; but a girl going to live with her married sister and agreeing to pay a reasonable sum to her married sister for her board and lodging is not generally regarded as a member of her brother-in-law's household.

8.3 THE POOR LAW
8.3.1 The Poor Law Under Stress
The extracts from annual reports of the Ministry of Health illustrate the inadequacy of poor law administration in the face of unprecedented problems, and the determined efforts to maintain the principles of 1834 in circumstances totally different from those of a century earlier. Living as they did among the people in need of relief, guardians in general stretched the regulations as far as they could.

Significantly, the report for 1921–2 made no reference to the ludicrous episode of 1921, when the borough council of Poplar, which had heavy unemployment and generous relief scales ('Wastrels' the *Daily Mail* called the Poplar guardians), went to prison in what proved to be a successful attempt to force more financial help out of the Metropolitan Common Poor Fund. George Lansbury was one of those involved.

The final extract from the report of 1926/27 reflects the quite wide-spread suspicion of 'love on the dole' (the title of Walter Greenwood's famous novel of 1933 would seem apt in this context). The reference to pre-1834 conditions reveals the hold of the legends that had grown up about the allowance system.

From the Third Annual Report of the Ministry of Health, 1921–2

POOR LAW: POLICY OF THE DEPARTMENT

By correspondence and through the General Inspectors every effort has been made to keep permanently before the Guardians the principles which should govern their actions. . . . In particular, reference may be made to the general pronouncements made in the circular letters issued. . . .

In the first of these letters emphasis was laid upon three principles of administration:

(1) The amount of relief given in any case, while sufficient for the purposes of relieving distress, must of necessity be calculated on a lower scale than the earnings of the independent workman who is maintaining himself by his labour.

(2) Relief should not be given without full investigation of the circumstances of each applicant.

(3) The greater proportion of the relief given in the case of able-bodied applicants should be given in specified articles of kind, and in suitable cases it should be made a condition that the relief shall be repaid by the recipient.

AREAS OF HIGH PAUPERISM

The proportion of the population chargeable to the poor rate at the end of March, 1922, varied from one in 200 in some Unions to nearly one in ten in Newcastle-upon-Tyne and Pontypridd, one in ten in South Shields and Stockton, one in nine in Middlesbrough, one in eight in Sheffield and Bedwellty, one in seven in Crickhowell, and one in six in Poplar. . . .

Many of the Unions which suffered severely at the time of the coal dispute were also affected at the time of the subsequent acute industrial depression. . . .

But even when every allowance has been made, it is difficult to attribute in every instance the fact that very large amounts have been expended in relief to the force of circumstances over which the Guardians had no control. It may be pointed out that in one of these Unions outdoor relief had, comparatively early in the dispute, reached the figure of £18,000 a week, when the Guardians decided that they must reconsider their policy and refused further outdoor relief except in cases of medical need. The weekly cost of outdoor relief dropped at once to £1,068. It is not certain what part the establishment of soup kitchens played in preventing any consequent distress, but such distress did not in fact arise, and the possibility of eliminating unconditional out-relief by the provision of meals only is worthy of consideration in times of pressure. . . .

In a certain number of Unions relief was given in the early part of the coal dispute to the miners themselves, and it was necessary to call the attention of the Guardians to the fact that such relief was unlawful. The judgment of the Court of Appeal in Attorney General v. Merthyr Tydfil (1900) . . . under which this advice was given, was to the following effect:

> 'Able-bodied men, who can, if they choose, obtain work which will enable them to maintain themselves, their wives and families, but who, by reason of a strike or otherwise, refuse to accept that work, are not entitled to relief, except that if they become physically incapable of work, the Guardians may, to prevent their starving, give them temporary relief . . .
>
> 'The wives and children of such men, however, are entitled to relief, though they themselves are not'.

From the Eighth Annual Report of the Ministry of Health, 1926–7

ADMINISTRATION OF THE POOR LAW

As a result of post-war conditions, including the industrial depression, and, still more, industrial disputes, there has been a great increase in the proportion of the population applying for assistance to the Guardians of the Poor. There has also been, in view of the size of the problem, and the comparative difficulty of any other means of dealing with it, a new and general tendency on the part of the Guardians themselves to grant, even to able-bodied persons, unconditional allowances of outdoor relief, in amounts which often approximate to, and may even exceed, the normal earnings of the applicant when he is in full work. In this way problems have arisen, new in character, and demanding new, rapid, and occasionally drastic measures. . . . The comparative extent of these new problems is indicated by the following figures:

Outdoor Relief

Years ended 31st March	Average daily number of persons in receipt of outdoor relief in the year		Amount of outdoor relief given in money and kind during the year	Total annual expenditure of all kinds on the relief of the poor (outdoor, indoor, maintenance of lunatics in asylums) and purposes connected therewith (excluding only sums spent out of loans on capital works)
	Number	Ratio per 10,000 of estimated population		
			£	£
1914	387,796	106	2,214,680	15,055,863
...	...	...	...	...
1925	912,139	235	13,374,653	36,841,768
1927	1,722,084	441	23,750,000 (estimated)	49,500,000 (estimated)

Even these figures, relating to the country as a whole, do not serve as any measure of the difficulties facing individual Boards of Guardians. The amount of unemployment and the other factors are unevenly distributed through the country, and the policies of administration adopted by the several Boards of Guardians also differ in degree and even in kind. The endeavours of successive Ministers have been directed to keeping prominently before the minds of the Boards of Guardians, and particularly those on whom a specially heavy portion of this burden has fallen, the principles on which they should exercise their discretion to grant or withhold relief. ...

Over the country as a whole these precautions have met with a reasonable measure of success, but

(1) The great increase in the expenditure on relief to unemployed persons which took place in 1921, and for which provision had not been made in the Guardians' estimates, necessitated legislation enabling Guardians to raise money by overdraft or short-term loans ... to meet their current expenditure. In the great bulk of cases steady progress was made with the repayment of the loans, but this reduction in the amount outstanding has been counterbalanced by large and recurring increases in a very limited number of Unions, and by the further borrowings resulting from the coal dispute of 1926. ...

(2) The use of Poor Law institutions as military hospitals during the War, increased pressure upon the beds available in voluntary hospitals, and the increase in the demand for institutional as opposed to home treatment of sickness have combined to bring about an expansion both in scope and character of the work formerly done by Boards of Guardians in providing treatment for the sick poor in institutions, and to relate the work, as part of the process of expansion, far more closely with other branches of hospital work and with the practice of medicine at large. Thus . . . there has been an increasing willingness on the part of patients needing surgical or medical care in an institution to look to the nature of the treatment open to them rather than the ownership of the institution in which it is given; and Boards of Guardians in urban areas possessing fully equipped infirmaries find themselves more and more catering for patients who would formerly have been treated at home or in the voluntary hospitals. . . .

REVIEW OF THE YEAR

(1) *Pauperism resulting from industrial disputes*

It is unfortunately impossible to distinguish with any certainty between the effects of the General Strike and those of the coal dispute in increasing the numbers of persons relieved. A study of the variations of the figures in areas of particular classes indicates that the consequences of the General Strike were still felt as late as the middle of June. After that date unemployment due, directly or indirectly, to the coal dispute was apparently the sole cause of the increases in numbers. . . .

The great bulk of the relief given in consequence of the dispute was domiciliary relief, and it is a question whether a proper use of the workhouse test would not have been effective in restraining a certain amount of fraud and concealment of resources which undoubtedly took place. . . .

As the dispute dragged out its length, an increasing number of Boards of Guardians declined to grant outdoor relief generally to the families of men engaged in the dispute, and at the end of the dispute there were 27 Unions in which this practice had been adopted. The number of orders of admission to the workhouse which were accepted in those Unions was very small indeed. . . .

In view of the depletion of the trade union funds, there was naturally some difficulty as regards the position of unmarried miners, who could neither receive relief themselves nor consume a share of the relief allowed for their dependants. In some Unions serious difficulty arose, and was accentuated by the attitude adopted by Medical Officers who issued wholesale, on application, certificates that single miners were so exhausted by privation as to be incapable of work. The necessary steps were taken to make the position clear to the medical staff, and substantial reductions in the numbers of certificates issued invariably followed. In one instance the Medical Officers were assaulted by miners in whose cases they had not been able to give certificates. . . .

The position of the relief staff was further made difficult in some Unions by the action either of Boards of Guardians, or of individual members of Boards, who, accepting unwillingly the limitations of the Merthyr Tydfil judgment, nevertheless endeavoured to secure an extended and illegal use of a Relieving Officer's discretion to grant the relief which they themselves had been required to abandon. . . .

It is commonly supposed that Poor Law relief is available only to meet the existing necessities of persons who have become destitute, and it is not generally realised that during the past six years numbers of young men, without employment and maintained on Poor Law relief, have married, securing thereby an increase in their income from relief, and have had families, each addition to the family bringing its addition to the family income. In this respect it may be doubted whether the present position can be paralleled since 1834.

The following cases have been selected from a longer list of cases of this kind identified in one large Union:

Occupation	Year of birth	Year of commencement of relief	Year of marriage	Number of children
Tinsmith	1902	1922	1922	2
Factory Hand	1903	1923	1924	1
Vanguard	1906	1923	1925	1

It has to be added that in many cases of this kind the marriage is a forced one.

8.3.2 The Guardians Default Act, 1926

In areas of high unemployment guardians used their powers of borrowing for relief to such an extent that a special Act was passed to set some of them aside. The guardians of West Ham, Bedwellty and Chester-le-Street were treated in this way.

From the Boards of Guardians (Default) Act, 1926

1. Where it appears to the Minister of Health ... that the board of guardians for any poor law union have ceased, or are acting in such a manner as will render them unable, to discharge all or any of the functions exercisable by the board, the Minister may by order under this Act appoint such person or persons, as he may think fit (whether qualified or not to be guardians for the union), to constitute the board in substitution for the then existing members of the board ... for such period, not exceeding twelve months, as may be specified in the order, and the persons so appointed shall be deemed for all purposes to constitute the board.

8.3.3 The End of the Guardians

Neville Chamberlain, as Minister of Health in Baldwin's government, carried through a reorganisation of local government in the Local Government Act 1929, which preserved the poor law as such but replaced the guardians, as the 1909 reports had proposed, by the local authorities.

The Act covered many aspects of local government, extending, for instance, powers for establishing hospitals, as well as providing for the taking over of the poor law hospitals by councils. As a minor footnote to history it also repealed the long since derelict Unemployed Workmen Act.

With the change in the administration of the poor law, policy at the centre at last moved away from deterrence and, as the report of the Ministry of Health for 1929–30 shows, a Relief Regulation Order was issued in 1930 stressing the need for a more constructive approach to the needy.

From the Local Government Act, 1929

PART I: TRANSFER AND ADMINISTRATION OF FUNCTIONS

1. On the appointed day the functions of each poor law authority, shall ... be transferred to the council of the county or county borough comprising the poor law area for which the poor law

authority acts . . . and as from the appointed day all then existing poor law authorities shall cease to exist. . . .

5. (1) A council . . . shall have regard to the desirability of securing that, as soon as circumstances permit, all assistance which can lawfully be provided otherwise than by way of poor relief shall be so provided.

6. (1) The council shall provide for the constitution of a committee of the council (hereinafter referred to as the public assistance committee) . . .

(2) All matters relating to the exercise by the council of the functions transferred to them under this Part of the Act, shall stand referred to the public assistance committee . . .

12. The Unemployed Workmen Act, 1905, shall, as from the appointed day, be repealed . . .

13. The council of every county and county borough shall, when making provision for hospital accommodation in discharge of the functions transferred to them under the Part of the Act, consult such committee or other body as they consider to represent both the governing bodies and the medical and surgical staffs of the voluntary hospitals providing services in or for the benefit of the county or county borough as to the accommodation to be provided and as to the purposes for which it is to be used. . . .

14. [The Local Government Act 1888 was extended to give to County Councils the same powers for providing hospitals as the Public Health Act, 1875, Section 131, gave to local authorities.

Section 131 of the latter Act was amended to allow the provision of maternity hospitals by Councils.]

Medical Officers of Health

58. The council of every county shall, after consultation with the councils of districts wholly or partly within the county, formulate arrangements for securing that every medical officer of health subsequently appointed for a district shall be restricted by the terms of his employment from engaging in private practice as a medical practitioner.

*From the Eleventh Annual Report of the Ministry of Health,
1929–30*

REVIEW OF THE YEAR

The question of the conditions which accompany the grant of relief
to the able-bodied came into great prominence, and since the conditions known as the 'workhouse test' and the 'modified workhouse
test' had either from design or necessity became practically obsolete,
the controversy centred around the subject of the remaining condition prescribed by the Relief Regulation Order, 1911, i.e. the
labour test. On this point the position was defined by the Minister
in the House of Commons in the following terms (reproduced in
circular 1069).

'While I am opposed to the wholesale application of test work
to men who are unfortunately in the position of being unable to
obtain work, I am of opinion that boards of guardians must have
some means, other than the offer of the House, for dealing with
the limited class whom they know to be undeserving of unconditional relief. In my view test work should as far as possible, be
adapted to the training and educating of men so that they may
be fitted to take on a new job when one offers. . . .'

The Poor Law Act, 1930, was passed on 20 March 1930. This
Act is merely a re-enactment of the Poor Law Act of 1927 (which
is itself a consolidating Act) with such amendments only as are
required by the passing of the Local Government Act, 1929.

Similarly, the Public Assistance Order, 1930, is a consolidation
of a large number of previous Orders. . . .

The Act and the Public Assistance Order of 1930, cover the
whole field of poor law administration except outdoor relief to the
able-bodied which formed the subject matter of the Relief Regulation Order, 1911. It was decided in the light of recent experience
that the latter Order was not a proper subject for consolidation
but required fundamental amendment, and the Relief Regulation
Order, 1930, which with the Public Assistance Order, 1930, and
the Poor Law Act, 1930, came into operation on 1 April 1930,
replaced the existing Order. The principal changes embodied in
the new Order are:

(1) That institutional relief is no longer to be regarded as
    exclusively the appropriate form of relief for the able-bodied.

(2) That the conditions to be attached to the grant of relief should have as their main object rather the improvement of employability both mentally and physically than mere deterrence, which is more appropriate for the limited class referred to in the Minister's answer quoted above. ...

FUTURE PROGRESS

Throughout the period under review occasion has been taken to emphasise the point that the abolition of *ad hoc* destitution authorities and the transfer of their functions to the major public health and local education authorities is not in itself sufficient to effect *per saltum* that 'break-up' of the poor law which has been the aim of reformers for many years. The ultimate aim should indeed be to continue to exercise under the poor law nothing but those residual functions which cannot by statute be exercised under any other powers. ...

But it is obvious that in nearly every area considerable reorganisation and development in the council's non-poor law services is required before this step can safely be taken. ...

The abolition of the boards of guardians which ... was a necessary and inevitable result of derating agriculture, productive industry and freight transport, has long been thought desirable because of the overlapping of their functions as separate independent authorities responsible for providing every kind of relief for the destitute, with the functions of public health and local education authorities. The great day of the *ad hoc* authority in English local government is past and the co-ordination of health functions in larger areas and in fewer hands should mark a definite step in social progress.

8.3.4 The Last Poor Law Acts

The poor law in its new administrative form was set out in the Act of 1930, the last major Act of the series that had been inaugurated nearly 350 years earlier. Sections already quoted [1.1.1, 1.2.5 and 5.1.2] are not repeated here.

The Act of 1934 made minor changes in the spirit of the Act of 1894 [5.1.5], and the last Poor Law Act of all, that of 1938, extended the indulgences of the 1890s by granting pocket money to old people in the workhouse.

From the Poor Law Act, 1930

PART I: CENTRAL AND LOCAL ADMINISTRATION

Central authority

1. The Minister of Health is charged with the direction and control of all matters relating to the administration of relief to the poor throughout England and Wales. . . .

Provided that nothing in this Act shall be construed as enabling the Minister to interfere in any individual case for the purpose of ordering relief. . . .

Local authorities

2. The law relating to the relief of the poor shall be administered locally by the councils of counties and county boroughs. . . .

Local administration

4. (1) The public assistance committee of the council of every county and county borough shall be constituted in such manner as may be provided by the administrative scheme for the county or county borough. . . .

(2) All matters relating to the exercise by the council of any county or county borough of their functions under this Act . . . shall stand referred to the public assistance committee. . . .

5. (1) Every county shall be divided into such areas as may be provided by the administrative scheme for the county. . . .

(2) For every such area there shall be a local sub-committee of the public assistance committee (to be called the guardians committee of the area). . . .

Outdoor relief

45. The Minister may declare, by such rules, orders or regulations as he may think fit, to what extent and for what period the relief to be given to able-bodied persons or to their families may be administered out of the workhouse, either in money or by the provision of food or clothing, or partly in one way and partly in the other. . . .

48. (1) In granting outdoor relief to a member of a friendly society, the council of a county or county borough shall not take into consideration any sum received from the friendly society as sick pay except so far as it exceeds five shillings a week: subject as aforesaid in estimating the amount of relief to be granted to any such

member it shall be at the discretion of the council whether they will or will not take into consideration the amount received by him from the friendly society.

(2) In granting outdoor relief to a person in receipt of or entitled to receive any benefit under the National Health Insurance Acts, the council of a county or county borough shall not take into consideration any such benefit, except so far as it exceeds seven shillings and sixpence a week.

From the Poor Law Act, 1934

1. Section forty-eight of the Poor Law Act, 1930 (which makes provision as to the matters to be disregarded in granting outdoor relief to members of friendly societies and certain other persons) shall have effect subject to the following amendments, that is to say:

(*a*) in subsection (1) of the said section after the words 'friendly society' wherever those words occur therein, there shall be inserted the words 'or trade union';

(*b*) at the end of the said section there shall be inserted the following subsections, that is to say:

(3) The last foregoing subsection shall not apply to maternity benefit and in granting outdoor relief to any person the council of a county or county borough shall not take into consideration any maternity benefit under the National Health Insurance Acts.

(4) In granting outdoor relief to any person the council of a county or county borough shall not take into consideration any wounds or disability pension received by any person whose resources are taken into account in relieving him, except so far as it exceeds one pound a week.'

From the Poor Law (Amendment) Act, 1938

1. The enactments relating to the relief of the poor shall have effect as if amongst the powers conferred on councils of counties and county boroughs there was included power to grant a personal allowance not exceeding 2/- a week to any person in receipt of relief from them in a workhouse or other poor law institution, being a person aged 65 years or upwards.

On this note poor law legislation came to an end, apart from the final reference in the National Assistance Act, 1948.

8.4 CONTRIBUTORY PENSIONS

8.4.1 Contributory Pensions, 1925

Pensions at sixty-five had long been considered desirable, but the increasing proportion of the elderly in the population made a contributory scheme seem essential. It was generally agreed, also, that something should be done for widows and orphans, as Lloyd George had intended before 1911, and Neville Chamberlain had a broad contributory scheme in mind on taking office in 1924. He was pressed to introduce his plans by Churchill, who wished to reduce taxation to stimulate economic recovery, and needed some balancing concession for the working-class. The Contributory Pensions Act was passed in 1925, and the new pensions began in 1926, apart from pensions at sixty-five, which were delayed for three years as an economy measure.

From the Widows', Orphans' and Old Age Contributory Pensions Act, 1925

CONTRIBUTORY PENSIONS

1. (1) Subject to the provisions of this Act relating to the payment of contributions . . . pensions shall be payable as follows,

   (a) to the widow of an insured man a pension at the rate of ten shillings per week, with an additional allowance in respect of children while under the age hereinafter specified, at the rate of five shillings per week for the eldest or only such child, and three shillings per week for each other such child (in this Act called a 'widow's pension');

   (b) in respect of the orphan children while under the age hereinafter specified of an insured man or of an insured widow, a pension at the rate of seven shillings and sixpence per week for each such child (in this Act called an 'orphan's pension');

   (c) to an insured man or an insured woman who has attained the age of sixty-five but has not attained the age of seventy, and to the wife of an insured man who has attained the age of sixty-five (such wife having attained the age of sixty-five but not having attained the age of seventy) a pension at the rate of ten shillings per week (in this Act called an 'old age pension').

   (2) The specified age in relation to any child shall be the age of fourteen or the age not exceeding sixteen up to which the child remains under full-time instruction in a day school.

(3) By way of contribution towards the cost of carrying this Act into effect there shall be paid such contributions as are hereinafter in this Act provided. . . .

10. (1) The contributions by or in respect of an insured person . . . payable under this Act and under the Insurance Act shall be paid as one contribution under the Insurance Act. . . .

43. (1) The Government Actuary shall in the year nineteen hundred and thirty-five, and in every succeeding tenth year, make a report to the Treasury on the general financial operation of this Act, the amount of contributions from the Exchequer which will be required to preserve the solvency of the treasury pensions account, and the value of the benefits conferred by this Act; . . .

(2) Unless Parliament otherwise determines, during the decennial period commencing the first day of January, nineteen hundred and thirty-six, the ordinary rates of contribution shall be increased in the case of men by twopence a week (of which in the case of employed persons one penny shall be payable by the employer and one penny by the employed person), and in the case of women by one penny a week (of which in the case of employed persons one halfpenny shall be payable by the employer and one halfpenny by the employed person).

First schedule : Ordinary rates of contributions

	Rate of contribution per week	By the employer	By the employed person
Contributions in case of men	9d	4½d	4½d
Contributions in case of women	4½d	2½d	2d

8.4.2 The 'Black-Coated Workers' Act, 1937

Chamberlain's contributory scheme was extended in 1937, on a voluntary basis, to lower-paid non-manual workers, then known as 'black-coated', but more commonly today as 'white-collar', workers.

From the Widows', Orphans' and Old Age Contributory Pensions (Voluntary Contributors) Act, 1937

SPECIAL VOLUNTARY CONTRIBUTORS

1. (1) A person . . . shall, if he gives notice in that behalf in the prescribed manner and if he fulfils the requirements hereinafter

mentioned, thereupon become insured for the purposes of the Widows', Orphans' and Old Age Contributory Pensions Act, as a voluntary contributor thereunder, and pensions shall become payable in respect of his insurance accordingly.

The said requirements are as follows, that is to say:

(a) in the case of a person who gives notice as aforesaid not later than twelve months after the commencement of this Act . . . that he was under the age of fifty-five at the commencement of this Act;

(b) in the case of a person who is not an initial entrant, that he is at the date of his notice under the age of forty; and

(c) in the case of any person, whether an initial entrant or not –

(i) that he is resident in Great Britain at the date of the notice and has been so resident for a period of not less than ten years . . .

(ii) that he has a total income not exceeding four hundred pounds a year in the case of a man, or two hundred and fifty pounds a year in the case of a woman . . .

(2) Men who are entitled under the preceding subsection to become voluntary contributors may elect to become insured as such contributors for the purpose of widows' pensions and orphans' pensions only.

8.5 PUBLIC HEALTH

8.5.1 National Health Insurance, 1926

Post-war economies led to discussion of doctors' capitation fees. A court of enquiry made an acceptable award, but recommended a Royal Commission, which was appointed by the Labour Minister of Health in 1924, John Wheatley.

The movement of opinion towards some form of national health service, in both majority and minority reports, should be noted.

From the Report of the Royal Commission on National Health Insurance, 1926: Majority Report

THE SCHEME OF NATIONAL HEALTH INSURANCE

14. The cost of the Scheme is shared between the insured persons, their employers and the National Exchequer. . . .

The total income received from contributions in the year 1924 amounted to £27,377,000, and a sum of about £5,000,000 was derived from interest on accumulated funds. The expenditure on benefits was £26,118,000, and the cost of administration of these benefits by Approved Societies and Insurance Committees was £3,804,000. The total expenditure from the Exchequer towards the cost of the Scheme, inclusive of the cost of the central Government Departments concerned in the administration, was £7,045,000. ...

THE GENERAL ATTITUDE TO THE HEALTH INSURANCE SCHEME

19. It will be remembered that, whereas the Scheme of National Health Insurance received a cordial reception on its first presentation to Parliament, a considerable volume of opposition was developed during the passage of the Bill and in the ensuing period before the Act came into full operation. ... It might have been expected that the appointment of the present Commission with its wide terms of reference and the publicity given to them, would have resulted in adverse representations being made to us on lines familiar to those who remember the exacerbation of spirit of 1911 and 1912.

20. In fact, however, we have received very little evidence directed against the Scheme as a whole, nor have we any reason to think that there now exists any considerable body of opinion adverse to the principle of National Health Insurance. ...

22. In contrast to the paucity of evidence directed against the general principles of the present Scheme, we received from many different quarters a large volume of evidence in its favour, testifying to the advantages in health and social security which had been derived under it. For instance, the British Medical Association said that 'the evidence as to the incidence of sickness benefit does point to the fact that the Scheme itself has almost certainly reduced national sickness, and we are quite sure that if the immense gain to national health includes immense gain to the comfort of the individual in knowing that he can have medical attention whenever he needs it, the gain is most marked. ...'

GENERAL SATISFACTION WITH THE SCHEME

28. We are satisfied that the Scheme of National Health Insurance has fully justified itself and has, on the whole, been successful in operation. ... We are convinced that National Health Insurance

has now become a permanent feature of the social system of this country, and should be continued on its present compulsory and contributory basis. At the same time, if the Scheme is to be made of the fullest advantage to the health and well-being of the nation, there are, in our opinion, various modifications and extensions that could, with advantage, be made, as and when opportunity offers and funds become available. . . .

138. . . . We feel sure that the wider the scope of the services, the more difficult will it be to retain the insurance principle. The ultimate solution will lie, we think, in the direction of divorcing the medical service entirely from the insurance system and recognising it along with all the other public health activities as a service to be supported from the general public funds. Consideration would have to be given to the question of the classes of society for whom the service would be available and whether it should be so available on a free basis or with payments by insurance or otherwise. These, however, are problems which need not – perhaps cannot – be solved now. . . .

THE FINANCIAL BURDEN OF THE EXISTING SOCIAL SERVICES
General conclusion

151. . . . Our country has chosen, and rightly as we think, to make several great schemes of social insurance an integral and permanent part of the national life. But while this principle may be accepted, it is clearly essential that a balance between the expenditure on these schemes and the productive capacity of the country should be struck. . . . It is small consolation to a bankrupt to be told that his doctor's bills have been the main cause of his disaster.

We feel that there may come a time, and that in fact there has come a time when the State may justifiably turn from searching its conscience to exploring its purse, and that in connexion with our present reference we are entitled to . . . frame our recommendations in the light – or the darkness – of the economic condition of the nation.

153. We therefore make the definite recommendation that only such extensions or modifications as involve no expenditure or can be met within the present financial resources of the scheme, should be considered as immediately practicable. . . .

THE APPROVED SOCIETY SYSTEM
Control by members

231. Although one of the main reasons advanced in support of the adoption of the Approved Society system was that it would place the management and control of National Health Insurance business in the hands of the insured persons themselves, yet in actual practice this has not been the result, so far, at any rate, as many millions of insured persons are concerned. We have had ample evidence ... that in some of the largest Societies ... there is no effective means whereby the members could exercise control over the affairs of the Societies, whilst in many others, where the rules do contain provision for enabling such control to be exercised, the vast majority of members ... do not avail themselves of their opportunities and evince little or no interest in the affairs of their Societies....

233. The situation surely is one which, however regrettable, is not merely wholly natural, but is in fact paralleled in nearly every department of the public life of the community. To expect that the great bulk of insured persons should display an active interest in the administration of the Act is to court disappointment. To put it no higher, it is not an attractive field of study and it is probably asking too much of insured persons to suggest that they should attend meetings to discuss, for example, the propriety of the claims for sickness benefit which some of their fellows, unknown to them personally, are making. ...

PROPOSALS FOR EXTENDING MEDICAL BENEFIT

260. In this and the following chapters we propose to deal with various matters which we consider are of immediate practical importance, the attainment of which is, moreover, within the financial bounds which we have regarded as prescribed for us by the general circumstances of the time. ...

261. The first of the questions to which we now turn is that of the extension of the scope of medical benefit. ... Medical benefit is at present a general practitioner service; but it cannot seriously be claimed that this is a satisfactory state of affairs. It means that the medical service given in respect of the insurance contribution stops short just where the need is greatest. In the serious and expensive cases the insured person is thrown back on his own resources or on the limited provision made by the general hospitals.

262. We feel very strongly that the completion of one, and that a highly important, element ought to take precedence over the introduction of new elements, however desirable in themselves the latter may be. . . .

DENTAL BENEFIT

348. Dental benefit is one of the most popular, if not the most popular, of the additional benefits, and as such it is available in some form or another to large numbers of insured persons. . . . The desirability of making it a normal benefit under the Act . . . has been urged upon us from many quarters. . . . The advantages to general health and the consequent beneficial reactions upon the benefit funds have been specially pressed upon our notice. Nevertheless we do not propose to recommend that any substantial change in the present arrangements should be made in the near future. . . .

349. It is mainly the question of cost which has caused us difficulty in this matter.

COST OF A STATUTORY DENTAL BENEFIT

350. The cost of providing a dental service for all insured persons cannot we are told be determined with any precision because of the impossibility of estimating accurately the number of persons who might apply for treatment. It is generally agreed that the dental condition of the industrial classes is deplorable. The proportion of insured persons needing some form of dental treatment is put at from 60 per cent to 80 per cent of the total. . . .

351. The other item in estimating the cost of a dental service is the cost per case treated. It is clear that the majority of persons now applying for treatment need dentures, and until the present arrears have been worked off, which would take some years, the proportion of denture cases is bound to be very large. The inevitable result is that the cost per case treated is high. . . .

EXTENSION OF MEDICAL BENEFITS TO DEPENDANTS

372. The National Conference of Friendly Societies . . . suggest that the best way of organising the provision of medical treatment is to merge all existing forms of public medical service (including medical benefit under the National Health Insurance Acts) into one National Medical Service, thereby creating one unified

organisation for the prevention and cure of disease. Under this system, the service would be provided for all persons below a given income limit. ...

We exclude the provision of medical benefit to dependants from our immediate recommendations on the Insurance Scheme, and suggest that the matter should be left over to be considered in connexion with any wider proposals for reorganising the health services of the community which may commend themselves to later students of the problem.

From the Report of the Royal Commission on National Health Insurance, 1926: Minority Report

GENERAL

3. The main questions of principle on which we differ from our colleagues are as follows:

(1) The evidence which we have heard, convinces us that it is undesirable to retain Approved Societies any longer as the agencies through which benefits paid in cash are distributed to insured persons; and

(2) We do not accept the view that it is either necessary or proper to assume that we are to recommend no development intended to provide, in the words of the Act of 1911 'for insurance against loss of health, and for the prevention and cure of sickness', which cannot be paid for out of the produce of the contributory scheme of Health Insurance as it stands. ...

RECOMMENDATIONS

8. That Local Authorities could and should take the place of Approved Societies. ...

10. That in considering the cost of proposed developments of health services there should be taken into account the loss to the nation resulting from neglect to provide sufficiently for the health of all persons who are or will be employable. ...

11. That an outlay which safeguards industrial well-being and conduces to efficiency should not be regarded as a burden on industry or on the community. ...

13. That medical benefit should be extended to include dental and ophthalmic advice and treatment. ...

14. That medical benefit should be provided for the dependants of insured persons. . . .

17. That the cost of the extension of medical benefit by the inclusion of a specialist and consultant service should be met under the provisions of the Act. . . .

21. [Allowances to dependents as under Unemployment Insurance.]

22–4. [Improvements in maternity services and extension of maternity benefit to uninsured wives.]

8.5.2 Public Health

The first major Public Health Act since 1875 extended the power of the local authorities to provide hospitals, including, for the first time, out-patients departments.

The problem of the place of the voluntary hospitals in the general provision was not to be solved until 1946, but as the 1929 Act had required local authorities to consult voluntary hospitals when making their own development plans, and few had complied, the clause was repeated.

From the Public Health Act, 1936

LOCAL ADMINISTRATION

1. . . . It shall be the duty of the following authorities to carry this Act into execution. . . .

   (i) in a county borough, the council of the borough;
   (ii) in an administrative county, as respects certain matters, the county council and, as respects all other matters, the councils of county districts. . . .

HOSPITALS, NURSING HOMES, ETC.

81. (1) A county council or a local authority may provide hospital accommodation for persons in their county or district who are sick.

(2) The power of a county council or local authority under this section to provide hospital accommodation for persons who are sick includes power to provide –

   (a) clinics, dispensaries and out-patient departments;
   (b) maternity homes.

82. A county council or local authority, when making provision for hospital accommodation under this Part of this Act, other than hospital accommodation for persons suffering from an infectious

disease, shall consult such committee or other body as they consider to represent both the governing bodies and the medical and surgical staffs of the voluntary hospitals providing services in, or for the benefit of, their county or district as to the accommodation to be provided and as to the purposes for which it is to be used.

8.5.3 The Hospitals

Owing to the depression there was comparatively little hospital development in the 1930s, and it was not until war came that it was realised how inadequate hospital facilities were over the country as a whole, and how low were the standards in many places, especially among voluntary hospitals.

Meanwhile, the voluntary hospitals were facing increasing financial difficulties, and, as they were receiving more and more of their funds from contributory schemes, were ceasing to be truly 'charitable'.

From B. Abel-Smith, The Hospitals, 1800–1948 *(1964) p. 440–*

THE DOCTORS' PLAN

The war had led to the first attempt to plan hospitals on a regional basis and the task of organising and operating the Emergency Medical Service had brought home to all concerned the failings of Britain's hospital system. In view of the vast anticipated demand for beds for war purposes, the unsatisfactory condition of the country's hospitals became a matter of national importance. Previously, Ministry officials had had little cause to visit hospitals particularly small and ill-equipped hospitals. The war was a major educative experience not only for the Ministry but also for the top doctors and many middle-class patients. . . .

Consultants from the best hospitals found themselves allotted beds in rural workhouses and mental hospitals. And they were shocked by what they found. . . .

This new awareness of the medical and social problems of Britain was not confined to doctors and administrators. Men and women of the higher social classes saw the medical care system of the Poor Law as VAD nurses, as voluntary and paid war workers and even as patients and patients' visitors. They saw also the evacuated children and mothers, the occupants of the public air raid shelters and the casualties of the air war. There was more communication between classes and there were more common problems.

From R. Pinker, English Hospital Statistics, 1861–1938 *(1966),*
pp. 48–9, 151–4

... In 1861 there were approximately 14,800 beds in the voluntary
hospitals of England and Wales. Over the next thirty years this
number of beds doubled, to be followed by an increase of very
similar proportions in the period 1891–1921. By 1938 voluntary
hospital provision had risen to over 87,000 beds. Each decade saw
not only the addition of new beds but the rapid conversion of
existing beds from quasi-convalescent to curative functions.

The public sector grew during the same period at an even more
striking rate. In 1861 there were roughly 50,000 beds in workhouse
sick wards. The quality of this poor law provision was at its best
makeshift and at its worst scandalous. By 1891 there were over
83,200 beds in public hospitals, and this figure more than doubled
in the succeeding twenty years. The 1921 total of 172,000 beds
was not greatly increased during the inter-war years. During the
years between 1921 and 1938 the total stock of public accommodation grew by a mere 4,000 beds. ...

The data for 1891 shows that in London 'Voluntary Gifts' and
'Income from Investments' accounted for nearly 90 % of all ordinary revenue in almost equal proportions.

'Voluntary Gifts' and 'Income from Investments' were also the
main sources (85 %) of the provincial revenue, but 'Voluntary
Gifts', with 60·3 % of the total, were by far the larger of the two.
After these sources the next largest was 'Workmen's Contributions
and Hospital Saturday Fund' which accounted for 8·5 % of all
ordinary provincial income. These sources produced only 1·8 % of
the income in London.

By 1911 'Voluntary Gifts' accounted for 53·1 % of all ordinary
income in London. The proportion of income from 'Investments'
had fallen from 43·7 % to 35·4 % of the total. 'Patients' Pay
ments' had increased slightly as a source of income, to 5·7 % of
the total.

In the provinces both 'Voluntary Gifts' and 'Investments' had
decreased slightly in importance although together they still
accounted for nearly 70 % of total ordinary income. Receipts from
'Patients' Payments' had risen slightly from 2·3 % to 3·7 %, but
the biggest increase of all was in revenue from 'Workmen's Contributions and Hospital Saturday Fund', which now amounted to
22·0 % of all provincial ordinary income. ...

By 1938 the trend away from a reliance on 'Voluntary Gifts' and 'Investments' to direct payments had gone still further. In London only 41·3% of all ordinary revenue came from 'Voluntary Gifts' and 'Investments', while 'Patients' Payments' was the largest single source, accounting for 39·4% of all ordinary income.

In the provinces this trend was even more in evidence. 'Voluntary Gifts' and 'Investments' accounted for only 33·2% of all ordinary income, compared with the 58·9% raised from 'Patients' Payments'. Meanwhile the proportion of 'Other Payments' to the total had fallen from 23·0% to 7·9%. At this time contributory schemes were becoming increasingly popular and these new sources of revenue were being classed as 'Patients' Payments' rather than 'Workmen's Contributions'. . . .

The general conclusion suggested by these data is that charity, as the Victorians understood the term, had long ceased to be the main financial mainstay of the voluntary movement. Payments, either in cash or from 'insurance' contributions, were the principal source of revenue.

8.6 HOUSING

8.6.1 The Commons Debate, 1923

After the shock of what was widely regarded as the extravagant Addison building programme it was 1923 before housing was tackled again. As Minister of Health, Chamberlain proposed a subsidy from the Treasury, but with no rate-aid, and mainly for private building.

Wheatley, who was one of the Independent Labour Party group of 'Clydesiders', and was to succeed Chamberlain as Minister of Health, had a far better understanding of housing needs from his origins in a Scottish mining village, and a better grasp of the realities of housing finance.

From the House of Commons Debate, 24 April 1923

THE MINISTER OF HEALTH (MR NEVILLE CHAMBERLAIN)

Of all the problems which the War has left behind it, there is none that is more obstinate or more persistent than that which concerns the housing of the people. As we look around us we see progress going on in many directions, and, although we may still be far from our goal, which is a return to normal conditions, yet at any rate it is perceptible that we are moving. But in housing, after four years, and in spite of a prodigious effort, the results of which were altogether disproportionate to the cost, we hardly seem to be any better off than we were. The census of 1921 shows that in the last ten years the average increase in the population of the country was a little over 181,000, and if you take the average family in the country as consisting of four and a half persons, which is rather more than the actual figure, it will be seen that of the 215,000 houses, which have been provided with State assistance, no fewer than 161,000 were required to meet the normal and ordinary increase in the population, leaving, therefore, only 54,000 as a contribution towards the reduction of the shortage. So we find ourselves today faced with the condition that great masses of our people are unable to find separate dwellings for themselves, and they have to be herded together, without privacy, without comfort, without almost the ordinary decencies of life. . . .

This is not entirely a war problem. To find the origin of the shortage, we have to go back further than 1914. We must go back to an historic year, the year 1909. If you take the houses under the annual value of £20, you will find that the net annual increase in the five years previous to 1909 was 80,000. In the five years after 1909, it fell to 46,000. . . .

After that came the War years, during which no houses were built at all. . . . Taking those facts into account, I think the House will see that it would be altogether unreasonable to suppose that these arrears which have been accumulating over a period of thirteen years could possibly be wiped out in the short period which is covered by this Bill. . . .

What is the situation today? Private enterprise is beginning to function once more. (Hon. Members: 'Where?') I am going to tell you where. I have been rather surprised to find how many houses have been built recently without any assistance from the State or from local authorities at all. . . . During the last six months upwards of 12,000 of such houses have been completed and a further 16,000 are in course of erection. It is perfectly true that most of these houses are of a superior class suitable for the middle-class, but there are two features about this operation which are worthy of notice. . . . The first is that these houses are all for sale, and for the most part they are being sold to the people who desire to occupy them. The second feature is that as cost has come down and as trade has improved, so there has been a gradual extension of the operations of the private builder from the better class to the less good class of house. In fact, gradually the enterprise of the private builder is approaching nearer and nearer to the type of house which is desired today by the working class. That provides me with a guide, because, if you can at the same time stimulate private enterprise and provide fresh facilities for financing his operations, you will be approaching nearer to the time when the private builder can cover the whole field of housing, and the more work that he undertakes the greater will be the attraction to labour to enter the building trade. . . . Having said so much, I am bound to recognise that this process is bound to be a very slow and gradual one, and that there still remains a considerable margin which for some years to come it will be impossible for private enterprise to touch. Therefore, I had to . . . initiate a new scheme of State subsidies to tide over the interval until these houses could be built without assistance . . . and . . . the only question left for me to decide was, what was the smallest subsidy which we must give, in order to obtain the hearty co-operation of the local authorities, upon which we have to rely to carry out our programme. . . .

Mr Wheatley: I am bound to say that as I listened to the right hon. Gentleman, I became more and more convinced that he does not understand the extent of the housing problem, that he does not understand the cause of the housing shortage, and that he does not understand the people and has no sympathy with the people for whom he is endeavouring to provide in this Measure. . . . May I say at the outset that the housing problem is not one of house building; it is really a problem of finance? . . .

I speak as one of the many people on this side of the House who has studied the housing problem from hard experience of living in the slums. I was one of eleven persons who lived, not merely for a month but for years in a single apartment dwelling in Lanarkshire. . . .

The rings and combines have been increasing their stranglehold on the housing industry. The type of house now proposed by the right hon. Gentleman could have been built in pre-War days for something in the neighbourhood of £200. . . . Before the War the money could have been borrowed quite easily at 3 per cent, with the result that the burden of interest on the rent in pre-War days for such a house would have been about £6 per annum. During the operation of the Addison scheme the cost of building houses of that description went up from £200 to the neighbourhood of £1,100, and the rate of interest on the capital went up from 3 per cent to 6 per cent. What was the result? On the £1,100 capital necessary for this small house, there had to be paid £66 in interest. ... The right hon. Gentleman takes the optimistic view that prices have fallen, and he is now going to escape the grip of the money-lender, but on that point I am not so optimistic. ...

The price of your housing capital will be at least 5 per cent. Even if you take it that you will be able to control the rings and compel them to deliver the houses at £500, and you get the money at 5 per cent, there is still a burden of £25 per annum to be placed by the money-lenders of this country on the rent of the smallest type of working-class house that even a Conservative Government can provide. ...

I wish the right hon. Gentleman would realise that everyone engaged in the industry, and every member of every political party outside Parliament is agreed that private enterprise is not in the future going to provide working-class houses as it did before the War, but that the provision of working-class houses will in the future be a public enterprise, and, realising that, will tell the people that we are going permanently into this industry and intend to remain in it.

8.6.2 The Chamberlain Act, 1923

From the Housing, etc. Act, 1923

TEMPORARY PROVISIONS FOR ENCOURAGING THE PROVISION
OF HOUSING ACCOMMODATION

1. – (1) The Minister of Health ... shall ... make or undertake to make contributions out of moneys provided by Parliament:

   (a) towards any expenses incurred by a local authority for the purposes of Part III of the Housing of the Working Classes Act, 1890 ... in promoting in accordance with section two of this Act the construction of houses of such type and size as is specified in this section and completed before the first day of October, nineteen hundred and twenty-five;

   (b) where the local authority satisfy the Minister that the needs of their area can more appropriately be met by the provision of such houses wholly or partly by the authority themselves, towards any expenses incurred by the authority in making such provision. A contribution under this section shall be the sum of six pounds for each house in respect of which the contribution is made, payable annually for a period of twenty years. . . .

(2) The houses in respect of which contributions may be given under this section shall be either –

(a) a two-storied house with a minimum of six hundred and twenty and a maximum of nine hundred and fifty superficial feet; or

(b) a structurally separate and self-contained flat or a one-storied house with a minimum of five hundred and fifty and a maximum of eight hundred and eighty superficial feet. . . .

Except where otherwise approved by the Minister on the recommendation of the local authority, every house or flat to which this section applies shall be provided with a fixed bath. . . .[1]

3. – Where a society, body of trustees, or company prove to the Minister that they are willing to undertake the construction of houses (of the type prescribed) without assistance from a local authority . . . the Minister may make contributions out of moneys provided by Parliament towards the expense of the like amount as he is authorised to make towards expenses incurred by a local authority in providing such houses.

8.6.3 The Wheatley Policy, 1924

Wheatley restored the principle of rate-aid, which, though often challenged, has not again been reversed, and maintained Treasury assistance. Even more important, he gave the building industry a guarantee of a regular demand for houses over fifteen years, which made possible the vast increase of house-building that was to take place by 1939.

From the House of Commons Debate, 3 June 1924

The Minister of Health (Mr Wheatley): The point on which we ought to be clear is as to what is the real ultimate problem. If I were to state it in my own words, possibly the statement would be suspect, as coming from a Socialist source, but no such suspicion will attach to anything coming from Birmingham. The housing committee of the city of Birmingham . . . have issued a report in criticism of my proposals and their real views upon housing overflow from the report. They say:

[1] An amendment of 1924 added the words 'in a bathroom'.

'The real problem is the provision of houses, not to sell but to let, and to let at rents which the working classes can afford to pay. Subsidies to private enterprise for houses to sell are good to the extent that they do get houses, but they do not touch the real problem and even larger subsidies would not get working men's houses built to be let. Let there be no mistake about that; no one will build these houses on any terms. . . .'

Taking the 1923 Act and subjecting it to this test of 'houses to let', I have no difficulty in proving that it has been a complete failure. On the 1 May of this year I find that in England, Scotland and Wales, under this Act there were 17,383 houses either completed or under construction by the local authorities for the purpose of letting. . . . I do not want to lay down any dogmatic figures, but I think that those who understand the problem will be inclined to agree that something like 100,000 new houses would be required annually to prevent the housing shortage from increasing. . . .

Perhaps I may be permitted to submit to the Committee an analysis of the rent of a working-class house, in order to see where relief may be obtained. Taking the case of a house at £500, I find that the amount which the land on which the house sits adds to the weekly rent of the house is only three-halfpence. . . . Taking the next item in the expenditure, the cost of materials and profits amounts to £280, and I find that that puts a weekly burden on the house of 1s 10d. Coming next to the cost of the people who build the house . . . the whole burden of the cost of building a house adds only 1s 3d a week. . . . How is it that we require a subsidy, seeing that the labour costs, the costs of the landlord, the manufacturer, the builder and the tradesmen and labourers engaged in producing a house only amount to a weekly rent of 3s 3d? It is when I come to the finance of it that I find where the burden comes in. Taking the rate of interest at 5 per cent for the loan periods, it requires 6s 6d a week from the house to meet the burden of finance. . . .

A great deal is being said about the total to be contributed in subsidy by the State and local authorities for the erection of these houses, and the impression is left upon the public mind that, somehow or other, the working class are the recipients of charity from the people who pay these subsidies. I find that the total subsidies are only half the interest charged. . . .

With that knowledge of the situation, I have approached the

building industry in a friendly manner, and I asked for their views in a national emergency as to the best manner of producing the necessary houses. Why had we such a shortage of skilled labour in the building industry? ... The explanation was that the industry was subject to violent fluctuations, and that sometimes, when money was comparatively cheap, the building industry would have a boom, would go on for a year or two, and then something would happen to disturb it, and there would be a slump extending over an almost corresponding period. During the slump period, the skilled men trained in the busy period were the victims of un-employment, and had to find relief in emigration.

In 1924 there are 62,090 fewer skilled men in the industry than were in it in 1913, although the demands of the nation are con-siderably greater today. . . .

In order to get the essential labour for the production of houses, it was necessary to stabilise the industry by the adoption of a long-term programme, and when the representatives of the men and the employers put to me a proposal for a long-term building programme, I said ... 'If you are prepared to accept from the State a 15-years' building programme on condition that you deliver a certain number of houses every year, then I am prepared to consider entering into such an agreement'. They went into the matter very carefully, and ultimately we fixed and made an agree-ment on that basis.

8.6.4 The Wheatley Act, 1924
From the Housing (Financial Provisions) Act, 1924

1. – (1) Sections one and three of the Housing, &c. Act, 1923 (which relate to contributions by the Minister of Health to the expenses of local authorities in assisting the construction of houses), shall extend to houses which are provided in pursuance of proposals approved by the Minister and are completed before the first day of October, nineteen hundred and thirty-nine. . . .

(2) The following paragraph shall be substituted for paragraph (*b*) of subsection (1) of section one of the Housing, &c. Act, 1923:

'(*b*) towards any expenses incurred by the local authority in the provision of such houses by the local authority them-selves.' . . .

2. – Where, in pursuance of proposals approved by the Minister after the passing of this Act, any houses are provided by a local

authority ... within the meaning of section three of the said Act ... then, if the houses are subject to special conditions as hereinafter provided in this Act, the contribution which the Minister may make or undertake to make in respect of each house, instead of being a contribution of six pounds payable annually for a period of twenty years –

(*a*) shall be a contribution of nine pounds or, if the house is situated in an agricultural parish, twelve pounds ten shillings; and

(*b*) shall be payable annually for a period of forty years. ...

3. – (1) Houses provided by a local authority themselves shall be deemed to be subject to special conditions if the local authority undertake that the following conditions will be complied with in relation to the houses:

(*a*) that the houses shall be let by the local authority for occupation to tenants who intend to reside therein:

(*b*) that it shall be a term of every such letting that the tenant shall not assign, sublet, or otherwise part with the possession of the house, or any part thereof, except with the consent in writing of the local authority ... and that such consent shall not be given unless it is shown that no payment other than rent has been or is to be received by the tenant. ...

(*d*) that a fair wages clause shall be inserted in all contracts for the construction of the houses;

(*e*) that the rents charged in respect of the houses shall not in the aggregate exceed the total amount of the rents that would be payable if the houses were let at the appropriate normal rents charged in respect of working-class houses erected prior to the third day of August, nineteen hundred and fourteen. ...

(*f*) that reasonable preference shall be given to large families in letting the houses.

8.6.5 Slum Clearance

An extensive programme of house-building having been put into effect, attention turned to slum clearance, and Arthur Greenwood, Minister of Health in the second Labour government, introduced Treasury subsidies for the purpose, while insisting on adequate re-housing.

The fall of the Labour government, and the imposition of economies by the 'National' government, caused delay, but Chamberlain got his tit-for-tat by winding up the Wheatley policy in 1933 so that authorities could concentrate on clearance, leaving other housing to private enterprise, which then carried out a spectacular building programme. An Act of 1935 extended the clearance policy to overcrowding (first declared a 'nuisance', be it remembered, in 1866), but sights had been set too low, and a great deal of disgraceful property remained in 1939, and had to wait for many more years.

From the Housing Act, 1930

PART I: PROVISIONS WITH RESPECT TO THE CLEARANCE OR IMPROVEMENT OF UNHEALTHY AREAS
Clearance areas

1. – (1) Where a local authority are satisfied as respects any area in their district –

   (i) that the dwelling-houses in that area are by reason of disrepair or sanitary defects unfit for human habitation or are by reason of their bad arrangement, or the narrowness or bad arrangement of the streets, dangerous or injurious to the health of the inhabitants of the area. . . .

   (ii) that the most satisfactory method of dealing with the conditions in the area is the demolition of all the buildings in the area.

the authority shall cause that area to be defined on a map . . . and shall pass a resolution declaring the area so defined to be a clearance area, that is to say, an area to be cleared of all buildings. . . .

Provided that, before passing any such resolution, the authority shall satisfy themselves –

   (*a*) that in so far as suitable accommodation available for the persons of the working classes who will be displaced by the clearance of the area does not already exist, the authority can provide, or secure the provision of, such accommodation in advance of the displacements which will from time to time become necessary as the demolition of buildings in the area, or in different parts thereof, proceeds; . . .

   (3) So soon as may be after a local authority have declared any area to be a clearance area, they shall secure the clearance of the area . . .

   (i) by ordering the demolition of the buildings in the area; or

   (ii) by purchasing the land comprised in the area and themselves undertaking the demolition of the buildings thereon. . . .

Improvement areas

7. – (1) Where a local authority are satisfied as respects any area in their district that the housing conditions in that area are dangerous or injurious to the health of the inhabitants by reason of the disrepair or sanitary defects of dwelling-houses therein, and also by reason either of overcrowding in the area or of the bad arrangement of the houses or of the narrowness or bad arrangement of the streets, and that those conditions can be effectively remedied, without the demolition of all the buildings in the area, by –

    (i) the demolition or repair, as the circumstances may require, of those dwelling-houses which are unfit for human habitation;

    (ii) the purchase by the authority of any land in the area which it is expedient for them to acquire for opening out the area . . .

    (iii) the abatement of overcrowding in the area,

the authority may pass a resolution declaring the area to be an improvement area. . . .

General

9. A local authority who have passed a resolution declaring any area to be a clearance area or an improvement area shall, before taking any action under that resolution which will necessitate the displacement of any persons of the working classes, undertake to carry out or to secure the carrying out of such re-housing operations as the Minister may consider to be reasonably necessary. . . .

Provisions with respect to the provision of housing accommodation and government assistance towards cost of re-housing operations

25. – (1) It shall be the duty of every local authority to consider the housing conditions in their area and the needs of the area with respect to the provision of further housing accommodation for the working classes . . . and to prepare and submit to the Minister proposals for the provision of new houses for the working classes, distinguishing those houses which the authority propose to provide for the purpose of rendering accommodation available for persons to be displaced by action taken by the authority under this Act. . . .

26. – (1) The Minister shall . . . make or undertake to make contributions out of moneys provided by Parliament towards any expenses incurred by a local authority in connection with any

action taken by them under this Act for dealing with clearance or improvement areas, or for the demolition of insanitary houses, or for the closing of parts of buildings, and in connection with the provision and maintenance of the housing accommodation rendered necessary by any action so taken.

(2) A contribution under this section shall be payable annually for a period of forty years, and shall be the appropriate sum (as hereinafter defined) multiplied by the number of persons of the working classes whose displacement is shown to the satisfaction of the Minister to have been rendered necessary by the action of the local authority.

Provided that the number of persons to be taken into account in calculating such contribution shall not exceed the number of persons of the working classes for whom suitable accommodation has been rendered available by the authority in new houses. . . .

(3) For the purposes of the last preceding subsection the expression 'appropriate sum' means –

(a) in the case of persons displaced from houses in an agricultural parish, the sum of two pounds ten shillings; and

(b) in the case of persons displaced from houses in other parishes, the sum of two pounds five shillings. . . .

Provision of houses in rural districts

32. – (1) It shall be the duty of the council of every county, as respects each rural district within the county, to have constant regard to the housing conditions of persons of the working classes, the extent to which overcrowding or other unsatisfactory housing conditions exist and the sufficiency of the steps which the council of the district have taken, or are proposing to take, to remedy those conditions and to provide further housing accommodation. . . .

37. The Minister, unless he is satisfied that owing to special circumstances some other standard of size or accommodation should be adopted –

(i) shall not approve the provision of any house which is not such a house as is specified in paragraph (a) or paragraph (b) of subsection (2) of section one of the Housing, &c., Act 1923, and

(ii) shall treat a house containing two bedrooms as providing accommodation for four persons, a house containing three bedrooms as providing accommodation for five persons, and a house containing four bedrooms as providing accommodation for seven persons.

38. A local authority in preparing any proposals for the provision of houses . . . shall have regard to the beauty of the landscape or countryside and the other amenities of the locality, and the desirability of preserving existing works of architectural, historic or artistic interest. . . .

46. If a local authority satisfy the Minister that, having regard to the demand for housing accommodation on the part of aged persons, there is a need in their area for houses of smaller dimensions than those specified . . . the Minister may reduce the minimum measurements specified.

8.6.6 The End of the Wheatley Policy, 1933
From the Housing (Financial Provisions) Act, 1933

1. No contribution shall be made by the Minister of Health under Section 1 or Section 3 of the Housing Act, 1923 or under the Housing (Financial Provisions) Act, 1924 towards expenses incurred in providing . . . any house not provided in pursuance of proposals submitted to him before 7 December 1932. [Some flexibility of date was permitted over plans which were substantially complete on the date named.]

8.6.7 Overcrowding, 1935
From the Housing Act, 1935

OVERCROWDING, REDEVELOPMENT AND RECONDITIONING
Abatement of overcrowding

1. – (1) It shall be the duty of every local authority before such dates as may be fixed by the Minister as respects their district to cause an inspection thereof to be made with a view to ascertaining what dwelling-houses therein are overcrowded, and to prepare and submit to the Minister a report showing the result of the inspection and the number of new houses required in order to abate overcrowding in their district, and, unless they are satisfied that the required number of new houses will be otherwise provided, to prepare and submit to the Minister proposals for the provision thereof. . . .

2. – (1) A dwelling house shall be deemed for the purposes of this

Act to be overcrowded at any time when the number of persons sleeping in the house either –

 (*a*) is such that any two of those persons, being persons ten years old or more of opposite sexes and not being persons living together as husband and wife, must sleep in the same room ...

 (*b*) is, in relation to the number and floor area of the rooms ... in excess of the permitted number. ...

 (2) In determining for the purposes of this section the number of persons sleeping in a house, no account shall be taken of a child under one year old, and a child who has attained one year and is under ten years old shall be reckoned as one half of a unit.

3. – (1) If after the appointed day the occupier or the landlord of a dwelling-house causes or permits it to be overcrowded, he shall be guilty of an offence. ...

Redevelopment areas

13. If the local authority for any urban area ... are satisfied, as a result ... that their district comprises any area in which the following conditions exist:

 (*a*) that the area contains fifty or more working-class houses;

 (*b*) that at least one-third of the working-class houses in the area are overcrowded, or unfit for human habitation and not capable at a reasonable expense of being rendered so fit, or so arranged as to be congested;

 (*c*) that the industrial and social conditions of their district are such that the area should be used to a substantial extent for housing the working classes; and

 (*d*) that it is expedient in connection with the provision of housing accommodation for the working classes that the area should be re-developed as a whole;

it shall be the duty of the local authority ... to pass a resolution declaring the area to be a proposed re-development area. ...

14. The authority shall prepare and submit to the Minister a re-development plan indicating the manner in which it is intended that the area should be laid out and the land therein used ... and in particular the land intended to be used for the provision of houses for the working classes, for streets and for open spaces. ...

18. In so far as suitable accommodation is not available for persons who will be displaced from working-class houses in the carrying

out of re-development in accordance with a re-development plan, it shall be the duty of the local authority to provide, or to secure the provision of, such accommodation in advance of the displacements from time to time becoming necessary as the re-development proceeds. . . .

Financial provisions

31. The Minister shall . . . undertake to make, and make, contributions out of moneys provided by Parliament towards any expenses incurred by a local authority in providing for the working classes housing accommodation which is either –

(a) required for the purpose of the abatement of overcrowding, or

(b) rendered necessary by displacements occurring in the carrying out of re-development in accordance with a re-development plan,

in so far as such accommodation is provided in blocks of flats on sites the cost of which as developed . . . exceeds one thousand five hundred pounds per acre. . . .

33. The Minister may . . . undertake to make, and make, contributions out of moneys provided by Parliament towards any expenses incurred by a rural district council in providing new housing accommodation required for members of the agricultural population for the purpose of the abatement of overcrowding in the rural district.

First schedule : Permitted number of persons

Rooms	Number of persons
1	2
2	3
3	5
4	7
5 or more	10, and 2 for each extra room

8.6.8 Final Report, 1939

The last report of the Ministry of Health before the outbreak of war in 1939 provided statistics of house-building under the various Acts since 1919.

From the Twentieth Annual Report of the Ministry of Health, 1938–9

HOUSING

Further steady progress has been made during the year in the drive against the slums, in the abatement of overcrowding and in the reconditioning of existing and the building of new houses. By the end of the year over a million persons had been removed from slum houses to new houses since the slum clearance campaign began in 1933, whilst the number of new houses erected since the Armistice by local authorities and private enterprise had reached 3,998,366.

Still further progress would no doubt have been made but for the international crisis in September, 1938. Despite this, however, the number of houses built by local authorities during the year was the highest in any year since 1927–8 and 23,774 more than in 1937–8. This increase was mainly due to the acceleration of building for slum clearance purposes in order to attract the subsidy payable under the Act. . . .

Although the Housing (Financial Provisions) Act, 1938, with its special provisions for the encouragement of the building of new houses for the agricultural population, became law at the end of March, 1938, the subsidies under the Act are normally payable only in respect of houses completed after 31 December 1938. It is not yet possible, therefore, to give a review of a full year's working of the Act. The figures available, however, show that a sufficiently good beginning has been made to justify the hope that the Act . . . will so improve the conditions of the workers in the agricultural industry that before long they will have no reason to envy the housing amenities enjoyed by workers in the towns.

Government contributions were made

Financial year	Housing, Town Planning, etc. Act, 1919	Housing (Additional Powers) Act, 1919	Housing, etc. Act, 1923	Housing (Financial Provisions) Act, 1924	Housing (Rural Workers) Acts, 1926 to 1938	Housing Act, 1936 (Sec. 105)	Housing Act, 1936 (Secs. 106, 108)	Housing (Financial Provisions) Act, 1938	Totals
1919–20	715	†	—	—	—	—	—	—	715
1920–21	17,597	11,208	—	—	—	—	—	—	28,805
1921–22	100,516	29,441	—	—	—	—	—	—	129,957
1922–23	159,002	39,179	—	—	—	—	—	—	198,181
1923–24	169,526	39,186	8,140	—	—	—	—	—	216,852
1924–25	172,428	39,186	70,421	2,486	—	—	—	—	284,521
1925–26	173,515	39,186	149,043	29,764	—	—	—	—	391,508
1926–27	174,397	39,186	241,649	90,055	—	—	—	—	545,287
1927–28	174,593	39,186	328,516	181,574	44	—	—	—	723,913
1928–29	174,603	39,186	381,972	232,900	836	—	—	—	829,497
1929–30	174,635	39,186	436,633	288,576	1,922	—	—	—	940,952
1930–31	174,635	39,186	436,633	343,639	3,377	—	—	—	997,470
1931–32	174,635	39,186	436,633	411,135	4,775	2,429	—	—	1,068,793
1932–33	174,635	39,186	438,047	460,718	5,787	8,491	—	—	1,126,864
1933–34	174,635	39,186	438,047	508,426	6,750	17,569	—	—	1,184,613
1934–35	174,635	39,186	438,047	520,298	8,280	41,231	—	—	1,221,677
1935–36	174,635	39,186	438,047	520,298	10,054	80,611	—	—	1,262,831
1936–37	174,635	39,186	438,047	520,298	11,875	136,044	1,070	—	1,321,155
1937–38	174,635	39,186	438,047	520,298	14,762	195,246	2,852	—	1,385,026
1938–39	174,635	39,186	438,047	520,298	18,482	261,875*	9,000*	16,000*	1,477,523*
Total contributions	£121,242,090	9,498,156	30,142,041	41,088,113	163,703	6,206,902	68,324	14,854	208,424,183

† These houses were the subject of lump sum grants and do not attract continuing annual payments

* These figures are provisional

9 The Impact of Total War

9.1 NEW POLICIES

9.1.1 Supplementary Pensions, 1940

The rise in the cost of living in the early months of the war led to the introduction of supplements to old age pensions in cases of need. Chamberlain had already promised to lower to sixty the age at which women became entitled to pensions, and the Bill for this measure was extended to give wider cover. When the new supplements became available 750,000 old people unexpectedly came forward who had obviously been unwilling, despite all the assurances of the Chancellor of the Exchequer, Sir John Simon, to apply to public assistance. The comment of *The Times* in August 1940 [9.1.2] on 'secret need' was apt.

From a Memorandum by Sir John Simon, Chancellor of the Exchequer, to the War Cabinet, January 1940
It is difficult to believe that there are still any very large number of old age pensioners who prefer destitution to the alleged indignity of applying for public assistance. Enquiries I have made seem to show that, while much is made by our opponents in the House of the stigma of public assistance, the great majority of industrial workers do not feel very strongly on this point.
[*History of the Second World War, Civil Series : Problems of Social Policy*, by R. M. Titmuss (1950), p. 516, n 5.]

From the House of Commons Debate, 23 January 1940
Sir J. Simon: There are nearly 3,000,000 old age pensioners over the age of 65 in this country. Most of them, of course, are drawing contributory pensions, but included in the total are 550,000 who are over 70 and whose pension is subject to a test of means. It is natural, when considering the need for improving the pensions system, to concentrate on the case of the pensioner who has no

additional resources other than public assistance. But investigation shows that this class of case, which certainly calls for our special consideration and with which I intend to deal, is exceptional. ...

Our latest information is that about 275,000 pensioners get additional relief from public assistance authorities and the annual cost of such relief is in the region of £5,250,000. We propose to take away altogether from the local authorities their present liability to supplement old age pensions, and to place this obligation upon central funds. ... Further, we propose that the present family needs test as administered by public assistance committees, which has regard to the income of all liable relatives wherever they reside, should be replaced by the household needs test as now applied in the case of applicants for unemployment assistance. ... The supplementary grant will really be of the nature of a supplementary pension. It will be paid through the Post Office as is the practice at present with the 10s. pensions. ...

It amounts to providing for regular payments through the Post Office for those people who feel and I think naturally feel a considerable sense of humiliation because they have to apply weekly for relief from local authorities.

9.1.2 The Pensions Act, 1940

Pensions for women at sixty and supplementary pensions were provided in this Act of 1940. Supplementary pensions became the responsibility of the Unemployment Assistance Board, which was renamed the Assistance Board.

From the Old Age and Widows' Pensions Act, 1940

PART I: WOMEN'S CONTRIBUTORY PENSIONS

1. (1) The age at which an old age pension under the Contributory Pensions Acts may become payable to a woman, whether as an insured woman or as the wife of an insured man who has attained the age of sixty-five, shall be reduced to sixty. ...

PART II: SUPPLEMENTARY PENSIONS

9. (1) A person shall be eligible for a supplementary pension under this Part of this Act who is a person entitled to receive weekly payments on account of an old age pension, or a person who has attained the age of sixty and is entitled to receive weekly payments on account of a widow's pension.

(2) Where it is proved that any person so eligible as aforesaid is in need of a supplementary pension, there may be granted to him a supplementary pension of an amount determined in accordance with the provisions of this Part of this Act.

(3) The sums required for the payment of supplementary pensions under this Part of this Act shall be defrayed out of moneys provided by Parliament. . . .

10. (1) The Board constituted under section thirty-five of the Unemployment Act, 1934, shall cease to be called the Unemployment Assistance Board and shall be called the Assistance Board. . . .

(3) The functions of the Assistance Board shall include the functions of granting supplementary pensions under this Part of this Act. . . .

(4) The administration of supplementary pensions shall be conducted in such manner as may best promote the welfare of pensioners.

From The Times, *14 August 1940*
Commenting on the fact that, although the standard rate of income for a single person dependent on a pension was only 19s 6d, for a married couple 32s, so many had come forward for supplementary pensions, *The Times* remarked in a leader:

> There has been a remarkable discovery of secret need. . . .
> The surprise of the investigation is that for so many old people the level of existence should have been so low.

9.1.3 The Means Test Abolished, 1941

The collapse of Chamberlain's ineffective war administration in May 1940 brought Labour into a coalition government under Churchill, and part of the price exacted by Labour for its support was the abolition of the household means test. Bevin, in moving the Bill to amend the Act, referred to the many devices adopted to evade the attentions of the Unemployment Assistance Board inspectors, the 'means test men', and circumvent what were felt to be the injustices of the Assistance policy.

By narrowing the basis of family responsibility the Act that followed brought nearer the abolition of the poor law and the creation of a new concept of assistance which were finally achieved in 1948.

From the House of Commons Debate, 29 April 1941
The Minister of Labour (Mr Ernest Bevin): I beg to move, 'That the Draft Unemployment Assistance (Determination of

Need and Assessment of Needs) (Amendment) Regulation, 1941 be approved.'

The approval by the House of these draft Regulations means that the household means test, as it used to be known, will be swept away and substituted by a test of personal need based on the circumstances in which the applicant is living. . . . There are two sets of Regulations. The first relates to unemployment assistance, made by the Minister of Labour and National Service, and the second to supplementary pensions made by the Minister of Health and the Secretary of State for Scotland jointly. . . .

The first important Regulation substitutes, in the case of household applicants, the fixed contribution from non-dependent members in place of the old rule of aggregating the resources. . . . This part of the Regulations at least removes what was a great grievance because of the difference in treatment of the family remaining at home and the son and daughter who left home. By placing them on exactly the same basis the old grievance of breaking up the home in order to get assistance or proper treatment will be removed. . . .

In dealing with this problem we have tried to devise a scheme that will remove the temptation to people to be cunning in order to get assistance. . . .

This subject has been one of very bitter controversy, and I am sure the House will be glad that we have arrived at what we, at least, believe to be the solution of a vexed problem. Somebody said the other day that the only thing now left of Queen Elizabeth was one toe sticking out of the ground and that, for the rest, the Poor Law was now buried.

9.1.4 Needs, Not Means, 1941

From the Determination of Needs Act, 1941

1. On and after the appointed day so much of subsection (3) of section thirty-eight of the Unemployment Assistance Act, 1934 as requires that in the case of an applicant for an allowance under that Act, or of an applicant for a supplementary pension under the Old Age and Widows' Pensions' Act, 1940, the resources of the applicant taken into account shall include the resources of all members of the household of which he is himself a member, shall cease to have effect.

1. Whether or not the applicant is the householder, the resources of members of the household, other than the applicant, the husband or wife of the applicant, and any member of the household dependent on the applicant, shall not be regarded as resources of the applicant.

9.1.5 Statistics of Assistance

From the Annual Report of the Ministry of Health, 1939–41 : Public Assistance

The break-up of the poor law received a notable impetus in August 1940, when supplementary pensions became payable ... in one month the number of persons in receipt of out-relief fell from 770,052 to 454,515.

From the Annual Report of the Ministry of Health, 1943–4 : Public Assistance

[The report noted that the number on out-relief had fallen to 291,826, and that the Determination of Needs Act had been applied to out-relief from 1 November 1943]:

The effect ... is to abolish the 'household means test', which had been a long established principle of the poor law.

From the Annual Report of the Assistance Board, 1944–5

[The 1944 report noted that the number on Assistance, which had been nearly 750,000 in 1935 and nearly 400,000 in 1939, had fallen to 16,200.

Supplementary pensioners in 1944 numbered 1,387,000, of whom 230,000 were over eighty.

The number of supplementary pensions rose in 1945, but fell to 500,000 in 1946 when the new old age pensions were introduced.]

9.2 THE BEVERIDGE REPORT, 1942

9.2.1 The Report

Arthur Greenwood was a minister without portfolio in the wartime cabinet from 1940–2, and was given a vague commission by Churchill to inquire into the practical development of social policies. He was pressed by the TUC to consider the adequacy of social insurance, and set up an inter-departmental committee of civil servants to survey existing schemes and make recommendations. Beveridge was appointed chairman, but saw possibilities of wider scope, and persuaded Greenwood to allow him to produce a report himself, using the civil servants only as advisers. The result was a major restatement of social policy on the now traditional lines of the Lloyd George – Churchill reforms, brought up to date to cope more adequately with the problems which the 1920s and 1930s had revealed.

From the Report on Social Insurance and Allied Services, 20 November 1942

THE WAY TO FREEDOM FROM WANT

11. The work of the Inter-departmental Committee began with a review of existing schemes of social insurance and allied services. The Plan for Social Security, with which that work ends, starts from a diagnosis of want – of the circumstances in which, in the years just preceding the present war, families and individuals in Britain might lack the means of healthy subsistence. During those years impartial scientific authorities made social surveys of the conditions of life in a number of principal towns in Britain, including London, Liverpool, Sheffield, Plymouth, Southampton, York and Bristol. They determined the proportions of the people in each town whose means were below the standard assumed to be necessary for subsistence, and they analysed the extent and causes of that deficiency. From each of these social surveys the same broad result emerges. Of all the want shown by the surveys, from three-quarters to five-sixths, according to the precise standard chosen for want, was due to interruption or loss of earning power. Practically the whole of the remaining one-quarter to one-sixth was due to failure to relate income during earning to the size of the family . . . abolition of want requires a double re-distribution of income through social insurance and by family needs.

15. The plan . . . takes account of two other facts about the British community. . . . The first . . . is the age constitution of the population, making it certain that persons past the age that is now regarded as the end of working life will be a much larger proportion of the whole community than at any time in the past. The second . . . is the low reproduction rate of the British community today; unless this rate is raised very materially in the near future, a rapid and continuous decline of the population cannot be prevented. The

first fact makes it necessary to seek ways of postponing the age of retirement from work rather than of hastening it. The second fact makes it imperative to give first place in social expenditure to the care of childhood and to the safeguarding of maternity. . . .

[After a list of changes involved in the plan:]
31. This considerable list of changes does not mean that, in the proposals of the Report, either the experience or the achievements of the past are forgotten. What is proposed today for unified social security springs out of what has been accomplished in building up security piece by piece. . . . The scheme proposed here is in some ways a revolution, but in more important ways it is a natural development from the past. It is a British revolution. . . .

Inclusion of universal funeral grant in compulsory insurance
157. All people when they die need a funeral. This need is now met for most though not quite all, people in Britain by voluntary industrial insurance, but at an excessive expense – certainly in administration, probably also in actual expenditure.

Substantial sums are distributed as death benefit by Friendly Societies other than collecting societies and Trade Unions, and some of these benefits are used for funeral expenses, but for the great majority of people provision for funeral expenses is undertaken through the Industrial Life Offices. The cost ratio of all the Industrial Life Offices taken together (including profits and tax) in 1937–40 was 37·2 per cent of the premiums, nearly 7/6 in the £.
158. As compared with this, the cost of administering a funeral grant as part of social insurance would be negligible. On the contribution side, it would mean adding one or two pence to the value of the insurance stamp, which would have to be affixed in any case to the insurance document; on the benefit side it would mean paying one claim only for each person in respect of a fact of which there could be no doubt and which must be formally recorded by the State for other purposes. . . . The administrative expenses of funeral grant in social insurance could not well be more than 2 or 3 per cent of the contribution, that is to say, more than about 6d in the £ of premiums in place of 7/6 in the £ under the present voluntary system. There can be no justification for requiring the public who need insurance for direct funeral expenses to pay the heavy tax involved in industrial assurance. . . .

PLAN FOR SOCIAL SECURITY
Assumptions, methods and principles

300. Scope of Social Security: The term 'social security' is used here to denote the securing of an income to take the place of earnings when they are interrupted by unemployment, sickness or accident, to provide for retirement through age, to provide against loss of support by the death of another person, and to meet exceptional expenditures, such as those connected with birth, death and marriage. Primarily social security means security of income up to a minimum, but the provision of an income should be associated with treatment designed to bring the interruption of earnings to an end as soon as possible.

301. Three assumptions: No satisfactory scheme of social security can be devised except on the following assumptions:

(a) Children's allowances for children up to the age of 15 or if in full-time education up to the age of 16;

(b) Comprehensive health and re-habilitation services for prevention and cure of disease and restoration of capacity for work, available to all members of the community;

(c) Maintenance of employment, that is to say avoidance of mass unemployment. . . .

302. Three Methods of Security: On these three assumptions, a Plan for Social Security is outlined below, combining three distinct methods: social insurance for basic needs; national assistance for special cases; voluntary insurance for additions to the basic provision. . . .

303. Six Principles of Social Insurance: The social insurance scheme embodies six fundamental principles:

Flat rate of subsistence benefit
Flat rate of contribution
Unification of administrative responsibility
Adequacy of benefit
Comprehensiveness
Classification. . . .

Abolition of want as a practicable post-war aim

445. The first step in considering the prospective economic resources of the community after the present war is to see what they were just before the war. The social surveys made by impartial investigators of living conditions in some of the main industrial centres of Britain between 1928 and 1937 have been used earlier

in this Report to supply a diagnosis of want. They can be used also to show that the total resources of the community were sufficient to make want needless. While, in every town surveyed, substantial percentages of the families examined had less than the bare minimum for subsistence, the great bulk of them had substantially more than the minimum. ... Want could have been abolished before the present war by a redistribution of income within the wage-earning classes, without touching any of the wealthier classes. This is said not to suggest that redistribution of income should be confined to the wage-earning classes; still less is it said to suggest that men should be content with avoidance of want, with subsistence incomes. It is said simply as the most convincing demonstration that abolition of want just before this war was easily within the economic resources of the community; want was a needless scandal due to not taking the trouble to prevent it.

446. The social surveys showed not only what was the standard of living available to the community just before the war but also that it had risen rapidly in the past thirty or forty years. The recent London and York surveys were designed to provide comparisons with earlier studies. They yielded unquestionable proof of large and general progress. When the New Survey of London Life and Labour was made in 1929, the average workman in London could buy a third more of articles of consumption in return for labour of an hour's less duration per day than he could buy forty years before at the time of Charles Booth's original survey. The standard of living available to the workpeople of York in 1936 may be put over-all at about 30 per cent higher than it was in 1899. This improvement of economic conditions was reflected in improvement of physical conditions. In London, the crude death rate fell from 18·6 per thousand in 1900 to 11·4 in 1935 and the infant mortality rate fell from 159 to 58 per thousand. In York the infant mortality rate fell from 161 per thousand in 1899 to 55 in 1936; in the same period nearly 2 inches was added to the height of schoolchildren and nearly 5lbs. to their weight. ... What has been shown for these towns in detail applies to the country generally. The real wages of labour, what the wage-earner could buy with his earnings just before the present war, were in general about one-third higher than in 1900 for an hour less of work each day. ...

447. [Yet] growing general prosperity and rising wages diminished want, but did not reduce want to insignificance. The moral is that new measures to spread prosperity are needed. . . .

PLANNING FOR PEACE IN WAR

455. There are some to whom pursuit of security appears to be a wrong aim. They think of security as something inconsistent with initiative, adventure, personal responsibility. That is not a just view of social security as planned in this Report. The plan is not one for giving to everybody something for nothing and without trouble, or something that will free the recipients for ever thereafter from personal responsibilities. The plan is one to secure income for subsistence on condition of service and contribution and in order to make and keep men fit for service. It cannot be got without thought and effort. It can be carried through only by a concentrated determination of the British democracy to free itself once for all of the scandal of physical want for which there is no economic or moral justification. When that effort has been made, the plan leaves room and encouragement to all individuals to win for themselves something above the national minimum, to find and to satisfy and to produce the means of satisfying new and higher needs than bare physical needs.

9.2.2 The Prime Minister's Broadcast, 1943

The Beveridge Report stimulated great public interest and enthusiasm, but was more coolly received in government circles. There was indignation at the delay in making a government pronouncement on the report, and on the coolness of the statement that was made in the Commons in February 1943, which led to a revolt among Labour MPs. Churchill therefore made this broadcast in March. In November Lord Woolton, who had been Minister of Food since 1940, was appointed Minister of Reconstruction, and plans began to be prepared.

From the Broadcast by the Prime Minister on the War and Future Social Policy, 21 March 1943

A good many people were so much impressed by the favourable turn in our fortunes which has marked the last six months that they have jumped to the conclusion that the war will soon be over and that we shall soon all be able to get back to the politics and party fights of peacetime. I am not able to share these sanguine hopes. . . .

We must beware of attempts to over-persuade or coerce H.M. Government to bind themselves or their unknown successors, in conditions which no one can foresee and which may be years ahead, to impose great new expenditure on the State without any relation to the circumstances which might prevail at that time. . . .

I am resolved not to give or to make all kinds of promises and tell all kinds of fairy tales to you who have trusted me and gone with me so far and marched through the valley of the shadow. . . .

However, it is our duty to peer through the mists of the future to the end of the war, and to try our utmost to be prepared by ceaseless effort, and forethought for the kind of situations which are likely to occur. . . .

We shall have to consider . . . how the inhabitants of this island are going to get their living at this stage in the world story, and how they are going to maintain and progressively improve their previous standards of life and labour. I am very much attracted to the idea that we should make and proclaim what might be called a Four Years' Plan. . . .

I personally am very keen that a scheme for the amalgamation and extension of our present incomparable insurance system should have a leading place in our Four Years' Plan. I have been prominently connected with all these schemes of national compulsory organised thrift from the time when I brought my friend Sir William Beveridge into the public service thirty-five years ago when I was creating the labour exchanges, on which he was a great authority, and when, with Sir Hubert Llewellyn Smith, I framed the first unemployment insurance scheme. The prime parent of all national insurance schemes is Mr Lloyd George. I was his lieutenant in those distant days, and afterwards it fell to me, as Chancellor of the Exchequer eighteen years ago, to lower the pensions age to sixty-five and to bring in the widows and orphans. The time is now ripe for another great advance, and anyone can see what large savings there will be in the administration once the whole process of insurance has become unified, compulsory and national. Here is a real opportunity for what I once called 'bringing the magic of averages to the rescue of the millions'. Therefore, you must rank me and my colleagues as strong partisans of national compulsory insurance for all classes for all purposes from the cradle to the grave. . . .

Next there is the spacious domain of public health. . . . We must establish on broad and solid foundations a National Health Service. Here let me say that there is no finer investment for any community than putting milk into babies. Healthy citizens are the greatest asset any country can have. . . . If this country is to keep its high place in the leadership of the world and to survive as a Great Power . . . our people must be encouraged by every means to have larger families. . . .

Following upon health and welfare is the question of education. The future of the world is to the highly educated races who alone can handle the scientific apparatus necessary for pre-eminence in peace or survival in war. I hope our education will become broader and more liberal. . . . No one who can take advantage of a higher education should be denied his chance. You cannot conduct a modern community except with an adequate supply of persons upon whose education . . . much time and money have been spent. . . .

We must make sure that the path to the higher functions throughout our society and Empire is really open to the children of every family. . . . All cannot reach the same level, but all must have their chance. I look forward to a Britain so big that she will need to draw her leaders from every type of school and wearing every kind of tie. . . .

I end where I began. Let us get back to our job. I must warn everyone who hears me of a certain, shall I say, unseemliness and also a danger of it appearing to the world that we here in Britain are diverting our attention to peace, which is still remote, and to the fruits of victory, which have yet to be won, while our Russian Allies are fighting for dear life . . . and while our thoughts should be with our armies and with our American and French comrades now engaged in decisive battle in Tunisia.

9.2.3 The 'White Paper Chase', 1944

Beveridge complained of the government's silence about his report, which was eventually followed in 1944, however, by a series of official policy statements on a national health service, employment policy and social insurance which he called 'the White Paper chase'.

From the White Paper on a National Health Service

INTRODUCTORY

The Government have announced that they intend to establish a comprehensive health service for everybody in this country. They want to ensure that in future every man and woman and child can rely on getting all the advice and treatment and care which they may need in matters of personal health; that what they get shall be the best medical and other facilities available; that their getting these shall not depend on whether they can pay for them, or on any other factor irrelevant to the real need – the real need being to bring the country's full resources to bear upon reducing ill-health and promoting good health in all its citizens. . . .

THE PRESENT SITUATION

The record of this country in its health and medical services is a good one. The resistance of people to the wear and tear of four years of a second world war bears testimony to it. Achievements before the war – in lower mortality rates, in the gradual decline of many of the more serious diseases, in safer motherhood and healthier childhood, and generally in the prospect of a longer and healthier life – all substantiate it. There is no question of having to abandon bad services and to start afresh. Reform in this field is not a matter of making good what is bad, but of making better what is good already. . . .

The immediate question is how far the present arrangements are inadequate and what are the reasons for altering or adding to them.

The main reason for change is that the Government believe that, at this stage of social development, the care of personal health should be put on a new footing and be made available to everybody as a publicly sponsored service. Just as people are accustomed to look to public organisation for essential facilities like a clean and safe water supply or good highways, accepting these as things which the community combines to provide for the benefit of the individual without distinction of section or group, so they should now be able to look for proper facilities for the care of their personal health to a publicly organised service available to all who want to use it – a service for which all would be paying as taxpayers and ratepayers and contributors to some national scheme of social insurance.

From the White Paper on Employment Policy

FOREWORD

The Government accept as one of their primary aims and responsibilities the maintenance of a high and stable level of employment after the war. This Paper outlines the policy which they propose to follow in pursuit of that aim.

A country will not suffer from mass unemployment so long as the total demand for its goods and services is maintained at a high level. But in this country we are obliged to consider external no less than internal demand. The Government are therefore seeking to create, through collaboration between the nations, conditions of international trade which will make it possible for all countries to pursue policies of full employment to their mutual advantage. . . .

If by these means the necessary expansion of our external trade can be assured, the Government believe that widespread unemployment in this country can be prevented by a policy for maintaining total internal expenditure. . . .

Unlike other Papers on post-war problems which the Government have presented or are preparing, this is not primarily an outline of projected legislation. For employment cannot be created by Act of Parliament or by Government action alone. Government policy will be directed to bringing about conditions favourable to the maintenance of a high level of employment; and some legislation will be required to confer powers which are needed for that purpose. But the success of the policy outlined in this Paper will ultimately depend on the understanding and support of the community as a whole – and especially on the efforts of employers and workers in industry; for without a rising standard of industrial efficiency we cannot achieve a high level of employment combined with a rising standard of living.

From the White Paper on Social Insurance

PART I

. . . On the social insurance scheme itself the Government have reviewed the questions of policy which were raised by the [Beveridge] Report and on which the Government's views as originally announced were and could only be provisional. Much time and labour have also had to be devoted to working out and fitting

247

together the details of the scheme – and as this Paper ampl
illustrates, social insurance is essentially a mosaic of detail. In th
result the Government are now in a position to put forward thei
proposals for a new scheme of social insurance. . . .

The underlying principles

6. Before the war, social studies had made it plain that in its mor
extreme form poverty affected households of two kinds – those i
which the bread-winner was ill or out of work or past working ag
and those in which the number of children strained overmuch th
available resources of the household. The Government therefor
conclude that there must be both an increased rate of sickness an
unemployment benefit and retirement pension, and a system
family allowances which will contribute substantially to the mai
tenance of growing children. The cost of these family allowanc
will be met wholly from the proceeds of taxation; they are th
outside the bounds of the scheme of social insurance properly s
called. With that one exception, the Government have adhered
the principle that freedom from want must be achieved in the fir
instance by social insurance – that benefits must be earned b
contributions. This has long been one of the essential features
British social legislation, and the Government believe that
reflects the desires and the characteristics of our people. . . .

The widened scope of social insurance

8. The Government have also decided that the scope of soci
insurance should be extended in two different senses – the rang
and amount of benefits provided and the number of people in
cluded. All the existing types of benefit will be increased, in mo
instances substantially, and they will be extended to include dea
grant. The scheme as a whole will embrace, not certain occupatio
and income groups, but the entire population. Concrete expressio
is thus given to the solidarity and unity of the nation, which in w
have been its bulwarks against aggression and in peace will be
guarantees of success in the fight against individual want and mi
chance. . . .

13. Benefits must be paid for, and a high level of benefit mu
mean a high level of contribution. The Government therefo
conclude that the right objective is a rate of benefit which provid
a reasonable insurance against want and at the same time tak

account of the maximum contribution which the great body of contributors can properly be asked to bear. There still remains the individual's opportunity to achieve for himself in sickness, old age and other conditions of difficulty a standard of comfort and amenity which it is no part of a compulsory scheme of social insurance to provide. And in reserve there must remain a scheme of National Assistance designed to fill the inevitable gaps left by insurance and to supplement it where an examination of individual needs shows that supplement is necessary. . . .

Conclusion

186. In conclusion the Government wish to place on record their gratitude to Sir William Beveridge for the great work which he did in preparing his comprehensive and imaginative Report. Their main tribute is the embodiment of so much of his plan in the proposals set out in this White Paper – proposals which will, in their belief, afford an adequate basis of social insurance for many years to come.

10 The 'Welfare State' Arrives

10.1 THE FIRST LEGISLATION

10.1.1 Family Allowances, 1945

Beveridge had made family allowances one of the three assumptions of his report, and they were accepted by the coalition government, the necessary legislation being introduced in the government's last weeks and carried by Churchill's 'caretaker' government in the summer of 1945. By a free vote the Commons decided that the allowances should be paid to the mother.

The first payments were made in August 1946.

From the Family Allowances Act, 1945

1. Subject to the provisions of this Act, there shall be paid by the Minister, out of moneys provided by Parliament, for every family which includes two or more children and for the benefit of the family as a whole, an allowance in respect of each child in the family other than the elder or eldest at the rate of five shillings a week.

2. A person shall be treated for the purposes of this Act as a child –

(*a*) during any period whilst he or she is under the upper limit of the compulsory school age; and

(*b*) during any period before the first day of August next following the day on which he or she attains the age of sixteen years whilst he or she is undergoing full-time instruction in a school, or is an apprentice. . . .

4. (1) Allowances for any family shall belong –

(*a*) in the case of the family of a man and his wife living together, to the wife. . . .

(2) Sums to be paid on account of an allowance for the family of a man and his wife living together shall be receivable either by the man or by the wife.

10.1.2 A New Policy for Deprived Children, 1948

The concern for children that was stirred by the war, and the revelation of inadequate care by some local authorities of children in their charge, led to the appointment of a Care of Children Committee, from which came a Central Training Council in Child Care and, in 1948, a new Children Act, which made a fresh start by breaking away from the old poor law concept (now altogether abandoned) and making the local authority fully responsible for the welfare of deprived children, with special departments and officers to care for them. At the same time the importance to child development of family life, so much disregarded by the poor law, was recognised.

The contrast in approach is illustrated by the different demands of section 15(c) of the Poor Law Act of 1930 [1.1.1] and section 12(1) of the Act of 1948.

From the Children Act, 1948

PART I: DUTY OF LOCAL AUTHORITIES TO ASSUME CARE OF CHILDREN

1. (1) Where it appears to a local authority with respect to a child in their area appearing to them to be under the age of seventeen –

   (a) that he has neither parent nor guardian or has been and remains abandoned by his parents or guardian or is lost; or

   (b) that his parents or guardian are, for the time being or permanently, prevented by reason of mental or bodily disease or infirmity or other incapacity or any other circumstances from providing for his proper accommodation, maintenance and upbringing; and

   (c) in either case, that the intervention of the local authority under this section is necessary in the interests of the welfare of the child,

   it shall be the duty of the local authority to receive the child into their care under this section.

   (2) Where a local authority have received a child into their care under this section, it shall be their duty to keep the child in their care so long as the welfare of the child appears to them to require it and the child has not attained the age of eighteen.

   (3) Nothing in this section shall authorise a local authority to keep a child in their care under this section if any parent or guardian desires to take over the care of the child, and the local authority shall, in all cases where it appears to them consistent with the

welfare of the child so to do, endeavour to secure that the care of the child is taken over either –

(a) by a parent or guardian of his, or

(b) by a relative or friend of his, being, where possible, a person of the same religious persuasion as the child or who gives an undertaking that the child will be brought up in that religious persuasion. . . .

PART II: TREATMENT OF CHILDREN IN CARE OF LOCAL AUTHORITIES

12. (1) Where a child is in the care of a local authority, it shall be the duty of that authority to exercise their powers with respect to him so as to further his best interests, and to afford him opportunity for the proper development of his character and abilities. . . .

20. (2) A local authority may make grants to persons who have attained the age of eighteen, but have not attained the age of twenty-one and who immediately before they attained the age of eighteen were in the care of a local authority, to enable them to meet expenses connected with their receiving suitable education or training.

10.2 NATIONAL INSURANCE

10.2.1 Commons Debates, 1946

Attlee's Labour government passed a comprehensive National Insurance scheme in 1946 and it came into effect in 1948, apart from old age pensions, now restyled retirement pensions, which were increased immediately.

Beveridge's term, 'social insurance', had been discarded earlier, under Conservative pressure, and replaced by 'national insurance', which was to remain, though a Ministry of Social Security such as Beveridge had wanted was established in 1966 (and has since been absorbed into a Department of Health and Social Security).

James Griffiths was Minister of National Insurance from 1945 to 1950. R. A. (Lord) Butler, best known at this time as the minister responsible for the Education Act of 1944, expressed Conservative support for the measure.

From the House of Commons Debate, 6 February 1946

Mr Griffiths: I believe this bringing of everybody into the scheme is one of the greatest things we are doing in this great Bill. . . .

The step is, I think, a long overdue logical development of the existing scheme. . . .

I now come to the benefits provided in the Bill. . . .

Before I deal with the individual benefits, however, I would touch upon the general question of the leading rates provided in the Bill. I would answer the question put to me why the figure of 26s was chosen and where we got it from. In the discussion on the Beveridge Report . . . and on the White Paper in November 1944, there was a good deal of argument and controversy about the practicability of adopting what is called the subsistence basis for benefits. . . .

We have given the most careful consideration to this question, which is vital and fundamental to the scheme. We are definitely of the view that it is undesirable, as well as impracticable, to have automatic adjustment. This method of pegging benefits to a specific cost of living and adjusting them automatically was tried at the end of the last war in war pensions, and broke down the first time it came to be applied. We are convinced, after examination, that it will break down again. It is equally clear that no general level of benefit can possibly cover all the varied individual needs of every person who would come within the scheme. If I may say a word on the problem of rent . . . we have discovered that, in the case of pensioners who get supplementation, rents vary from 2s 6d to 20s a week. We therefore came to the conclusion that it is, in our view, impossible to have a general level that excludes some kind of supplementation to meet those three points.

Having said that, let me add, the Government feel very strongly indeed that, in order that the benefit and pension rates may be soundly based, they must satisfy two essential requirements. In the first place, the leading rates must be fixed initially at figures which can be justified broadly in relation to the present cost of living. Secondly, we believe that definite arrangements should be made for a review of the rates from this point of view at periodic intervals. It will be remembered that Sir William Beveridge, in order to arrive at the rates of benefit which he proposed, first estimated the cost of the requirements of various classes of persons in terms of 1938 prices. To these basic figures he added amounts sufficient to allow for a rise of rather more than 25 per cent in the cost of necessaries, including rent, and it was in this way that he arrived at the provisional rates of benefit and pension of 24s single and 40s joint. . . .

The House will be aware that the Chancellor of the Exchequer has expressed the Government's intention to hold the cost of living at about 31 per cent over the September, 1939, level. We decided, therefore, to review the leading rates proposed in the White Paper and in the Beveridge Report on the basis of an overall addition of 31 per cent instead of 25 per cent. The result was, to establish a basic rate of 42s for a couple living together, with 26s for a single adult, for unemployment, sickness, widows' pension and retirement pension, 16s for an adult dependant and 7s 6d as the child's allowance for the first child in any family, the others to be covered by family allowances. I believe that we have in this way, endeavoured to give a broad subsistence basis to the leading rates. Further, the Bill places a statutory duty upon the Minister to review every five years the rates of benefit payable under the scheme. . . . This provision imparts a new and valuable criterion into our scheme of national insurance. It is the beginning of the establishment of the principle of a National Minimum Standard.

From the House of Commons Debate, 30 May 1946
Mr R. A. Butler: I think we should take pride that the British race has been able, at this time in our history, shortly after the terrible period through which we have all passed together, to show the whole world that we are able to produce a social insurance scheme of this character. . . . We look forward not only to an all-in insurance scheme but to an all-in society, in which this Bill will be a feature, just as other Measures – educational, health and others – will take their place in a society in which, if differentiations are to go, ignorance must also go, the ignorance of one section of the community about the lives of the others. . . .

We have heard a great deal, since the early days of that great pioneer Sir William Beveridge, of those words 'social security'. . . . The word 'security' gives a rather negative impression. I should prefer to call it 'social certainty'. There should be, at the basis of everyone's life in this country, certainty about certain things, and, upon that certainty, people should be able to build a fuller and better life. I have never taken the view . . . that, because a person has certainty over some aspects of his life, he will necessarily sink back into a negative position, undertaking no creative work whatever. It is much wiser to put a basis into the lives of people, so that they may be enabled to have more time to devote to the creative things of life, and to help the country through the difficult times ahead.

10.2.2 The National Insurance Act

From the National Insurance Act, 1946

An Act to establish an extended system of national insurance providing pecuniary payments by way of unemployment benefit, sickness benefit, maternity benefit, retirement pension, widows' benefit, guardian's allowance and death grant, to repeal or amend the existing enactments relating to unemployment insurance, national health insurance, widows', orphans' and old age contributory pensions and non-contributory old age pensions, to provide for the making of payments towards the cost of a national health service.

PART I: INSURED PERSONS AND CONTRIBUTIONS

1. (1) Every person who on or after the appointed day, being over school leaving age and under pensionable age, is in Great Britain, and fulfils such conditions as may be prescribed as to residence in Great Britain, shall become insured under this Act and thereafter continue throughout his life to be so insured.

(2) For the purposes of this Act, insured persons shall be divided into the following three classes:

(*a*) employed persons, that is to say persons gainfully occupied in employment in Great Britain, being employment under a contract of service;

(*b*) self-employed persons, that is to say persons gainfully occupied in employment in Great Britain who are not employed persons;

(*c*) non-employed persons, that is to say persons who are not employed or self-employed persons. . . .

2. (1) For the purpose of providing the funds required for paying benefit . . . contributions shall be payable by insured persons, by employers and out of moneys provided by Parliament. . . .

3. (1) Where it appears to the Treasury expedient so to do with a view to maintaining a stable level of employment, they may by order direct that contributions, instead of being paid at the rates set out in the First Schedule to this Act, shall, for such periods as

may be specified . . . be paid at such higher or lower rates . . . as may be so specified or determined. . . .

PART II: BENEFIT
Preliminary

10. (1) Benefit shall be of the following descriptions:
   (*a*) unemployment benefit.
   (*b*) sickness benefit.
   (*c*) maternity benefit, which shall include maternity grant, attendance allowance and maternity allowance.
   (*d*) widow's benefit, which shall include widow's allowance, widowed mother's allowance and widow's pension.
   (*e*) guardian's allowance.
   (*f*) retirement pension.
   (*g*) death grant . . .

Retirement pensions

20. (1) A person shall be entitled to a retirement pension if
   (*a*) he is over pensionable age and has retired from regular employment; and
   (*b*) he satisfies the relevant contribution conditions. . . .

   (4) The weekly rate of a retirement pension shall be increased by one shilling for every twenty-five contributions as an employed or self-employed person paid by the beneficiary in respect of the period after his attaining pensionable age. . . .

21. A woman over pensionable age shall be entitled to a retirement pension by virtue of the insurance of her husband.

Death grant

22. (1) A person shall be entitled to a death grant in respect of the death of any person if
   (*a*) he has reasonably incurred or reasonably intends to incur, in connection with the deceased's death, expenses to which this section applies.
   (*b*) the deceased either himself satisfied the relevant contribution conditions, or was at death the husband, wife, widower, widow, or a child of the family, of a person satisfying the said conditions. . . .

   (6) Not more than one person shall be entitled to a death grant in respect of the same death. . . .

Additional rights to benefit

23. The weekly rate of unemployment benefit, sickness benefit, a retirement pension or a widow's allowance shall, for any period for which the beneficiary has a family which includes a child or children, be increased in respect of that child or the elder or eldest of those children by the amount set out in the third column of Part I of the Second Schedule to this Act. . . .

24. The weekly rate of unemployment benefit, sickness benefit or a retirement pension shall be increased by the amount set out in the fourth column of Part I of the Second Schedule to this Act for any period during which the beneficiary is residing with or is wholly or mainly maintaining his wife who is not engaged in any gainful occupation or occupations from which her weekly earnings exceed twenty shillings.

10.3 NATIONAL HEALTH

10.3.1 Public Health During the War

The section on Food and Nutrition in this survey of the war years reported evidence still noticeable of past shortages due to earlier long-term unemployment.

From On the State of the Public Health During Six Years of War, *Report of the Chief Medical Officer of the Ministry of Health, 1939–45 (Sir Wilson Jameson)*

INTRODUCTION

This is the 21st report of a Chief Medical Officer of the Ministry of Health. It is no ordinary Annual Report covering a single year of peace. Its pages tell of the state of the public health . . . during the trials, the mercies, the efforts and the final triumphs of six years of the grimmest struggle Britain has endured since the Conquest. . . . That, after these six years of unprecedented strain alike upon the nation and upon the medical resources of the realm, the state of the public health should be as good as it is today is indeed a miracle. . . .

Vital statistics. The vital statistics during the war period . . . have been phenomenally good. The birth rate, rising from 1941 onwards, reached 17·7 in 1944, the highest it has been since 1926. . . .
An outstanding feature has been the low mortality of children from disease. . . . .

Considerable reductions in infant mortality rates occurred in many large towns between 1938 and 1944, examples being Liverpool from 74 to 58, Nottingham 71 to 57, Manchester 69 to 54, Newcastle-on-Tyne 66 to 51, Birmingham 61 to 42, Sheffield 50 to 42, Greater London 50 to 43 and Bristol 42 to 35. The rates of 23 in 1939 and 25 in 1944 recorded by Oxford demonstrate how great are the possibilities of further improvement. . . .

New low records of both cases and deaths from diphtheria have been established in each successive year since the immunisation campaign started in 1941. In 1944 diphtheria deaths were less than one-third of the pre-war average, and the number of cases notified 30,000 below the pre-war average and 6,000 lower than the previous low record. Nevertheless it is a sad reflection that in this country during the war far more children under 15 were killed by this preventable disease than by enemy bombs. . . .

GENERAL EPIDEMIOLOGY
The future of public vaccination

The machinery of public vaccination built up by the Vaccination Acts was suitable to the times and for its enlarging purpose, but in the opinion of many who administer the Acts it is now cumbersome and out of date . . . it is reasonable to consider whether vaccination against smallpox should be brought administratively into line with immunisation against diphtheria by the participation of all medical practitioners in the work of public vaccination. . . .

Since 1898, when the Vaccination Act of that date enacted that exemption of a child from vaccination could be claimed by the parent or guardian on the ground of conscientious objection, the annual numbers of infant vaccinations have decreased except at times of the prevalence of smallpox. . . . For some time before 1939 the enforcement of the Vaccination Acts against those parents or guardians who did not comply with the law had been falling into abeyance, and in the war years it has been abandoned. Compulsion is now a dead letter. . . .

MATERNITY AND CHILD WELFARE
Nutrition

To safeguard the nutrition of expectant mothers and young children a National Milk Scheme was introduced in 1940 by the Ministry of Food in consultation with the Ministry of Health to supply liquid milk, free or at a reduced price, to expectant mothers and children under five, who were entitled to receive one pint daily, or, in the case of infants under one year, its equivalent in dried milk. During the winter months the supply was secured by restricting the allowance of milk to the general public. In April, 1941, arrangements were made to supply a half cream as well as a full cream dried milk under the National Scheme.

The Ministry of Food, in consultation with this Department, also introduced a scheme for supplying cod liver oil and fruit juices sufficient to meet the needs of all children under two, so far as vitamins A, D and C were concerned. . . .

During the winter of 1941–2 an allocation of four eggs was made for expectant and nursing mothers and children under five, against one to the ordinary consumer, and oranges were reserved for children under six years of age. Many welfare authorities also provided meals for necessitous expectant mothers in recognised communal centres. . . .

The take-up of the vitamin supplements was, however, very disappointing in spite of all the efforts to make mothers realise the importance of obtaining these supplements for themselves and for their children. The average percentage take-up in England for fruit juices has not exceeded 45·7 per cent . . . for cod liver oil the corresponding figure is only 21 per cent; and for vitamin A and D tablets, 34·3 per cent. . . .

The national provision of milk and vitamin supplements to the priority groups has probably done more than any other single factor to promote the health of expectant mothers and young children during the war, and this scheme, together with rationing and the greatly improved nutritional qualities of the national loaf has contributed to the gradual decline in the maternal, neonatal and infant mortality and stillbirth rates, so noteworthy in the last five years. The scheme has resulted in the consumption of more milk per head by these priority groups to whom milk is of vital importance particularly those 'under-privileged classes' who, before the war, could not afford enough milk. . . .

FOOD AND NUTRITION
Assessment

In order to be able to advise on matters of nutritional policy it was necessary for the Ministry of Health to keep a continuous watch on the nutritional state of the people. . . .

Clinical surveys. – In 1942 Professor Sydenstricker of the U.S.A. was sent to the Ministry by the Rockefeller Foundation, and was employed in making a rapid clinical examination of some five thousand persons in different parts of the country. He had a large experience of deficiency diseases in the southern states of America and was particularly well qualified for work of this kind, which was outside the experience of most doctors in this country. Later he was succeeded by Drs Stannus and Hawes, both with long colonial experience of deficiency diseases, and later by Drs Adcock and Fitzgerald, also of the Colonial Service.

With the co-operation of medical officers of health they were able to examine many hundreds of persons a week, and to look for those clinical signs which were thought to indicate a deficiency of some particular nutrient. Their findings were unexpectedly satisfactory, for even although they paid most attention to poor areas they found surprisingly little evidence of under-nourishment or malnutrition which could not be attributed to past shortages. In districts which before the war had been subject to long periods of unemployment, many of the adults and adolescents, and particularly the women, showed that they had suffered severely, but only occasionally could evidence of a present deficiency be found.

10.3.2 The National Health Service

Aneurin Bevan, Minister of Health from 1945 to 1951, introduced the National Health Service Bill in 1946, and it came into effect, with the National Insurance Act, in 1948, though only after a fierce contest with the doctors, reminiscent of Lloyd George's experience some thirty-five years earlier. Bevan hints at the difficulties at some points of his speech.

The health centres referred to are, of course, only now becoming general.

From the House of Commons Debate, 30 April 1946
The Minister of Health (Mr Aneurin Bevan): In the last two years there has been such a clamour from sectional interests in the field of national health that we are in danger of forgetting why these proposals are brought forward. . . . The first reason why a health scheme of this sort is necessary at all is because it has been the firm conclusion of all parties that money ought not to be permitted to stand in the way of obtaining an efficient health service. Although it is true that the national health insurance system provides a

general practitioner service and caters for something like 21 million of the population, the rest of the population have to pay whenever they desire the services of a doctor . . . and therefore tend to postpone consultation as long as possible (while) there is the financial anxiety caused by having to pay doctors' bills. . . . In the second place, the national health insurance scheme does not provide for the self-employed, nor, of course, for the families of dependants. . . . Furthermore, it gives no backing to the doctor in the form of specialist services. . . . Our hospital organisation has grown up with no plan, with no system; it is unevenly distributed over the country and indeed it is one of the tragedies of the situation that very often the best hospital facilities are available where they are least needed. . . . One of the first merits of this Bill is that it provides a universal health service without any insurance qualifications of any sort. It is available to the whole population and . . . it is intended that there shall be no limitation on the kind of assistance given – the general practitioner service, the specialist, the hospitals, eye treatment, spectacles, dental treatment, hearing facilities, all these are to be made available free. There will be some limitation for a while, because we are short of many things . . . so it will be some time before the Bill can fructify fully in effective universal service. . . . There are, of course, three main instruments through which it is intended that the Health Bill should be worked. There are the hospitals; there are the general practitioners; and there are the health centres. . . . The voluntary hospitals of Great Britain have done invaluable work. When hospitals could not be provided by any other means they came along. . . . But they have been established often by the caprice of private charity. They bear no relationship to each other [and] are, very many of them, far too small, and therefore to leave them as independent units is quite impracticable.

Furthermore . . . I believe it is repugnant to a civilised community for hospitals to have to rely upon private charity. I believe we ought to have left hospital flag days behind. . . . I have been forming some estimates of what might happen to voluntary hospital finance when the all-in insurance contributions fall to be paid by the people of Great Britain. . . . The estimates I have got show that between 80 and 90 per cent of the revenues of the voluntary hospitals . . . will be provided by public funds. . . . Of course, in many parts of the country it is a travesty to call them voluntary hospitals. In the mining districts, in the textile districts, in the districts where there are heavy industries, it is the industrial population who pay the weekly contributions for the maintenance of the hospitals. When I was a miner ... I was on the hospital committee ... and when I looked at the balance-sheet, I saw that 97 per cent of the revenues were provided by the miners' own contributions. ...

It is an impossible situation for the State to find something like 90 per cent of the revenues of these hospitals and still to call them voluntary. So I decided, for this and other reasons, that the voluntary hospitals must be taken over. ...

When I considered what to do with the voluntary hospitals ... I had to reject the local government unit ... because the local authorities are too small, because their financial capacities are unevenly distributed. ... I decided that the only thing to do was to create an entirely new hospital service, to take over the voluntary hospitals, and to take over the local government hospitals, and to organise them as a single hospital service. ... A number of investigations have been made ... from time to time, and the conclusion has always been reached that the effective hospital unit should be associated with the medical school. If you grouped the hospitals in about 10 to 20 regions around the medical schools, you would then have within those regions the wide range of disease and disability which would provide the basis for your specialised hospital service. Furthermore, we should be providing what is very badly wanted, and that is a means by which the general practitioners are kept in more intimate association with new medical thought and training. ... When we come to the general practitioners ... the proposal which I have made is that [they] shall not be in direct contract with the Ministry of Health, but in contract with new bodies. There exists in the medical profession a great resistance to coming under the authority of local government. ... This proposal ... puts the doctor in contract with an entirely new body, the local executive council, on [which] the dentists, doctors and chemists will have half the representation. In fact, the whole scheme provides a greater degree of professional representation for the medical profession than any other scheme I have seen. ... One of the advantages of that proposal is that the doctors do not become – as some of them have so wildly stated – civil servants.

One of the chief problems that I was up against in considering this scheme was the distribution of the general practitioner service throughout the country. The distribution at the moment is most uneven. In South Shields before the war there were 4,100 persons per doctor; in Bath 1,590. . . . If the health services are to be carried out, there must be brought about a re-distribution of the general practitioners throughout the country. . . . One of the first consequences of that decision was the abolition of the sale and purchase of practices . . . it would, I think, be inhuman, and certainly most unjust, if no compensation were paid for the value of the practices destroyed. The sum of £66,000,000 is very large. In fact, I think that everyone will admit that the doctors are being treated very generously. . . .

I cannot at the moment explain to the House what are going to be the rates of remuneration of doctors. . . . Some of my hon. Friends on this side of the House are in favour of a full salaried service. I am not. I do not believe that the medical profession is ripe for it, and I cannot dispense with the principle that the payment of a doctor must in some degree be a reward for zeal. . . . Therefore it is proposed that capitation should remain the main source . . . but it is proposed that there shall be a basic salary . . . a young doctor entering practice for the first time needs to be kept alive while he is building up his lists. . . . I have also made a concession which I know will be repugnant in some quarters. The doctor, the general practitioner, and the specialist, will be able to obtain fees, but not from anyone who is on any of their own lists. . . . I think it is impracticable to prevent him having any fees at all. To do so would be to create a black market. . . . The same principle applies to the hospitals. Specialists in hospitals will be allowed to have fee-paying patients . . . unless we permit some fee-paying patients in the public hospitals there will be a rash of nursing homes all over the country. If people wish to pay for additional amenities . . . like privacy in a single ward, we ought to aim at providing such facilities . . . but while we have inadequate hospital facilities, and while rebuilding is postponed, it inevitably happens that some people will want to buy something more than the general health service is providing. If we do not permit fees in hospitals, we will lose many specialists . . . for they will go to nursing homes. . . .

The third instrument to which the health services are to be articulated is the health centre, to which we attach very great importance indeed. The general practitioner cannot afford the apparatus necessary for a proper diagnosis in his own surgery. This will be available at the health centre. The health centre may well be the maternity and child welfare clinic of the local authority also. The provision of the health centre is, therefore, imposed as a duty on the local authority. . . .

There you have the three main instruments through which it is proposed that the health services of the future should be articulated. . . . Some have said that the preventive services should be under the same authority as the curative services. . . . What are the preventive services? Housing, water, sewage, river pollution prevention, food inspection – are all these to be under a regional board? If so, a regional board of that sort would want the Albert Hall in which to meet. This is paper planning. It is unification for unification's sake.

10.4 NATIONAL ASSISTANCE

10.4.1 The Commons Debates, 1947–8

It fell to Bevan also to launch the National Assistance scheme which at last replaced the poor law and was happily less controversial than the National Health Service. The hope expressed by Tom Steele, Parliamentary Secretary to the Ministry of Labour, in moving the third reading of the Bill, that National Assistance would eventually have little to do has been belied by events.

From the House of Commons Debate, 24 November 1947

The Minister of Health (Mr Aneurin Bevan): I am presenting to the House of Commons the last of the Measures which the Government have adopted for the expansion of the social services of this country. The House will be aware that in the last few years a number of substantial steps have been taken in transforming and enlarging the social services. . . . However, there will still remain . . . 400,000 persons on outdoor relief, and 50,000 in institutions. There thus remain, after we have bitten into the main body of the Poor Law, these residual categories which have to be provided for. . . .

The Government approach the problem from the angle that they wish to see the whole residual problem in two special categories. They wish to consider assistance by way of monetary help made a national responsibility and welfare a local responsibility. Where the individual is immediately concerned, where warmth and humanity of administration is the primary consideration, then the authority which is responsible should be as near to the recipient as possible. Therefore, it is proposed that we shall transfer to the Assistance Board, to be renamed the National Assistance Board, the responsibility for providing the financial help which will still be needed. . . . .

There are a number of persons for whom special provision will have to be made. There are, for example, the blind. Their welfare will be the responsibility of the principal local welfare authorities. . . .

We propose to place upon the Assistance Board the duty of providing maintenance of the blind and upon the local authorities a duty to make special schemes for their training and welfare. . . .

The National Assistance Board will provide its assistance on the basis of a determination of needs. . . . I have spent many years of my life in fighting the means test. Now we have practically ended it. In the future only the resources of the man and dependent children – that is, children under 16 years of age – will be taken into account in determining their need. Where there are other members of the household, they will be regarded as making some contribution towards the payment of rent, as at present. . . .

There is another category of persons for whom we shall have to accept an even larger measure of responsibility than we have had in the past, and these are old persons. By 1970, old persons – that is, persons reaching pensionable age – will be one in five of the total population. It is a staggering figure; indeed, it can be said that, in some respects, the proper care and welfare of the aged is the peculiar problem of modern society. We have, of course, gone a long way towards it by making provision for increased old age pensions. . . .

The Nuffield Foundation Survey reports that 95 per cent of old people live independent lives in their own homes or the homes of their children, but it does not always follow that old folk want to live in the homes of their children. . . .

Therefore, we have decided to make a great departure in the treatment of old people. The workhouse is to go. Although many people have tried to humanise it, it was in many respects a very evil institution. We have determined that the right way to approach this problem is to give the welfare authorities, as we shall now describe them, the power to establish special homes.

From the House of Commons Debate, 5 March 1948

The Parliamentary Secretary to the Ministry of National Insurance (Mr Steele): We hope that this Debate today will conclude consideration by this House of a Measure which is itself the culmination of a series of Measures of social legislation. . . .

The broad effect of these Measures is greatly to extend provision through insurance against the ordinary emergencies of life, and greatly to narrow the field in which needs not otherwise provided for will arise. But there will always remain the need for a residuary service against want. . . . For many years, too, we shall have with us those who cannot benefit from the new insurance provisions. This need is met by the National Assistance scheme. . . .

When the new regulations have been approved, the Board will have to review, in the light of their provisions, the allowances at present being paid by way of supplementary pensions and unemployment assistance. In addition, they must make arrangements with local authorities for putting national assistance into payment at 5 July 1948, to about a quarter of a million households which are now being maintained by outdoor relief, blind domiciliary assistance, or tuberculosis treatment allowances. . . .

Lastly the Board must be ready to deal with the applications which will, no doubt, be received from persons who are struggling hard to make both ends meet, but who at present refuse to apply for outdoor relief for the various reasons which formerly influenced the million old age pensioners who refused to apply for outdoor relief, although they readily applied for supplementary pensions from the Board. I think it would be inappropriate to wish the National Assistance Board an active future. Our hope is that the extensions of insurance, and eventually a rising level of prosperity for all, will in the long run leave it with little to do.

10.4.2 The End of the Poor Law, 1948

Section 1 of the National Assistance Act formally brought the poor law to an end after three and a half centuries. The provisions of the Act of 1601, some of which had been restated as recently as 1930, may be compared with sections 4, 16, 17, 21, 29 and 42.

From the National Assistance Act, 1948: An Act to Terminate the Existing Poor Law and to Provide in lieu Thereof for the Assistance of Persons in Need by the National Assistance Board and by Local Authorities

PART I: INTRODUCTORY

1. The existing poor law shall cease to have effect, and shall be replaced by the provisions of Part II of this Act as to the rendering, out of moneys provided by Parliament, of assistance to persons in need, the provisions of Part III of this Act as to accommodation and other services to be provided by local authorities, and the related provisions of Part IV of this Act.

PART II: NATIONAL ASSISTANCE
The National Assistance Board

2. (1) The Assistance Board shall be known as the National Assistance Board. . . .

(2) The National Assistance Board shall exercise their functions in such manner as shall best promote the welfare of persons affected by the exercise thereof.

(3) For the purpose of securing the prompt discharge of their functions under this Act, the Board shall by regulations provide for the local administration of their said functions, and in particular, for the discharge by local officers of the Board of the functions of the Board in relation to applications for assistance and the decision of all questions arising thereon. . . .

3. For the purpose of securing that full use is made of the advice and assistance, both on general questions and on difficult individual cases, of persons having local knowledge and experience in matters affecting the functions of the Board, the Board shall arrange for the establishment of advisory committees throughout Great Britain. . . .

Giving of assistance by board

4. It shall be the duty of the Board in accordance with the following provisions of this Part of this Act to assist persons in Great Britain who are without resources to meet their requirements, or whose resources (including benefits receivable under the National Insurance Acts, 1946) must be supplemented in order to meet their requirements.

5. The question whether a person is in need of assistance, and the

nature and extent of any assistance to be given to him, shall be decided by the Board. . . .

Re-establishment centres and reception centres

16. For the re-establishment of persons in need thereof through lack of regular occupation or of instruction or training the Board may provide centres, to be known as re-establishment centres, where . . . such persons may attend or may be maintained by the Board, and in either case may be afforded by the Board the occupation, instruction or training requisite to fit them for entry into or return to regular employment.

17. (1) It shall be the duty of the Board to make provision whereby persons without a settled way of living may be influenced to lead a more settled life, and the Board shall provide and maintain centres, to be known as reception centres, for the provision of temporary board and lodging for such persons. . . .

PART III: LOCAL AUTHORITY SERVICES
Provision of accommodation

21. (1) It shall be the duty of every local authority to provide –
  (a) residential accommodation for persons who by reason of age, infirmity or any other circumstances are in need of care and attention which is not otherwise available to them;
  (b) temporary accommodation for persons who are in urgent need thereof, being need arising in circumstances which could not reasonably have been foreseen or in such other circumstances as the authority may in any particular case determine.

2. In the exercise of their said duty a local authority shall have regard to the welfare of all persons for whom accommodation is provided, and in particular to the need for providing accommodation of different descriptions suited to different descriptions of such persons as are mentioned in the last subsection. . . .

Welfare services

29. A local authority shall have power to make arrangements for promoting the welfare of persons to whom this section applies, that is to say persons who are blind, deaf or dumb, and other persons who are substantially and permanently handicapped by illness, injury, or congenital deformity or such other disabilities as may be prescribed by the Minister. . . .

Recovery of expenses

42. (1) For the purposes of this Act –

   (*a*) a man shall be liable to maintain his wife and his children, and

   (*b*) a woman shall be liable to maintain her husband and her children.

10.4.3 National Assistance Board Statistics

The report of the Assistance Board for 1947 recorded the practice of sending congratulations to pensioners who were 100 or more. There were fifty-four of these in 1947, twenty-four of them over 100 and one actually 105. The report commented that 'staff at the Board's local offices take a lively personal interest in these anniversaries'.

(This agreeable practice, it is understood, is still – 1972 – continued, and the successors to the Assistance Board staff also, where necessary, send information to Buckingham Palace for the Queen's telegrams.)

From the Annual Report of the National Assistance Board, 1949

Numbers on Assistance
(in round figures)

Group	1948 On Public Assistance	1948 On Assistance Board	1949 On NAB
Separated wives:	14,500	1,300	34,000
Unmarried mothers:	4,000	300	9,000

The report noted that the rise in numbers when the NAB took over from the Assistance Board and the Public Assistance committees of the local authorities probably represented earlier reluctance to go to the Relieving Officer.

In all, the NAB made in 1949 1,150,000 weekly allowances. The report added that this number represented only half the proportion of the population on out-relief in the 1840s, though a larger proportion than in 1900.

11 New Practice and New Concepts

11.1 THE NATIONAL HEALTH SERVICE

11.1.1 The Cost of the National Health Service, 1956

Bevan had been shocked at the cost of the NHS, which by 1950 was already twice that of the necessarily speculative estimate of 1946, and shuddered to think of the 'cascade of medicine' pouring down British throats. He resigned from Attlee's government in 1951, however, over a proposal to introduce charges, and took with him two other notable ministers, John Freeman and Harold Wilson.

The Conservative government of Churchill that followed the 1951 election introduced prescription charges, and in 1953 appointed a committee under the economist C. W. Guillebaud, to consider how costs could be kept down without detriment to the service. Contrary to many expectations, the Guillebaud report, when it appeared in 1956, cleared the NHS of charges of extravagance, and showed indeed that the proportion of the national product spent on it had actually declined. The committee argued, in fact, that more needed to be spent, especially on hospitals. Two-thirds of the country's hospitals, it is true, dated from the nineteenth century, nearly half of them from before 1891 and one-fifth from before 1861, but it was not until 1962 that a substantial building programme was launched, and by that time Britain was seriously lagging behind other countries with a national health service.

From the Report of the Committee of Enquiry into the Cost of the National Health Service (the Guillebaud Report), 1956, pp. 49–50, 268–9

THE GENERAL STRUCTURE OF THE NATIONAL HEALTH SERVICE
Our remaining terms of reference are 'to suggest means, whether by modifications in organisation or otherwise, of ensuring the most effective control and efficient use of such Exchequer funds as may be made available; to advise how, in view of the burdens on the

Exchequer, a rising charge upon it can be avoided while providing for the maintenance of an adequate Service; and to make recommendations'.

An 'Adequate Service'

Before we can deal with the many questions implied in these terms of reference, we must consider at the outset what is meant by the provision of an 'adequate service'.

If the test of 'adequacy' were that the Service should be able to meet every demand which is justifiable on medical grounds, then the Service is clearly inadequate now, and very considerable additional expenditure (both capital and current) would be required to make it so. . . .

But even if it were possible, which we very much doubt, to attach a specific meaning to the term 'an adequate service' at a given moment of time, it does not follow that it would remain so for long with merely normal replacement. There is no stability in the concept itself: what might have been held to be adequate twenty years ago would no longer be so regarded today, while today's standards will in turn become out of date in the future. The advance of medical knowledge continually places new demands on the Service, and the standards expected by the public also continue to rise.

We conclude that in the absence of an objective and attainable standard of adequacy the aim must be, as in the field of education, to provide the best service possible within the limits of the available resources. . . .

Our Final Comment

Having concluded that in practice there is no objective and attainable standard of 'adequacy' in the health field, and that no major change is needed in the general administrative structure of the National Health Service, we have sought to ascertain where, if anywhere, there is opportunity for effecting substantial savings in expenditure, or for attracting new sources of income, within the existing structure of the Service; but we have found no opportunity for making recommendations which would either produce new sources of income or reduce in a substantial degree the annual cost of the Service. In some instances – and particularly with regard to the level of hospital capital expenditure – we have found it necessary, in the interests of the future efficiency of the Service, to make recommendations which will tend to increase the future cost. ...

There are defects in the present organisation and administration of the National Health Service to which we have drawn attention throughout our Report; but these weaknesses apart, we have reached the conclusion that the Service's record of performance since the Appointed Day has been one of real achievement. The rising cost of the Service in real terms during the years 1948–54 was kept within narrow bounds; while many of the services provided were substantially expanded and improved during the period. Any charge that there has been widespread extravagance in the National Health Service, whether in respect of the spending of money or the use of manpower, is not borne out by our evidence.

11.1.2 The Finances of the National Health Service, 1970

The cost and sources of the finance of the NHS are here analysed in roughly round figures. The Service is mainly financed from taxation, but from the first a contribution, explicitly described since 1957 as the NHS contribution, has been levied on insured persons through their National Insurance payments. The individual weekly levy has been increased by stages, but owing to the increasing cost of the service the proportion of the total cost met by this NHS contribution, though it has fluctuated, has averaged about ten per cent.

From the Annual Report of the Department of Health and Social Security, 1970, pp. 5, 152–3

THE FINANCE OF THE HEALTH AND WELFARE SERVICES

Total Cost	*£ million* *(round figures)*	*percentage* *of total*
Central administration	$9\frac{1}{2}$	$\frac{1}{2}$
Hospital services – current	843	51
– capital	$106\frac{1}{2}$	$6\frac{1}{2}$
Executive Councils' administration	$10\frac{1}{2}$	$\frac{3}{4}$
General medical services	121	$7\frac{1}{4}$
Pharmaceutical services	$162\frac{1}{2}$	$9\frac{3}{4}$
General dental services	78	$4\frac{3}{4}$
General ophthalmic services	$23\frac{1}{2}$	$1\frac{1}{2}$

Total Cost	£ million (round figures)	percentage of total
Welfare foods	33½	2
Local Health Authority services	152	9¼
Local welfare services	92	5½
Others	19	1¼
Total	1,651	

Sources of Finance		
Treasury (excluding grants to Local Authorities)	1,200	72¾
NHS contributions	152	9¼
Payments by persons using the service	83	5
Rates and grants to Local Authorities	212	12¾
Other income	4	¼
Total	1,651	

11.2 THE END OF BEVERIDGE

11.2.1 Sharing Prosperity, 1959

The Ministry of Pensions, created in 1916 to deal with war pensions, was combined with National Insurance in 1953. John Boyd-Carpenter was appointed to the joint Ministry in 1955, and remained there until made Paymaster-General in Macmillan's famous reshuffle in 1962.

The increase of scale rates which Boyd-Carpenter announced in 1959 marked a new and significant turn in policy. Hitherto rates had been based, according to Beveridge's principles, on what he called in his report 'subsistence needs'. They had risen with the cost of living, but were now to be raised higher so that recipients of Assistance could have some share in the country's increasing prosperity.

Many had lived below subsistence levels before the war. Beveridge had insisted on such levels for all, but now something more was to be added: the Beveridge period had ended.

From the House of Commons Debate, 24 June 1959 (1)
The Minister of Pensions and National Insurance (Mr John Boyd-Carpenter): . . . The proposal to increase the scale rates is, unlike

273

that on any previous occasion, not the result of, or necessitated by, changes in the cost of living. On the contrary, it embodies a proposal by the Government to raise the actual standards of Assistance and, therefore, to improve the standards of life of the recipients of Assistance. . . .

It is, and I would stress this, the stability of prices, in part at any rate, which offers us the opportunity to take this step and make this advance in standards. It is, plainly, difficult to make a deliberate advance in standards at a time when one is competing with rising prices and when, particularly in view of the fact that National Assistance is, as it has often been called, the long-stop of the social services, it is necessary to move its scales to compete with price changes.

When, however, we have achieved, as we have over recent months and particularly over the recent year, a considerable measure of stability, it then becomes much more practicable to make an advance in standards. It is also, as the House will appreciate, a great deal easier for my right hon. Friend the Chancellor of the Exchequer to face the substantial increase in expenditure which is involved for this purpose at a time when the national economy is strong and resilient. . . .

It is possible to appreciate the extent of the improvement in standards if one compares the results which will be achieved, if the House approves the proposals, with the change in prices since the scales were first fixed in 1948. The Index of Retail Prices has moved over that period by 55 per cent, but if the House approves the proposals, the scale for the single householder will be, in cash terms, 108 per cent above the July, 1948 level; for a married couple it will be 113 per cent; and for a child between the ages of 11 and 15 it will be 119 per cent. Another possibly useful comparison is with the change in earnings over the period. Taking the nearest dates that are available, earnings between April, 1948, and October, 1958 have risen on the average by about 90 per cent. These Assistance proposals will, as I have already indicated, carry the various National Assistance scales to levels in excess of 100 per cent. . . .

It is often the case that when we are discussing National Assistance scales, only the scale rates are given, but for a realistic appreciation of what they are worth, what they mean for those who have to live on them, it is necessary to remember that to the scales are added, in the majority of straightforward cases, the actual rents and rates paid.

The latest figure I have had for the average rent and rates paid by recipients of National Assistance is 18s 6d a week. That is an average; there are, of course, wide differences in individual cases. When that figure is added to the 50s single and 85s married scales which we propose, it is clear that for those concerned, who are the poorest section of the community, these are substantially beyond proposals which in other spheres have been made in respect of pension or other analogous benefit rates. . . .

I commend these proposals to the House at this time as being proposals designed to help the poorest section of our community to share in the rising standards of an increasingly prosperous nation.

11.2.2 Exorcising the Poor Law Spirit, 1959

In this same speech of 1959 Boyd-Carpenter dealt with the lingering memory of the shame of the poor law.

From the House of Commons Debate, 24 June 1959 (2)

I come now to the question of the often alleged feeling that one's pride is hurt or one's self-respect is damaged by making an application for National Assistance. That such a feeling exists it would be foolish to deny, but it has been enormously diminished in recent years and to some extent is now more the product of historical memories than of actual facts. . . .

I agree that it would be a tragedy if anyone who was in need and was suffering was deterred from applying for assistance by this thought. . . . It is therefore important that we should analyse its causes . . . it is to a considerable degree the product of ignorance. It is ignorance of the point that one does not need to be penniless to be assisted. . . . There is a belief that the applicant for assistance has to come cap in hand. . . . It is perhaps felt that an applicant has to face some hard-faced committee. That is not the procedure. . . . A call is . . . made at home and a discussion takes place which is concerned as much with needs as with means. . . . The more that procedure is realised the more it will be clear that no one has the slightest reason for failing to exercise the rights which this House has given them in respect of National Assistance.

There is an idea that this is charity and, as such, derogatory.

This is no more charity than any other social service for which Parliament votes the money. Family allowances are financed in exactly the same way, and I have never heard of any unwillingness to apply for them.

I am certain that if we make it clear that this is a social service like any other, more flexible, perhaps, more exactly designed to deal with varying cases of hardship, but financed by the taxpayer in the same way as others, the more we can put paid to the idea that one loses one's self-respect by exercising the rights which a Christian and civilised society gives of ensuring that no one should fall below the levels that Parliament has laid down.

11.2.3 The 'Beveridge Revolution' Ended, 1964

The Beveridge Plan had been based on the principle, established in 1911, of flat-rate contributions for flat-rate benefits. With increasing prosperity this was inadequate, and in any case inflation was reducing the value of contributions paid. The Labour party in 1957 put forward plans for earnings-related pensions, which the Conservative government adopted in a limited and inadequate form in 1961.

On taking office in 1964 the Labour government indicated its intention of generally relating benefits to earnings, while adjusting them in accordance with changing values and standards. Earnings-related supplements to unemployment and sickness benefits were introduced, as a first step, in 1966 [11.2.4(1)], and in 1969 R. H. S. Crossman, Secretary of State for the Social Services, presented proposals for a completely new scheme of national superannuation and social insurance, with contributions and benefits related to earnings [11.2.4(2)]. These proposals had to be abandoned, however, on the defeat of the government in the general election of 1970.

The new Conservative government put forward its own proposals for a broader pensions scheme in 1971 [11.2.4(3)]. The pensions element in the Labour plan was for a state system covering everyone, to which the occupational pension schemes which had so much increased in recent years would be subsidiary. The Conservative plan, on the other hand, proposed a partnership of the two systems.

From the House of Commons Debate, 10 November 1964
The Chancellor of the Duchy of Lancaster (Mr D. Houghton): . . . On the longer-term reform of the scheme of National Insurance we must be clear about our aims. The Beveridge revolution spent itself some years ago. . . .

Poverty is unfortunately still to be found amongst many casualties of the affluent society but the modern concept of social security goes far beyond the sort of national minimum which the Webbs and Beveridge thought about.

The social services to me, and I believe to all Socialists, are a means of achieving greater equality. I have already said that, and I believe that this must govern our whole approach to the recasting of the social security scheme. All the social services are an expression of political and moral judgment and also of economic judgment. Hon. Members opposite ... stressed the fact that we have now had 20 years of the Beveridge concept and that it was time to define its place in modern society, but they did not do it. . . .

As far as I know, hon. and right hon. Members opposite have never as a party got further than to talk loosely about pensioners and others having a share of the prosperity of the nation. To us they are part of the nation – one nation. They should be fully integrated with the social and economic fabric of the whole nation. If we accept, as we do on these benches, that there should be some compulsory redistribution in our social services, the first question which we have to answer is, how much? . . .

Is the contributory principle for social security outmoded? The answer is 'No', not in this country with our traditions of the contributory principle. But the so-called insurance principle, so long an illusion, is outmoded. It has been purely of psychological advantage in the past and it has had no real substance ever since the present scheme was started. The fundamental change which I should like to see in social security would be social security as a right of citizenship with simple conditions replacing the bewildering, intricate, anomalous and unfair jungle of conditions which we have today.

In these days no scheme of social security can be satisfactory which fails, first, to provide benefits bearing some reasonable relationship to the actual amount of income lost by sickness, unemployment and on retirement, and so on, and, secondly, which fails to keep those benefits abreast of changing values or standards. This suggests to me that although contributions would be payable it would be quite unsound to relate benefits solely to the number or even the amounts of contributions actually paid.

Our concept for the 1970s is that all should pay according to their means and should receive in return an assurance of income-related social security. . . .

The future role of the National Assistance Board and the work it does will be considered with great care and understanding. . . . Whether the Board remains separate or is merged with the Ministry is largely a matter of administration and presentation.

11.2.4 Earnings-Related Benefits

From the Annual Report of the Ministry of Social Security, 1966, p. 20

EARNINGS-RELATED SUPPLEMENT TO UNEMPLOYMENT AND SICKNESS BENEFIT

From 6 October 1966 an earnings-related supplement became payable to people over 18 and under minimum pension age who are entitled to flat-rate unemployment or sickness benefit. The supplement is also payable to people drawing industrial injuries injury benefit or unemployability supplement instead of sickness benefit. It can also be paid to certain widows who normally work even though they have no title to flat-rate unemployment or sickness benefit because they have chosen not to pay flat-rate contributions. The supplement is normally payable after the first twelve days of unemployment or sickness . . . for up to 156 days (six months) of unemployment or sickness in a period of interruption of employment. The rate of supplement is broadly one-third of that part of average weekly earnings between £9 and £30 a week but regulations provide for benefit to be related to bands of annual earnings. It is paid in addition to flat-rate sickness or unemployment benefit, including increases for dependants subject to a maximum total benefit of 85 per cent of average weekly earnings. The maximum weekly supplement is thus £7, payable on average earnings of £30 a week or more.

From National Superannuation and Social Insurance: Proposals for Earnings-Related Social Security (Cmnd 3883, 1969)

1. The Government are proposing the most fundamental changes in social security since the present national insurance scheme was introduced soon after the Second World War.

2. The present scheme is clearly inadequate. Nearly 30 per cent of all pensioners are dependent in some degree on supplemen-

tary benefit. The existing flat-rate scheme has failed, despite the effort made in 1961 to shore it up by introducing an element of graduated contribution and pension. And the extent of this failure will grow unless the whole system is radically reconstructed.

3. This White Paper sets out the Government's proposals for replacing the present national insurance scheme by a new scheme of national superannuation and social insurance, in which both contributions and benefits will be related to the earnings of the individual employee. The new earnings-related contributions will mostly be higher than the present-scheme contributions, especially for higher earners. In return, those who pay the new contributions will earn new and higher personal pensions and other benefits – personal in two particular senses. First, national superannuation pensions will be related to the individual's personal earnings record; the uniform flat-rate pension will go. Secondly, unlike pension rights under most private superannuation schemes, those under national superannuation will never be lost, however many times or for whatever reason the individual changes his job.

4. The new earnings-related pensions and other benefits will only be available to those who have paid the new contributions. Twenty years of new-scheme contributions will be required before the first pensions at the full new-scheme rates are paid, to people reaching pension age then. These full rates will normally be adequate, even for those whose earnings have been relatively low, to live on without other means. Contributors who reach pension age during the twenty-year build-up period will earn pensions at intermediate rates. As more and more people draw the higher pensions which they will have earned by their new-scheme contributions, the proportion of pensioners needing supplementary benefit will gradually decline.

5. The new earnings-related pensions will not be available to those who are pensioners already. But they will continue to share in the nation's rising living standards, through periodical increases in their pensions. . . .

6. The income of the new scheme will automatically rise as earnings rise. . . . The Government will be required by law to undertake a review every two years of the main rates of

benefits in payment, both under the present scheme and under the new. The increases made will, as a minimum, compensate for any rise in prices during the two-year period. . . .

THE NEED FOR CHANGE
The financial position of pensioners today

9. There are about 7,000,000 people drawing national insurance pensions today. Until the middle 1960s, comprehensive information on the financial position of pensioners (apart from those receiving national assistance) was lacking, although independent research had provided evidence that a substantial number were entitled to receive national assistance but had not applied for it. This evidence was confirmed by a survey which was carried out in 1965 by the Ministry of Pensions and National Insurance with the co-operation of the National Assistance Board. This survey indicated that while about 1,450,000 pensioners were being helped by national assistance, there were about a further 850,000 who could have qualified for some payment of assistance at that time but had not applied – and of these roughly 300,000 were living appreciably below national assistance standards. The survey also showed that a very large number were only just above national assistance levels. If those levels had been £2 a week higher, about three-quarters of all pensioners would have been within the scope of national assistance. . . .

13. How has it happened that the present scheme of national insurance founded on the principles of the Beveridge Report, fails to provide an adequate income in retirement? In 1948 the Report seemed a great step forward for Britain and a model for many other countries. Our 'Welfare State' became more comprehensive than that of any other country. . . .

17. The basic reason for this failure was undoubtedly the acceptance . . . of Beveridge's recommendation that the scheme should be based on a system of flat-rate contributions and benefits; but there were four other factors –
   (a) In the first place there was the increasing proportion of the population over pension age. . . .
   (b) Secondly, the Government decided that existing pensioners should receive the full rate of pension straight away. . . .

(c) Thirdly ... there was a continuing need to improve the real value of pensions and to keep them moving upwards in step with the rising living standards of those in work.

(d) Fourthly, when the national assistance scheme came into operation in 1948 its levels (including allowances for rent) were in most cases substantially above the level of national insurance pensions and benefits. From the start, therefore, hundreds of thousands of old people needed to supplement their national insurance pension with an allowance from the National Assistance Board. ...

18. Underlying these factors was the basic weakness of the flat-rate system itself. A flat-rate contribution falls equally on the incomes of rich and poor. It is easily borne by the better-off, but hits the poorest hardest. The flat-rate contribution had to be set, therefore, at a level which the lowest wage-earner could afford. Experience has shown that under this system the level of contribution necessary to provide adequate pensions would place too great a burden on the lowest-paid contributors. ...

19. These were the problems which led to the introduction of the graduated pension scheme in 1961. ...

20. The pensions provided in return for graduated contributions, combined with the flat-rate pensions, still offer no prospect of achieving the original objectives of the Beveridge plan. The graduated pension scheme fails in two respects: its pensions are left unprotected against inflation and it cannot be adjusted for economic growth. ...

Conclusion

22. Neither the flat-rate scheme by itself, nor the present combination of flat-rate and graduated schemes, has succeeded in providing adequate pensions by right of contribution. For those without occupational pensions or private means, it is not the national insurance scheme which provides security in old age, but the supplementary benefits scheme. The latter is not, as was intended, just a 'safety net' for the exceptional case. Instead it is a vast platform which now helps to support some two million people over pension age.

From Strategy for Pensions: the Future Development of State and Occupational Provision (Cmnd 4755, 1971)

1. This White Paper sets out the Government's proposals for implementing their policy on pensions. It is a plan for action which recognises the different purposes of the State basic scheme and of occupational pension schemes and the importance of establishing a framework within which each can fulfil its own function. . . .

2. There are nearly twice as many retirement pensioners today as there were when the present national insurance scheme started in 1948 and the number is still rising. This means that costs are going up all the time. And since the number of pensioners is rising faster than the number of people at work these higher costs must fall even more heavily on the current working population. A scheme based on flat-rate contributions cannot meet the cost without causing hardship to workers on low earnings. It is time to face these facts squarely. The cost must be shared fairly and realistically. There must be no promises that depend on our children doing more for us than we are willing to do now for our parents.

3. Over the same period an equally remarkable growth has taken place in the provision of occupational pensions: about twice as many people today have pensionable jobs. More and more employers and employees have seen the wisdom of contributing to schemes which will lead to better living standards in retirement. Higher earnings have made this possible for many people who would formerly have been wholly dependent upon the State when they retired. The occupational pensions movement is an established and healthy part of our social system and through the savings they generate occupational pension schemes are playing a valuable part in our economy. It is time to welcome them into full partnership with the State scheme and to develop the scope they offer for greater independence in retirement.

4. From this background of rising costs in the State scheme and growing opportunities for occupational provision two clear objectives emerge. First, we must establish the State scheme on a sound financial basis which will enable rising costs to be met without hardship to contributors with low earnings. This means that contributions must be related to earnings. But to

induce acceptance of earnings-related contributions by promising earnings-related pensions on a pay-as-you-go basis would simply force the percentage rates of contribution to rise higher and higher to meet the emerging cost. This would be to solve the present financial problem by creating an even bigger one for the future. In the Government's view an equitable and enduring solution can only be found in a system of earnings-related contributions for basically flat-rate pensions. Secondly, we must secure, primarily through the growth of occupational pension schemes based on funding principles, that everyone has the opportunity of saving for a pension related to his earnings and we must ensure that a change of job does not lead to the loss of occupational pension rights.

5. People are more likely to understand and accept the social rights and obligations that lie at the heart of the State scheme and to take full advantage of the opportunity for personal saving that occupational schemes offer if the essential difference between the two forms of pension is clearly recognised. The contrast is between, on the one hand, a State scheme through which today's contributors support today's pensioners and, on the other, occupational schemes through which today's contributors by their savings can make their own personal provision for their own individual retirement over and above the basic State pension. . . .

7. Following [a] period of consultation the Government will present a Bill to Parliament to give legal effect to their proposals. Their aim is to bring the main structural changes into operation from April 1975. Meanwhile, within the limits of the existing structure, the Government will press on with developing the State scheme. . . .

87. Opportunities for higher earners to secure higher living standards in retirement do not depend upon the State. For people of working age, access to a decent occupational scheme should become a matter of course. Personal savings, buying a house, personal insurance – these are additional ways in which people today can decide to make provision for their retirement. The Government's aim is to encourage more and more people to take these opportunities. But while the social obligations set out in this White Paper are the responsibility of the State the opportunities are the responsibility of individuals and

employers. It is by personal enterprise and foresight, and not by reliance on an ever-widening extension of State commitments, that better living standards for our people in the later years of life will be secured.

11.2.5 Social Security and Supplementary Benefits, 1966

In accordance with the general plan announced in 1964 a reorganisation of pensions, national insurance and national assistance was undertaken in 1966, combining them in one Ministry (later to be amalgamated with the Ministry of Health in a Department of Health and Social Security). To overcome the distinction between insurance and assistance, which still left with the latter, in many minds, a flavour of the poor law, the two services were brought together, and new names devised. Assistance was converted to Supplementary Benefits, consisting of 'supplementary pensions' and 'supplementary allowances', while the National Assistance Board, which had been an independent body, became the Supplementary Benefits Commission, within the new Ministry. The association of insurance and assistance was not, in practice, complete, but Beveridge's aim of a single Ministry was at last realised.

The Ministry of Social Security Act, which created the new organisation, also restated family liabilities, in the same terms as the 1948 Act, thereby retaining a tenuous statutory connection with the Act of 1601. The second schedule of the new Act provided for what became known as the 'wage stop', the limitation of supplementary allowances for the unemployed and sick to their normal earnings.

From the Ministry of Social Security Act, 1966

An Act to provide for the appointment of a Minister of Social Security and the transfer to him of the functions of the Minister of Pensions and National Insurance and of certain functions of the National Assistance Board; to replace Part II of the National Assistance Act 1948 by provisions giving rights to non-contributory benefit; and for purposes connected with those matters.

PART I: THE MINISTER OF SOCIAL SECURITY AND THE COMMISSION

1. – (1) It shall be lawful for Her Majesty to appoint a Minister of Social Security having the functions provided for by the following provisions of this Act. . . .

2. – (1) The Ministry of Pensions and National Insurance is hereby dissolved and the National Assistance Board shall cease to exist on such date as the Minister of Social Security

may by order appoint; and there are hereby transferred to the Minister of Social Security –

(a) ... the functions of the Minister of Pensions and National Insurance;

(b) ... the functions of the National Assistance Board. ...

3. – (1) There shall be established ... a Commission, known as the Supplementary Benefits Commission, which shall exercise the functions conferred on them by this Act in such manner as shall best promote the welfare of persons affected by the exercise thereof.

PART II: NON-CONTRIBUTORY BENEFIT
Right to and amount of benefit

4. – (1) Every person in Great Britain of or over the age of sixteen whose resources are insufficient to meet his requirements shall be entitled, subject to the provisions of this Act, to benefit as follows, that is to say –

(a) if he has attained pensionable age, to a supplementary pension,

(b) if he has not attained pensionable age, to a supplementary allowance. ...

PART III: RECOVERY OF EXPENSES

22. – (1) For the purposes of this Act –

(a) a man shall be liable to maintain his wife and his children, and

(b) a woman shall be liable to maintain her husband and her children;

and in this subsection the reference to a man's children includes a reference to children of whom he has been adjudged to be the putative father and the reference to a woman's children a reference to her illegitimate children. ...

SCHEDULE 2

Provisions for Determining Right to and Amount of Benefit Adjustment to Normal Earnings.

5. – (2) ... the weekly amount of any supplementary allowance payable to [a] person shall not ... exceed what would be his net weekly earnings if he were engaged in full-time work in his normal occupation.

*From the Annual Report of the Ministry of Social Security, 1966,
pp. 50, 60–1*

SUPPLEMENTARY BENEFITS
Introduction

The Ministry of Social Security Act 1966 established a new scheme
to provide non-contributory benefits as of right for people whose
resources are less than their requirements by the standards laid
down in the Act. This scheme of supplementary benefits replaced
the National Assistance Scheme set out in the National Assistance
Act 1948, and also the obsolescent Non-Contributory Old Age
Pensions which were still available for people over age 70 in
September 1961. For the first time the control and administration
of contributory and non-contributory benefits were brought
together in one Ministry, the new Ministry of Social Security. . . .

The new scheme provides higher levels of benefits than were
available under the National Assistance Scheme. It also provides
for the first time a specific entitlement to benefit for those people
who satisfy the conditions laid down in the Act and its regulations.
These conditions, which are substantially different from those that
governed the National Assistance Scheme, have been designed to
remove features which tended to discourage some people from
claiming, and to make the scheme easier for people to understand
and fairer as between one person and another. The prime object
of the Act was to establish a new scheme which would encourage
as many as possible of those who might be entitled to benefit to
claim it. . . .

Adjustment to normal earnings

Unless there are exceptional circumstances, the Supplementary
Benefits Commission are required by the Ministry of Social
Security Act to restrict the amount of supplementary benefit payable to a person whose right to supplementary allowance is subject
to the conditions of section 11 of the Act, i.e. registration for
employment, so that his total income when unemployed is not
greater than it would be if he were in full-time employment. . . .

At the end of the year the restriction known as the 'wage-stop'
was being applied to some 25,000 allowances; of these 22,000 were
in respect of unemployed persons, and the remaining 3,000 in
respect of persons temporarily out of the employment field, mainly
because of sickness. . . . Many of the allowances subject to wage-

stop were being paid to claimants with large families. The amounts by which such allowances were restricted ranged from a few shillings to several pounds.

Although a person whose allowance is subject to 'wage-stop' is no worse off financially while he is unemployed than when he is working, the Commission recognise that the family could suffer hardship. Their officers, therefore, keep a special lookout for hardship to the family where the allowance is substantially restricted, and where necessary make an additional lump-sum grant to alleviate serious hardship. Officers also keep allowances under review to make sure that they move in line with increases in the level of earning. . . .

Welfare

The Ministry of Social Security Act places on the Commission a duty to exercise their functions 'in such manner as shall best promote the welfare of persons affected by the exercise thereof'. A similar requirement existed in the National Assistance Act. The Commission's officers are of course expected to ensure that the supplementary benefit awarded is adequate to meet the requirements of the person concerned, including in particular any special requirements not covered by the long-term addition. Equally they are required to be continuously on the alert to recognise cases in which there is a need for services to be provided by other statutory, or voluntary, services, e.g. the need for a home help or 'meals on wheels'. Where such needs are found to exist, the officer will either advise and help the person to get into touch with the appropriate authority or, where necessary, will make direct contact with the authority on his behalf.

From the Annual Report of the Ministry of Social Security, 1967, p. 36

CONCLUSION

This is the first Annual Report of the Supplementary Benefits Commission, and they wish to place on record on this occasion their appreciation of the help they have had from all the officials concerned in any way with the administration of the Supplementary Benefit Scheme, and their warm appreciation of the exceptional effort so willingly made during a difficult year by the staff in local offices dealing directly with the public, often under great pressure. . . .

Society is not made up of work-shys and abusers of supplementary benefits. Of course there are bound to be some of these exploiting the social services, but the very large majority of people for whom the Supplementary Benefits Scheme caters are people in difficulty and genuine need.

12 Poverty Continues

As in the USA in the same period, the 1960s saw a rediscovery of poverty, bringing the realisation that, for all the measures taken, the greater prosperity of the country as a whole still left considerable pockets of poverty and distress, relatively worse off in some respects than ever before. Social surveys in the 1930s had shown two main causes of serious poverty, low incomes and large families. Families in the sixties were generally smaller, but special investigations in 1966 into family circumstances and the effects of the wage stop revealed how much poverty was still due to low earnings.

This situation must be seen against the broad social and economic background. Despite all the changes that have taken place in the present century, there has been little alteration in the overall ownership of wealth, and the pay structure has retained considerable rigidity as between classes and occupations.[1]

12.1 THE WAGE-STOP

From Administration of the Wage-Stop, *Report by the Supplementary Benefits Commission* (*1967*)

1. Great concern has been felt in recent years about the position of families living on low incomes. . . .

2. . . . the wage-stop provisions contained in the Ministry of Social Security Act 1966 have been the target of considerable criticism. . . .

4. The purpose of the wage-stop is not to provide an incentive to a man to get work. The wage-stop does not require a man to get less when receiving Supplementary Benefit than he would get when working. What it does is to ensure that an unemployed man's income is *no greater* than it would be if he were in full-time employment. . . .

[1] G. Routh, *Occupation and Pay in Great Britain, 1906–60*, p. x.

7. As benefit cannot be paid to bring the income of a man in full-time employment up to Supplementary Benefit levels, the statutory provisions recognise that it would be wrong in equity to bring the income of a man of low earning capacity up to these levels because he happened to be unemployed or temporarily sick when there was nothing which could be done for his counterpart in full-time work. Here it may be noted that, on the basis of the Enquiry into the Circumstances of Families ... it has been estimated that, had the November 1966 Supplementary Benefit rates been in force in June 1966, there would then have been 160,000 families living below the level of those rates, of whom 20,000 would actually have been receiving Supplementary Benefit which was wage-stopped and the remaining 140,000 would have been families of men in full-time work.

8. The wage-stop is not, therefore, a cause of family poverty: it is a harsh reflection of the fact that there are many men in work living on incomes below the Supplementary Benefit standard. ...

9. Against this background the Commission decided to make some detailed field enquiries to obtain a clearer picture of the actual living conditions of wage-stopped claimants. ...

21. The general impression derived ... was not so much one of grinding poverty in any absolute sense as one of unrelieved dreariness with, in some cases, little hope of improvement in the future. ...

23. The information obtained from the Report reinforced the Commission in its conviction that it was necessary to undertake a thorough review of the whole administration of the wage-stop, with a view to ensuring that every wage-stopped claimant should receive the maximum permissible payment while at the same time preserving, as the Commission have a duty to do, the general intentions of the wage-stop provisions of the Act. ...

24. Although the principles underlying the wage-stop are basically simple, its operation gives rise to a number of practical difficulties. To conform with the requirements of the Act, the wage-stop needs to be related to the earnings which a man is likely to receive in the work he could get, rather than to what he may have earned in the past. The estimate of future earnings

must take account not only of the basic wages payable to men in their usual occupations but also of the possibility of over-time, bonus payments, etc. There is also the question of what expenses should be deducted to arrive at a true figure for take-home pay. . . .

12.2 FAMILY CIRCUMSTANCES

From Circumstances of Families, *Report of the Ministry of Social Security* (1967)

FOREWORD

This Report presents the results of an enquiry into the circum-stances of families with two or more children, made in June and July, 1966, by what was then the Ministry of Pensions and National Insurance with the co-operation of the National Assistance Board, under the guidance of a committee representing both academic and administrative experience. . . .

3. The enquiry was designed primarily to show the number of families whose resources were less than their requirements on the basic national assistance standards and the extent to which their needs could not be met by national assistance allowances. At a later stage estimates were also made by reference to the standards of supplementary benefit laid down by the Ministry of Social Security Act 1966. . . .

6. For the purpose of the enquiry a sample was taken from the Ministry's records of families with two or more children. Since there is no comprehensive register of families with one child, it was impracticable to include them but it is possible to make rough estimates of the numbers whose resources did not match their requirements, to supplement the information provided by the enquiry. In the summer of 1966 there were in all about seven million families with children. Of these – including those with one child – it seems probable that approaching half a million families, containing up to 1¼ million children, had incomes from earnings, contributory benefits, family allowances, or other sources (but excluding national assistance which was paid to a substantial pro-portion of them) amounting to less than would now be paid to a family which qualified for supplementary benefit. About 145,000 of these families were fatherless; 160,000 were those of men who

were sick or unemployed; and 140,000 of men in full-time work. The remainder were a miscellaneous group of families including, for example, families where there was no mother or where the father worked away from home. Virtually all the fatherless families received national assistance in full. Six out of ten of the sick and unemployed received it, the proportion being substantially higher among those whose absence from work had been prolonged. About two-thirds of the miscellaneous group of families received assistance. Altogether it seems likely that out of the half-million families whose resources were less than their requirements about 350,000 were receiving assistance or could have received it if they had applied. If the supplementary benefits scheme had been in operation the number would have been larger.

7. Those which cause particular concern are a group of about 160,000 families, with half a million children in them, whose fathers were disqualified by the Acts from receiving national assistance because they were in full-time work, or who were men receiving an allowance because they were unemployed or temporarily sick but who, because of the wage-stop, could not be paid enough to bridge the gap between their income and their requirements measured by supplementary benefits standards. . . .

9. Since the enquiry was carried out, the Government have introduced changes in the Social Security scheme which have benefited some families. From 6 October 1966, earnings-related supplements became payable with sickness or unemployment benefit after an absence from work lasting two weeks and these supplements can be paid for a period of up to six months' interruption of employment. Similar supplements based on a deceased husband's earnings are now paid with widow's allowance for the first six months of widowhood. Further, the Government's rate rebate scheme was only just under way at the time of the enquiry, and is now fully in operation. It is more than probable that as a result of these developments the resources of a number of families, including some where the father is in full-time work or subject to the wage-stop, have risen above the supplementary benefit level.

10. But the hard core of the problem remains. . . .

13 Statistics of Social Policy

The statistics that follow illustrate various aspects of the financing and operation of social services.

13.1 PUBLIC EXPENDITURE, 1951–70

The first tables summarise expenditure on the social services both in figures and as percentages of the total public expenditure over the years 1951–70, with certain other items for comparison.

The second and third tables show more comparative figures over the years 1921–69 and 1948–69.

13.1.1 Public Expenditure Summary: Analysis by Function (in £ million and percentages)

UNITED KINGDOM

	1951	1961	1966	1970
Social services:				
Social security	707	1,628	2,577	3,908
Welfare services	96	158	262	364
National health service	498	930	1,395	2,089
Education	398	1,013	1,768	2,592
Housing	404	555	975	1,213
Defence and external relations	1,411	1,859	2,512	2,796
Debt interest	687	1,257	1,553	2,105
Expressed as a percentage of total public expenditure:				
Social security	*12·1*	*15·8*	*16·8*	*18·1*
National health service	*8·4*	*9·0*	*9·1*	*9·7*
Education	*6·8*	*9·8*	*11·5*	*12·0*
Housing	*6·9*	*5·4*	*6·4*	*5·6*

[Source: *Social Trends*, No. 2, 1971, Table 134]

13.1.2 Public Expenditure at 1963 Prices (in £ million)

	1948	1951	1966	1969
National Health Service	449	771	1,097	1,157
Education	483	540	1,008	1,135
Defence	1,599	1,836	1,805	1,618

[Source: *National Income and Expenditure, 1970*, Table 14]

13.1.3 Expenditure on Social Services, including Housing, 1921–69 (in £ million, current prices)

1921	1931	1938	1950	1969
396	465	516	1,595	7,900

[Source: *The British Economy: Key Statistics, 1900–1970*, Table I]

13.2 NET INCOME AND SOCIAL SECURITY, 1951–70

13.2.1 Net Income: At Work or Sick, Unemployed or Retired (in £ and percentages)

Great Britain	October			
	1951	1961	1966	1970
Married couple with two children aged under 11				
At work:				
Average earnings	8·30	15·34	20·30	28·05
Family allowance	0·25	0·40	0·40	0·90
less national insurance contributions	0·25	0·78	1·12	1·65
less income tax	0·06	0·59	1·35	4·11
Net income – (*a*)	8·24	14·37	18·23	23·19
Sick or unemployed:				
Standard rate of sickness or unemployment benefit	2·73	5·97	8·35	10·30
Family allowance	0·25	0·40	0·40	0·90
Net income – (*b*)	2·98	6·37	8·75	11·20
(*b*) *as percentage of* (*a*)	36·1	44·4	48·0	48·3
Standard rate of sickness or unemployment benefit *plus* earnings-related supplement	—	—	12·10	15·95
Family allowance	—	—	0·40	0·90
Net income – (*c*)	—	—	12·50	16·85
(*c*) *as percentage of* (*a*)	—	—	68·6	72·7

[Source: *Social Trends*, No. 2, 1971, Table 40]

13.3 NATIONAL INSURANCE AND NATIONAL ASSIST-ANCE/SUPPLEMENTARY BENEFITS, 1951–70

13.3.1 Persons Receiving National Insurance Benefits and Extent Supplemented (in thousands and percentages)

Great Britain	31 December			
	1951	1965	1968	1970
National insurance beneficiaries:				
Unemployment benefit	207	166	294	302
Sickness benefit	906	975	1,037	1,060
Retirement pensions and contributory old age pensions *plus* widows aged 60–4 receiving widows' benefit	4,146	6,529	7,141	7,693
Percentages of national insurance beneficiaries also receiving national assistance/supplementary benefit:				
Unemployment benefit (percentage of persons)	*16*	*13*	*20*	*19*
Sickness benefit (percentage of persons)	*13*	*12*	*14*	*15*
Retirement pensions plus *widows aged 60–4 receiving widows' benefit (percentage of pensioners)*	*22*	*22*	*28*	*27*
Percentages of male national insurance beneficiaries also receiving earnings-related supplement:				
Unemployment benefit			*35*	*37*
Sickness benefit			*29*	*29*

[Source: *Social Trends*, No. 2, 1971, Table 43]

13.4 STATISTICS OF NATIONAL ASSISTANCE/ SUPPLEMENTARY BENEFITS, 1948-70

Table 1 shows the categories of those receiving assistance/benefits. Retirement pensioners predominate throughout, and this is further shown in tables 2 and 3.

13.4.1 Persons Receiving Supplementary Benefits (in thousands)

Great Britain

	National Assistance			Supplementary benefits	
	1948	1951	1965	1966	1970
Retirement pensioners and national insurance widows 60 years and over	495	767	1,239	1,631	1,745
Others over pension age	143	202	196	187	156
Unemployed with national insurance benefit	19	33	34	77	73
Unemployed without national insurance benefit	34	33	78	102	166
Sick and disabled with national insurance benefit	80	121	149	156	164
Sick and disabled without national insurance benefit	64	98	138	142	159
Women under 60 with dependent children	32	41	108	125	191
National insurance widows under 60	81	86	55	59	63
Others	63	81	15	16	20
Total persons receiving supplementary benefit	1,011	1,462	2,012	2,495	2,738
of which					
Wage stopped (unemployed)	—	—	16	22	32

[Source: *Social Trends*, No. 2, 1971, Table 44]

13.4.2 Supplementary Benefits: Age of Men Receiving Regular Weekly Payments (in thousands)

November 1970

	Total	16–17 years	18–20 years	21–29 years	30–39 years	40–49 years	50–59 years	60–64 years	65–69 years	70–74 years	75–79 years	80–84 years	85–89 years	90 years and over
All supplementary benefits	998	12	21	63	58	72	97	97	212	173	107	55	25	7
All supplementary pensions	576	—	—	—	—	—	—	—	210	172	107	55	25	7

[Source of 2 and 3: *Annual Report of the Department of Health and Social Security, 1970*, Tables 115 and 116]

13.4.3 Supplementary Benefits: Age of Women Receiving Regular Weekly Payments (in thousands)

November 1970

	Total	16–17 years	18–20 years	21–29 years	30–39 years	40–49 years	50–59 years	60–64 years	65–69 years	70–74 years	75–79 years	80–84 years	85–89 years	90 years and over
All supplementary benefits	1,740	11	28	95	76	76	126	173	267	319	280	169	88	32
All supplementary pensions	1,325	—	—	—	—	—	—	172	266	319	280	169	88	32